More Than the Law

The LAW AND PUBLIC POLICY: PSYCHOLOGY AND THE SOCIAL SCIENCES series includes books in three domains:

Legal Studies—writings by legal scholars about issues of relevance to psychology and the other social sciences, or that employ social science information to advance the legal analysis;

Social Science Studies—writings by scientists from psychology and the other social sciences about issues of relevance to law and public policy; and

Forensic Studies—writings by psychologists and other mental health scientists and professionals about issues relevant to forensic mental health science and practice.

The series is guided by its editor, Bruce D. Sales, PhD, JD, ScD(hc), University of Arizona; and coeditors, Bruce J. Winick, JD, University of Miami; Norman J. Finkel, PhD, Georgetown University; and Valerie P. Hans, PhD, University of Delaware.

* * *

More Than the Law

BEHAVIORAL AND SOCIAL FACTS IN LEGAL DECISION MAKING

PETER W. ENGLISH
BRUCE D. SALES

AMERICAN PSYCHOLOGICAL ASSOCIATION
WASHINGTON, DC

Published by
American Psychological Association
750 First Street, NE
Washington, DC 20002
www.apa.org

To order
APA Order Department
P.O. Box 92984
Washington, DC 20090-2984
Tel: (800) 374-2721; Direct: (202) 336-5510
Fax: (202) 336-5502; TDD/TTY: (202) 336-6123
Online: www.apa.org/books/
E-mail: order@apa.org

In the U.K., Europe, Africa, and the Middle East, copies may be ordered from
American Psychological Association
3 Henrietta Street
Covent Garden, London
WC2E 8LU England

Typeset in Goudy by Stephen McDougal, Mechanicsville, MD

Printer: United Book Press, Baltimore, MD
Cover Designer: Berg Design, Albany, NY
Technical/Production Editor: Peggy M. Rote

The opinions and statements published are the responsibility of the authors, and such opinions and statements do not necessarily represent the policies of the American Psychological Association.

Library of Congress Cataloging-in-Publication Data

English, Peter W.
    More than the law : behavioral and social facts in legal decision making /
Peter W. English and Bruce D. Sales.
        p. cm. — (The law and public policy)
    Includes bibliographical references and index.
    ISBN 1-59147-255-5 (hardcover)
    1. Law—United States—Psychological aspects. I. Sales, Bruce Dennis. II. Title.
III. Series.

KF385.E54 2005
349.73'01'9—dc22   2005000158

British Library Cataloguing-in-Publication Data
A CIP record is available from the British Library.

Printed in the United States of America
First Edition

To my wife, Kathy Ebalo English, and my parents, John and Josephine English, for their love and support in all things great and small.

—Peter W. English

To Justin, Heather, and Jon, who made salient for me the importance of excellence in education.

—Bruce D. Sales

CONTENTS

ACKNOWLEDGMENTS

We appreciate the efforts of our colleagues Norman Finkel, Daniel Krauss, Roger Levesque, and Daniel Shuman, who read and commented on an early draft of this book. We tried to address all of their excellent recommendations, but if we failed the blame is solely our own. We also appreciate the research assistance of our students Brian Carreon, Scott Christensen, Lori Cohen, Timothy Geiger, Frank Johnson, Matt Meeker, and Sara Ransom.

More Than the Law

1

INTRODUCTION

This is a book of short stories, although not in the tradition of American literary masters. Rather, these are stories written by modern American legal experts like the justices on the U.S. Supreme Court. These stories concern far more than just the characters that inhabit them because they are about issues that can affect us all. With the exception of the example in chapter 5, the stories are taken from actual court cases. Although most of them were discussed in the national media, they all had their origin locally, when, for example, some individual, perhaps from your state, city, or neighborhood, took a dispute to the local school board, then to state court, then to federal court, and finally to the U.S. Supreme Court, where the local dispute was ultimately decided.

In this book, we show that the law is not a fortress guarded by lawyers using inaccessible and arcane rules of law to fend off the average citizen. Rather, it is a dynamic forum where legal rules interplay with conflicts between people and groups and where disagreements about what are the relevant behavioral and social facts must be decided by the legal decision maker before those legal rules can be applied to reach a resolution (ending to the story). Indeed, each story exemplifies a lesson about the law's use of behavioral and social facts. Unlike stories found in popular literature, these stories and their lessons cannot be easily dismissed because they affect the most fundamental aspect of our lives: how we may behave and the consequences of deviating from the legally accepted behavior or norm. Thus, the stories are nonfiction and important. But they are one thing more as well. They teach us that the people who make our laws can rely on behavioral and social facts to help them make their decisions. How these facts are identified, analyzed, used, misused, or not used when they should be is critical to understanding and appreciating how legal decision makers carry out their responsibilities.

You might wonder why judges, for example, need to bother with these facts when they have such a rich and complex set of rules (i.e., the law) to rely on. The answer is simple. The law provides the rules of the game—the rules that will determine how, indeed whether, the facts will be used. But the rules are not the story. The facts make the story, and it is this story, contentious though it often may be, that needs an ending, a legal resolution.

In most cases, the stories presented by the competing parties (litigants in a court case or parties representing different interests before a legislature or a governmental agency) are quite different, although the parties purport to be talking about the same event. This leaves the legal decision maker with the task of deciding what are the proven facts as opposed to those that are assumed by one of the parties. It is easy to say, "I know the truth about a set of events," but when you say it, are you sure that you have all of the necessary information to make the statement? Is your statement based on opinions, hunches, or educated guesses that go beyond the facts and ultimately are not reflective of them?

Knowing the proven facts is complex because there are many sources for factual knowledge. Most of us do not fix our own automobile, plumbing, or household appliances because we do not understand them well enough. A similar problem occurs for legal decision makers. Complex issues often involve contested facts that only experts are knowledgeable about. Thus, legal decision makers need factual knowledge and often look to experts representing fields as diverse as the behavioral, social, biomedical, or physical sciences to help settle disputes.

What legal decision makers do with this expert factual knowledge, however, cannot always be easily predicted. The mere presence or availability of proven factual knowledge does not mean that the facts will be understood and used appropriately to form the basis of a decision. Indeed, the stories in this book illustrate the range of ways that legal decision makers use, abuse, and ignore relevant factual knowledge in their work. The stories also include situations in which the facts that the legal decision maker needs are not yet known or are only partially proven. We have selected 11 different stories to present, each containing an important and different lesson. Collectively, these stories establish the fact that behavioral and social facts are used in legal decision making, why this factual knowledge is used, and the problems related to the use or attempted use of that factual knowledge.

Each chapter presents one story that considers such diverse topics as forced testing of high school student athletes for use of illegal drugs, abortion, murder, and allegations by preschool children of sexual abuse by their teacher. You may not like the way all of the stories end because some of the outcomes conflict with your preconceptions and expectations of what is just and fair. But keep an open mind. When reading each story, do not limit yourself to asking whether you agree or disagree with a particular decision or law. Also ask the questions that will help you discover why you reached your conclusion and how the legal decision maker (e.g., the judge) reached her or his result. For example, how important was factual knowledge in the legal decision? Did the court (the term lawyers often use when referring to a judge in a case) rely on some facts that you were unaware of? Did it fail to consider other important factual knowledge? Was the factual knowledge incomplete? Did the decision maker use the right facts? Were the facts "tailored" to fit a preconceived decision, or did the facts determine the outcome? Were the facts scientifically derived or the result of expert opinion? And would a decision in a similar case likely be different in the future if new facts emerge?

Before reading these stories, some background information is helpful. You need to briefly consider what law is, what behavioral and social facts are, and how the two are related.

THE LAW

The law is found in the U.S. and state Constitutions; statutes passed by Congress and state legislatures; decisions of federal and state court judges; rules, regulations, and decisions of state and federal governmental agencies (e.g., a state department of mental health, a state department of corrections, or the U.S. Federal Trade Commission); and county and municipal codes (e.g., local traffic laws or local building codes). This body of law forms the basis for the operation of all of our legal systems that so pervasively influence our lives. These legal systems are organizations created by the law and operated according to its mandates to fulfill governmental responsibilities. These systems include state and federal governmental departments and agencies (e.g., the courts and departments of corrections, education, environmental protection, parks and recreation, transportation, or revenue and taxation).

Law and legal systems have a human side. In addition to people being regulated by the law, it is people who make the systems work. Thus, to understand law, you must also understand the people who are regulated by it and who participate in the operation of the legal systems. These people include prosecutors (i.e., the legal actor who represents the government in criminal proceedings), plaintiffs (i.e., the individual or entity who sues another in civil court), defendants (i.e., the individual or entity who is sued in civil or criminal court by the plaintiff in a civil case and the prosecutor in a criminal case), judges, lawyers, lay witnesses, expert witnesses, legislators, and all other persons who interact with the law. How these legal participants affect and are affected by the law and legal systems is the legal process in action, and you should not be overly surprised to learn that the law in action often differs from the written law because of the decisions of legal actors.

Constitutional Law

All laws, regardless of their source, must not conflict with the supreme law of the land, the U.S. Constitution, including its 27 Amendments. The first 10 Amendments, known as the Bill of Rights, guarantee certain rights to the people. Of these, the first 8 Amendments describe what the federal government is prohibited from doing (e.g., enacting laws that place restrictions on individual liberties). The Ninth Amendment reserves for the people rights not specifically enumerated in the Constitution but nonetheless protected by it. The Tenth Amendment reserves for the states any powers not assigned to the federal government; the constitutional principle of "state's rights" is derived from this Amendment. The Fourteenth Amendment limits state's rights assured by the Tenth Amendment by constraining states from abridging individual rights without due process of law and by guaranteeing all citizens the equal protection of the laws.

The U.S. Constitution is an elegant document, remarkable for its brevity and simplicity. When disputes do arise as to its meaning, they usually center on trying to determine the original intent of the drafters and how to apply a document that is more than 200 years old (at least the first 10 amendments) to today's world. What is generally not disputed is that federal law reigns supreme over conflicting state law in those areas that the constitution has expressly granted authority to the federal government (e.g., the right to regulate interstate commerce, federal taxation, national defense, and foreign relations). State or local laws prevail (a) in those areas that the federal government has not been authorized to act or (b) where the federal government has chosen not to act, and the topic is one that is not exclusively limited to federal control.

Finally, all states have their own constitutions. State action must conform to the state constitution but can never violate the federal Constitution.

Statutory Law

Statutory law (also known as legislative law) arises from the federal and state legislatures. Legislatures are bodies of elected representatives whose primary duty is to enact law. The U.S. Congress and most state legislatures comprise two houses: a Senate and a House of Representatives or Assembly. Each has slightly different responsibilities, but both have equal power to propose legislation. For a piece of legislation to become law, it must be approved by both houses of the legislature and signed by the Chief Executive—the

President of the United States for federal legislation and the state's Governor for state legislation. When both houses approve a piece of legislation but the Chief Executive vetoes it, there are rules for allowing the legislature to override that veto. Legislatures are not limited to proposing and passing only new laws, however. They may also revise or repeal existing laws. At the local level, city councils and county boards of supervisors can also be considered legislative bodies because they have authority to make laws affecting local jurisdictions.

Similar to constitutional law, federal statutory law is supreme over state statutory law that conflicts with federal mandates. In addition, both state and federal statutes must conform to U.S. constitutional mandates, and state statutory law must also conform to state constitutional mandates.

Case Law   *like on t.v. Judge Judy etc*

The Judicial Branch of the federal and state governments is responsible for interpreting and applying the relevant law to disputes that are brought before its courts. Its decisions are collectively known as case law but also referred to as the common law.

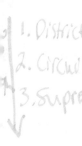

There are separate federal and state court systems. Among other things, the federal courts hear cases that involve federal and constitutional questions and disputes between states. The federal judiciary is divided into a three-part hierarchy. The U.S. District Courts (the federal trial courts) assume the lowest level of the system and thus have original jurisdiction in cases presented to them. There is at least one district court in each state and in the District of Columbia and Puerto Rico. The more populous states have several district courts. Overseeing the district courts are 13 U.S. Circuit Courts of Appeals. They serve as an intermediate court hearing appeals from the district courts within their assigned region and have original jurisdiction to hear a very limited number of cases. There is no reason to discuss the original jurisdiction of appellate courts further for purposes of this book. Sitting at the top of the federal court hierarchy is the U.S. Supreme Court. It has original jurisdiction in a limited number of cases (e.g., controversies between two or more states) and hears appeals from the U.S. Circuit Courts of Appeals. This latter jurisdiction typically arises when the issues transcend the immediate parties to the litigation and the federal appellate courts have issued conflicting opinions on an issue (U.S. Supreme Court, 2003). It also hears appeals from the state supreme courts when a U.S. constitutional issue is involved. Its interpretation of whether federal and state laws conform to the U.S. Constitution is final. Finally, the U.S. Supreme Court has original jurisdiction in a very limited number of cases that, once again, are not worth considering for purposes of this book.

Getting the U.S. Supreme Court to hear an appeal is not automatic. Indeed, the justices only hear arguments in about 100 of the approximately

7,000 cases that are submitted to them each year (U.S. Supreme Court, 2001). Whether an appeal is heard by the U.S. Supreme Court is a matter for its own discretion; at least four of the nine Supreme Court justices must agree to hear an appeal. If a case is denied a hearing before the U.S. Supreme Court, the lower court ruling stands.

Court systems at the state level generally follow the hierarchical model of the federal system. Cases are first heard in civil or criminal trial courts. These may include municipal and traffic courts for petty cases and superior courts for more serious civil and criminal cases. Appeals can be made first to an intermediate appellate court and then finally to the state's highest court, which is typically referred to as the supreme court. There is nothing sacrosanct in the use of this terminology, however. New York, for example, refers to its highest appellate court as the New York State Court of Appeals. Finally, note that according to prevailing legal convention, the word court is spelled with a capital C when used to refer to the U.S. Supreme Court.

Administrative Law

The Executive Branch of government is led by the President at the federal level and the Governor at the state level. Among other things, the Chief Executive is responsible for representing the government, suggesting new laws to the legislature and carrying out the laws that the legislative branch has enacted. To help the Chief Executive in these tasks, the legislature has created various administrative agencies (e.g., a state department of corrections or the U.S. Environmental Protection Agency) that have the power to issue administrative rules, regulations, decisions, orders, and opinions relevant to carrying out their functions as assigned to them by the Chief Executive and the legislature. These agencies have the ability to enforce the administrative law, resolve disputes that arise under the administrative law, and clarify and interpret statutes and policies that pertain to that agency. These administrative rules, regulations, decisions, orders, and opinions have the force of law but cannot conflict with constitutional, statutory, or case law.

Interactions Between the Different Sources of Law

Although each branch of government (Legislative, Judicial, and Executive) has distinct responsibilities, they do not function independently of one another when they make law. For example, when Congress or a state legislature enacts a statute, an administrative agency may have to issue new rules and regulations to implement the statute. If there are no constitutional problems with the law, then the courts are obligated to use the law when deciding cases. If a legislature does not like the way courts or administrative agencies have interpreted or used a particular law, the legislature may amend or repeal that law to prevent further misunderstandings or misuse. Similarly, in the context of a case, courts may need to examine a law made by the Legislative Branch (i.e., a statute) or the Executive Branch (e.g., an administrative rule) to make sure it passes constitutional muster. If, in the court's opinion, a law violates constitutional provisions, the court will declare the law void or its offending part void. There are a number of books available that can teach you how to find a law or laws relevant to a topic of interest to you (e.g., Morris, Sales, & Shuman, 1997; Sales & Shuman, 2005).

BEHAVIORAL AND SOCIAL FACTS

A fact is something that is proven. So when we refer to a behavioral or social fact, we are referring to proven facts (as opposed to assumed facts that subsequently may be proven to be false) about human behavior and human social interactions. How these facts come to be known is a bit more complicated. People often assume that they can recognize the facts and often are so confident in their beliefs that they confuse confidence with accuracy. Prejudice and bias are steeped in such confidence.

So where can one turn to find proven facts? The answer is most obvious when the facts are hidden from our senses. In those situations, one unhesitatingly turns to the sciences for answers. For facts about space and cosmology, one turns to physics and astrophysics. For facts about human disease, one turns to biomedical science. And for facts about human behavior, one turns to the behavioral and social sciences. Although many people assume that they are "students of human nature," the facts that they believe underlie their assumptions and conclusions may be wrong. They have no proof for them. As with other hidden facts, if people want the accurate behavioral and social facts, they must turn to the behavioral and social sciences that study the topic. When it comes to behavioral and social facts in legal decision making, these sciences comprise psychology, sociology, criminology, family studies, communications, economics, linguistics, anthropology, and political science.

It is reasonable to wonder why the sciences, including the behavioral and social sciences, have this unique ability to discover the facts. The answer is simple. It is the method that the sciences use to uncover facts that makes their discoveries accurate. The hallmark of this approach is that hypotheses about the facts are proposed and then subjected to empirical tests in an attempt to determine whether the hypotheses can be disproved. Typically, such research is then submitted to scientific journals for publication, a process that involves peer review of the work. Peer review is a process whereby other scientists, also expert in the topic, critically review the scientific work for accuracy. There are other important tests for the quality of the scientific work, but one can learn more about these in a course or courses on research methods and statistics. To further explore the scientific method, see Popper (1965, 1992) and Ziman (1991).

Scientific knowledge is neither static nor discoverable all at once. The scientific method allows scientists to discover facts within the confines of the conditions in which these facts were studied. For example, scientific research on how a new drug works can provide needed facts, but not all of the facts, about the drug. The acquisition of such knowledge typically takes years of scientific work. For instance, once one learns how the drug works, one has to study how the drug operates when in the presence of other drugs in the body and in an aging body that is subjected to the drug over a long period of time.

INTEGRATING BEHAVIORAL AND SOCIAL FACTS IN LEGAL DECISION MAKING

In the rest of this book, readers will learn that behavioral and social fact knowledge is directly relevant to legal decision making. To prove this point, in Part I, we set the stage by demonstrating that behavioral and social factual knowledge is used in legal decision making and that there may be multiple sources for this factual knowledge (e.g., cognitive psychology and sociology) in legal decisions.

In Part II, we then ask and answer why behavioral and social factual information is used. We consider five primary uses: identifying and evaluating the validity of the behavioral and social factual assumptions underlying a law, helping to set the goals for new law or the goals for a revision of an existing law, aiding in the resolution of disputed facts, aiding in the resolution of factual disputes relating to the constitutionality of a law, and educating legal decision makers about behavioral and social knowledge so that they can perform their responsibilities more effectively.

Despite the potential uses for behavioral and social factual knowledge, in Part III we demonstrate that there may be problems with legal decision makers trying to use it. For example, the legal decision maker may choose not to rely on the information for policy or other legal reasons. Even when the judge, legislator, or administrative agency decision maker wants to rely on behavioral and social facts, there can still be problems. The needed factual knowledge may not yet exist, or although research exists in the area of concern, it may not directly address the specific concerns of the legal decision maker or it may suffer from methodological or statistical flaws.

For laypersons, these chapters teach a series of essential lessons—lessons that will help them understand and appreciate the importance that behavioral and social knowledge bring to legal decision making. Empirical researchers who previously were unfamiliar with the relationship of behavioral and social science to law will recognize new and vast opportunities for research, which, if done correctly, can have a real impact in the courts, legislatures, and administrative agencies throughout our land. Behavioral and social science experts will come to understand both why the law seeks their information and the special burden they bear as experts to provide legal decision makers with the most accurate behavioral and social facts relevant to the legal issue under consideration.

ORGANIZATION OF THE BOOK

To achieve these goals, in subsequent chapters we consider original legal materials (one per chapter). Each chapter starts with an introduction that will familiarize you with the chapter's lesson and how it will be represented in the excerpted legal reading. The introduction is followed by the excerpted legal reading (e.g., a U.S. Supreme Court case) and a discussion (entitled Analysis and Implications) in which we review, elaborate on, and critically explore the behavioral and social facts relevant to the legal issue under consideration. We intentionally take these discussions beyond simply proving the lesson of each chapter. We use our analysis in every chapter to demonstrate the rich relationship between law and behavioral and social facts.

The 11 lessons (one per chapter) presented in this book transcend the particular legal excerpt presented in each chapter. The excerpts were selected because they educate in an interesting way. However, there are many other legal issues and materials that could have been chosen for each lesson.

To make the book more readable, we have edited the excerpted legal materials presented in each chapter. Citations to earlier legal cases and statutes are eliminated; citations to (but not the content of) the original behavioral and social science literature are omitted; unnecessary footnotes are deleted, and the content of important footnotes is placed within the text; names of the behavioral and social scientists who served as experts are deleted; quotation marks are deleted when their only purpose is to show who first made the point; the language of the legal text is revised if it could be written more clearly and if rewriting was necessary to help nonlegal readers understand the case; and legal discussions that were irrelevant to the purposes of this book are deleted. For this reason, we also do not include the name of the judge who wrote the opinion nor how many judges concurred in the opinion or dissented from it. We do have an excerpt from both a Concurring Opinion in chapter 10 and a Dissenting Opinion in chapter 12 because they are necessary to fully appreciate the lessons of those chapters. If readers wish to find the full, unedited text, the citation for the legal excerpt in each chapter is listed in the References at the end of the chapter. This citation can be used to find the unedited legal excerpt in a law or university library or on the World Wide Web.

The Analysis and Implications section in each chapter does not attempt to discuss all of the legal issues that a case raises nor every behavioral and social science research study relevant to the legal excerpt. To do so would expand most of the chapters into separate book-length manuscripts. But even if doing so only substantially expanded the length of this book, it would create the real possibility of losing many of our potential readers who do not plan to become experts in the field. Rather, the goal is to teach the lessons of this book and demonstrate within each chapter the relationship between law and behavioral and social facts.

Finally, one may ask why not simply write a nonfiction book about this topic? The answer is that the information would not have been as compelling or as educational as reading the original legal materials. The law represents a dynamic process composed of real controversies, lawyers who are passionate about winning for their clients, and legal decision makers who must be fair and impartial if they are to execute their responsibilities faithfully. Add to this, the need of legal decision makers for accurate behavioral and social factual knowledge, and the result is a compelling set of stories that teach interesting and important lessons.

REFERENCES

Morris, R., Sales, B. D., & Shuman, D. W. (1997). *Doing legal research: A guide for social scientists and mental health professionals.* Thousand Oaks, CA: Sage.

Popper, K. R. (1965). *Conjectures and refutations: The growth of scientific knowledge.* New York: Basic Books.

Popper, K. R. (1992). *Logic of scientific discovery.* New York: Basic Books.

Sales, B. D., & Shuman, D. W. (2005). *Experts in court: Reconciling law, science, and professional knowledge.* Washington, DC: American Psychological Association.

U.S. Supreme Court. (August 20, 2003). *A brief overview of the Supreme Court.* Retrieved June 14, 2004, from http://www.supremecourtus.gov/about/briefoverview.pdf

U.S. Supreme Court. (2001). *The justices' caseload.* Retrieved June 1, 2004, from http://www.supremecourtus.gov/about/justicecaseload.pdf

Ziman, J. M. (1991). *Reliable knowledge: An exploration of the grounds for belief in science.* New York: Cambridge University Press.

I

BEHAVIORAL AND SOCIAL FACTS ARE USED IN LEGAL DECISION MAKING

2

FACTUAL KNOWLEDGE IS CRITICAL IN LEGAL DECISION MAKING

EXAMPLE: MANDATORY TESTING FOR DRUG USE BY STUDENT ATHLETES

Drug abuse is one of the most serious problems facing our nation. Federal, state, and local governments are spending billions of dollars in a war on drugs, which includes a law enforcement presence on our borders, special drug courts to handle the many thousands of drug cases each year, and educational programs designed to deter children from ever using drugs. One tactic to deter drug use that is increasingly used by school districts is to require certain categories of students, like athletes, to take a drug test if they want to participate in a school sport.

As one can imagine, some parents, children, and civil liberties groups object to this practice and have challenged these policies. This was the situation with a 12-year-old named James Acton. James was an Oregon boy who wanted to play football but could not unless he agreed, like all other potential football players, to be subject to random drug tests. James and his parents sued their school district over the policy, and their case eventually was heard in the U.S. Supreme Court.

We start with the Supreme Court's opinion because it demonstrates the importance of behavioral and social facts in legal decision making. For the Court to find in favor of the school district, it needed to find that the government had a compelling interest in protecting student athletes, the other students, and the school personnel from harm. The Court did this by finding that there was a behavioral and social fact basis for concluding that the drug problem was epidemic, that athletes were leaders of the drug culture and role models in the community, that drugs can lead to injuries in athletes, and that athletes have lowered expectations of privacy that would lower the intrusiveness of the mandatory drug test (i.e., which the law considers a search of the person). Without such facts, it is unlikely that the Supreme Court would have ruled that the district's drug-testing policy was constitutional under the Fourth and Fourteenth Amendments to the U.S. Constitution.

VERNONIA SCHOOL DISTRICT V. ACTON

United States Supreme Court

Vernonia School District (henceforth District) operates one high school and three grade schools in the logging community of Vernonia, Oregon. As elsewhere in small-town America, school sports play a prominent role in the town's life, and student athletes are admired in their schools and in the community.

Drugs had not been a major problem in Vernonia schools until the mid-to-late 1980s when teachers and administrators observed a sharp increase in drug use. Students began to speak out about their attraction to the drug culture and to boast that there was nothing the school could do about it. Along with more drugs came more disciplinary problems. Between 1988 and 1989, the number of disciplinary referrals in Vernonia schools rose to more than twice the number reported in the early 1980s, and several students were suspended. Students became increasingly rude during class; outbursts of profane language became common.

Not only were student athletes included among the drug users but athletes were the leaders of the drug culture. This caused the District's administrators particular concern because drug use increases the risk of sports-related injury. Expert testimony at the trial confirmed the deleterious effects of drugs on motivation, memory, judgment, reaction, coordination, and performance. High school coaches witnessed a severe sternum injury suffered by a wrestler, and various omissions of safety procedures and misexecutions by football players, all attributable in their belief to the effects of drug use.

Initially, the District responded to the drug problem by offering special classes, speakers, and presentations designed to deter drug use. It even brought in a specially trained dog to detect
drugs, but the drug problem persisted. According to the trial court
where the case was heard:

> The administration was at its wits end and a large segment of
> the student body, particularly those involved in interscho-
> lastic athletics, was in a state of rebellion. Disciplinary prob-
> lems had reached epidemic proportions. The coincidence of
> an almost three-fold increase in classroom disruptions and
> disciplinary reports along with the staff's direct observations
> of students using drugs or glamorizing drug and alcohol use
> led the administration to the inescapable conclusion that
> the rebellion was being fueled by alcohol and drug abuse as
> well as the students' misperceptions about the drug culture.

The District's Drug-Testing Policy

In response to the problem, District officials considered a
drug-testing program. They held a parent "input night" to discuss
the proposed Student Athlete Drug Policy (henceforth Policy or
District Policy), and the parents in attendance gave their unanimous approval. The school board approved the Policy for implementation in the fall of 1989. Its expressed purpose was to prevent
student athletes from using drugs, to protect their health and safety,
and to provide drug users with assistance programs.

The Policy applied to all students participating in interscholastic athletics. Students wishing to play sports had to sign a form
consenting to the testing and obtain the written consent of their
parents. Athletes were tested at the beginning of the season for
their sport. In addition, once each week of the season the names
of the athletes were placed in a pool from which a student, with
the supervision of two adults, blindly drew the names of 10% of
the athletes for random testing. Those selected were notified and
tested that same day, if possible.

The student to be tested completed a specimen control form
with an assigned number. Prescription medications that the student was taking were identified by providing a copy of the prescription or a doctor's authorization. The student then entered an
empty locker room accompanied by an adult monitor of the same
sex. Each boy selected produced a sample at a urinal, remaining
fully clothed with his back to the monitor, who stood approximately 12 to 15 feet behind the student. Monitors could (though

do not always) watch the student while he produced the sample, and they listened for normal sounds of urination. Girls produced samples in an enclosed bathroom stall, so that they could be heard but not observed. After the sample was produced, it was given to the monitor, who checked it for temperature and tampering and then transferred it to a vial.

The samples were sent to an independent laboratory, which routinely tested them for amphetamines, cocaine, and marijuana. Other drugs, such as LSD, could also be screened at the request of the District, but the identity of a particular student did not determine which drugs would be tested. The laboratory's procedures were 99.94% accurate. The laboratory did not know the identity of the students whose samples it tested. It was authorized to mail written test reports only to the superintendent and to provide test results to District personnel by telephone only after the requesting official recited a code confirming his authority. Only the superintendent, principals, vice principals, and athletic directors had access to test results, and the results were not kept for more than one year.

If a sample tested positive, a second test was administered as soon as possible to confirm the result. If the second test was negative, no further action was taken. If the second test was positive, the athlete's parents were notified, and the school principal convened a meeting with the student and his parents, at which the student was given two options: (a) participate for 6 weeks in an assistance program that includes weekly urinalysis or (b) be suspended from athletics for the remainder of the current season and the next athletic season. The student was then retested prior to the start of the next athletic season. A second offense resulted in automatic imposition of Option b. A third offense resulted in suspension for the remainder of the current season and the next two athletic seasons.

The Constitutional Claim

In the fall of 1991, James Acton, then a seventh grader, signed up to play football at one of the District's grade schools. He was denied participation, however, because he and his parents refused to sign the drug-testing consent form. The Actons filed this lawsuit on the grounds that the District's policy violated the Fourth and Fourteenth Amendments to the U.S. Constitution.

The Fourth Amendment to the U.S. Constitution provides that the federal government shall not violate "[t]he right of the people to be secure in their persons, houses, papers, and effects, against unreasonable searches and seizures." The Fourteenth Amendment extends this constitutional guarantee to searches and seizures by state officers such as public school officials, and includes state-compelled collection and testing of urine such as that required by the District's Policy.

As the text of the Fourth Amendment indicates, the ultimate measure of the constitutionality of a governmental search is its reasonableness. Whether a particular search is reasonable is judged by balancing its intrusiveness against its promotion of a legitimate, compelling governmental interest.

The Privacy Interest of Student Athletes

The first factor to be considered in deciding the reasonableness of the District's Policy is the nature of the student athlete's privacy interest upon which the search intrudes. The Fourth Amendment does not protect all subjective expectations of privacy but only those that society recognizes as legitimate. What expectations are legitimate varies, of course, with context, depending, for example, on whether the individual asserting the privacy interest is at home, at work, in a car, or in a public park. In addition, the legitimacy of certain privacy expectations vis-à-vis the state may depend on the individual's legal relationship with the state. The subjects of the Policy are children, who have been committed to the temporary custody of the state as schoolmaster.

Unemancipated minors lack some of the most fundamental rights of self-determination, including the right of liberty in its narrow sense (i.e., the right to come and go at will). They are subject, even as to their physical freedom, to the control of their parents or guardians. When parents place minor children in schools for their education, the teachers and administrators of those schools stand in loco parentis over the children entrusted to them.

The nature of that power is custodial and tutelary, permitting a degree of supervision and control that could not be exercised over free adults. A proper educational environment requires close supervision of schoolchildren as well as the enforcement of rules against conduct that would be perfectly permissible if undertaken by an adult. Thus, while children assuredly do not shed their constitutional rights at the schoolhouse gate, the nature of those rights is what is appropriate for children in school.

Fourth Amendment rights are different in public schools than elsewhere; an evaluation of the reasonableness of a search cannot disregard the school's custodial and tutelary responsibility for children. For their own good and that of their classmates, public school children are routinely required to submit to various physical examinations and to be vaccinated against various diseases. Particularly with regard to medical examinations and procedures, therefore, students within the school environment have a lower expectation of privacy than members of the general population.

The legitimate privacy expectations of student athletes are even less. School sports are not for the bashful. They require "suiting up" before each practice or event and showering and changing afterward. Public school locker rooms, the usual sites for these activities, are not notable for the privacy they afford. The locker rooms in Vernonia are typical: no individual dressing rooms are provided; shower heads are lined up along a wall, unseparated by any sort of partition or curtain; not even all the toilet stalls have doors. There is an element of communal undress inherent in athletic participation.

In addition, by choosing to go out for the team, student athletes voluntarily subject themselves to a degree of regulation even higher than that imposed on students generally. In Vernonia's public schools, student athletes must submit to a preseason physical exam, including the giving of a urine sample, acquiring adequate insurance coverage or signing an insurance waiver, maintaining a minimum grade point average, and complying with any rules of conduct, dress, training hours, and related matters, as may be established for each sport by the head coach and athletic director with the principal's approval.

This Court previously recognized that collecting the samples for urinalysis intrudes upon an excretory function, which is traditionally shielded by an individual's great privacy interest. But the degree of intrusion depends on the manner in which production of the urine sample is monitored. Under the District's Policy, male student athletes produce samples at a urinal along a wall. They remain fully clothed and are only observed from behind, if at all. Female student athletes produce samples in an enclosed stall, with a female monitor standing outside listening only for sounds of tampering. These conditions are nearly identical to those typically encountered in public restrooms, which men, women, and especially school children, use daily. Under such conditions, the privacy interests compromised by the process of obtaining the urine sample are negligible.

The other privacy-invasive aspect of urinalysis is the information it discloses concerning the state of the subject's body and the materials the student athlete has ingested. In this regard, it is significant that the tests at issue here look only for drugs and not for whether the student is, for example, epileptic, pregnant, or diabetic. Moreover, the drugs for which the samples are screened are standard, and do not vary according to the identity of the student. The results of the tests are disclosed only to a limited class of school personnel who have a need to know and are not turned over to law enforcement authorities.

Requiring advance disclosure of medications is not unreasonable per se, nor is it a significant invasion of privacy. In addition, although the practice of the District seems to have been to have a school official take medication information from the student at the time of the test, that practice is not set forth in, or required by, the Policy. It may well be that if and when James was selected for random testing at a time that he was taking medication, the District would have permitted him to provide the requested information in a confidential manner, for example, in a sealed envelope delivered to the testing lab. Nothing in the Policy contradicts that, and when Acton chose, in effect, to challenge the Policy as it appears in writing, we will not assume the worst. Accordingly, we conclude that the invasion of privacy was not significant.

The Compellingness of the District's Interest

The government's interest motivating a search must be compelling. Whether there is a compelling state interest is determined by asking whether the interest is important enough to justify the particular search in light of other factors that show the search is relatively intrusive upon a genuine expectation of privacy.

That the nature of the government's concern is important—indeed, perhaps compelling—can hardly be doubted. Deterring drug use by our nation's schoolchildren is at least as important as enhancing efficient enforcement of the nation's laws against the importation of drugs. School years are the time when the physical, psychological, and addictive effects of drugs are most severe. Maturing nervous systems are more critically impaired by intoxicants than mature ones are; childhood losses in learning are lifelong and profound; children grow chemically dependent more quickly than adults, and their record of recovery is depressingly poor. And, of course, the effects of a drug-infested school are visited not just on the users but on the entire student body and faculty when the educational process is disrupted. In the present case, the necessity for the state to act is magnified by the fact that this evil is being visited not just on individuals at large but on children for whom it has undertaken a special responsibility of care and direction.

Finally, the District's Policy is narrowly directed at drug use by school athletes, for whom the risk to themselves or their competitors is particularly high. Apart from psychological effects, which include impairment of judgment, slow reaction time, and a lessening of the perception of pain, the particular drugs screened by the District's Policy have been demonstrated to pose substantial physical risks to athletes. Amphetamines produce an artificially induced heart rate increase, peripheral vasoconstriction, blood pressure increase, and masking of the normal fatigue response, making it a very dangerous drug when used during exercise of any type. Marijuana causes irregular blood pressure responses during changes in body position, reduction in the oxygen-carrying capacity of the blood, and inhibition of the normal sweating responses resulting in increased body temperature. Cocaine produces vasoconstriction, elevated blood pressure, and possible coronary artery spasms and myocardial infarction.

As to the immediacy of the District's concerns, this Court is not inclined to question the trial court's conclusion that a large segment of the student body, particularly those involved in interscholastic athletics, was in a state of rebellion, that disciplinary actions had reached epidemic proportions, and that the rebellion was being fueled by alcohol and drug abuse as well as by the students' misperceptions about the drug culture. It seems to us self-evident that a student-athlete drug problem is particularly dangerous to the athletes involved, and results in dangerous role models for other athlete and nonathlete students. These problems are effectively addressed by making sure that athletes do not use drugs.

Acton argues that a less intrusive means to the same end was available, namely, drug testing on suspicion of drug use. We have repeatedly refused to declare that the least intrusive search is the only reasonable one under the Fourth Amendment. It may be impracticable, for one thing, simply because the parents who are willing to accept random drug testing for athletes may not be willing to accept accusatory drug testing for all students because it transforms the process into a badge of shame. Acton's proposal also brings the risk that teachers will impose testing arbitrarily on troublesome, but not drug likely, students. It generates the expense of defending lawsuits that charge such arbitrary imposition or that simply demand greater due process protections (e.g., a lawyer to represent the accused student) before accusatory drug testing is imposed. And not least of all, testing on suspicion of drug use adds to the ever-expanding diversionary duties of schoolteachers (i.e., the new function of spotting and bringing to account

Facts on drugs, peril to athletes

drug abuse), a task for which they are ill prepared and which is not readily compatible with their vocation. A drug-impaired individual will seldom display any outward signs detectable by the layperson or, in many cases, even a physician. Teaching requires an ongoing relationship, one in which the teacher must occupy many roles—educator, adviser, friend, and, at times, parent substitute. The relationship is rarely adversary in nature. In many respects, therefore, testing based on suspicion of drug use would not be better, but worse.

Conclusion

Taking into account all the factors considered above—the decreased expectation of privacy, the relative unobtrusiveness of the search, and the severity of the need met by the search, Vernonia's Policy is reasonable and hence constitutional.

This does not mean that suspicionless drug testing will readily pass constitutional muster in other contexts. The most significant element in this case is that the Policy was undertaken in furtherance of the government's responsibilities, under a public school system as guardian and tutor of children entrusted to its care. When the government acts as guardian and tutor, the relevant question is whether the search is one that a reasonable guardian and tutor might undertake. Given the findings of need made by the trial court, we conclude that in the present case it is.

The primary guardians of Vernonia's schoolchildren appear to agree. The record shows no objection to this district-wide program by any parents other than the couple before us here—even though a public meeting was held to obtain parents' views. There is insufficient basis to contradict the judgment of Vernonia's parents, its school board, and the trial court, as to what was reasonably in the interest of these children under the circumstances.

Supreme Cts Final ruling in Favor of school district

ANALYSIS AND IMPLICATIONS

A government-ordered drug test is considered a search, and the Fourth Amendment to the U.S. Constitution will only allow searches that are reasonable. The U.S. Supreme Court noted that the way to determine the reasonableness of the search was to balance James Acton's right to privacy against any legitimate interest the government might have, and the compellingness of that interest, in allowing the drug tests. The Court considered three general factors in balancing these interests: a student's expectation of privacy, the nature of the search (drug test), and the school's interest in conducting the search.

Expectation of Privacy

The Court began by noting that not all subjective expectations of privacy are protected. In other words, we do not get to decide for ourselves which aspects of our lives are private. Rather, we are entitled only to those subjective expectations that society deems legitimate. Whether an expectation is legitimate depends in part on the nature of the relationship between the individual and the state. The individuals subject to the testing in this case are children who are in the temporary custody of the state while they are playing sports in school. And, as the court noted, the school district assumes parental responsibilities as guardian and tutor while the children are in school. This is a critical point because the Court is really deciding if there are a set of circumstances that would lead a reasonable guardian to submit his or her child to a search of this type (i.e., a drug test).

The Court also noted that certain school experiences leave children with a lower expectation of privacy than adults. For example, children periodically have to take physical exams and be vaccinated against disease. Children who also are student athletes, the Court reasoned, must have an even lower expectation of privacy. After all, much of what athletes do in preparation for their sports is communal; they must change into and out of their uniforms together and then shower together, all in the closed confines of a locker room. The fact that student athletes must also take preseason physical exams, offer proof of insurance, maintain a minimum grade point average, and agree to follow any rules of conduct or dress that the administration sets, further diminish their expectation of privacy.

Despite the Court's belief that it determined the privacy expectations of student athletes, there are no empirical data in the scientific literature that specifically address relevant questions, such as, Do student athletes have a lower expectation of privacy? Does their expectation of privacy become violated when an authority figure is present to collect a urine sample? Do all athletes perceive privacy and their expectations for it similarly? We do know that there are different types of privacy (e.g., withholding personal information from others, avoiding others, and not being seen; Westin, 1967). We also know that people who have different personality characteristics often prefer a particular kind of privacy (Pedersen, 1982, 1987). Although athletes no doubt share some characteristics that drew them to participate in a particular sport, they may also be different enough from one another for them to have differing views and expectations of privacy. Thus, although the court perceived all athletes similarly, it may be scientifically inappropriate to do so.

It would have been possible to provide the Court with empirically based information about these issues. There are several techniques for measuring privacy that could be adapted for measuring the student athletes' expectations of privacy. Stewart and Cole (2001) had backpackers keep a daily diary while they camped. The diaries were turned over to the researchers at the conclusion of the backpackers' trip and analyzed for perceptions of crowding and privacy. A similar method could be used to measure the expectations of privacy among student athletes. Contemporaneous reports could provide compelling evidence regarding student athletes' true feelings about the drug testing and the degree to which they felt their privacy was violated, if at all. In a study of 500 college athletes, Coombs and Coombs (1991) found that some test takers were embarrassed, humiliated, upset, and anxious about the experience. Several researchers have also devised specific inventories for measuring preferences for privacy (e.g., Marshall, 1974; Pedersen, 1979) that could be administered to students and compared to those of other students to determine whether the athletes displayed a lesser preference for privacy.

Expectations of privacy among other groups may shed some light on the importance of conducting research on this issue. For example, federal courts have mandated that institutionalized patients with mental illness are entitled to certain standards in their physical environment to ensure their privacy. Unfortunately, no one thought to ask the patients what their expectations of privacy were until O'Reilly and Sales (1987) did so and discovered that the changes ordered by the courts (e.g., screens or curtains around beds, toilets, and showers) did not adequately ensure the sense of overall privacy that the patients sought. Might a similar result occur if student athletes were surveyed?

Even if yes, however, other studies suggest that there are conditions under which people will lower their privacy expectations. For example, job seekers are less likely to apply to companies that test for drugs and have weak confidentially policies. However, the applicants' reluctance to apply to such companies is mediated by the applicants' positive attitude toward the company and a perception that the testing procedure is fair (Sujak, Villanova, & Daly, 1995). Perhaps a similar phenomenon occurs in student athletes. That is, a higher initial expectation of privacy may be lowered because of their knowledge that they will enjoy the benefit of athletic participation and the testing procedure is fairly carried out. In addition, Coombs and Ryan (1990) found that athletes were deterred from using drugs because of their sense of team loyalty (i.e., getting caught by the drug test would hurt the team) and their belief that testing improved their athletic performance. Testing also gave the athletes a socially acceptable excuse to refuse drugs if offered them by friends (Coombs & Coombs, 1991; Coombs & Ryan, 1990). These studies suggest that student athletes may be willing to maintain a lowered expectation of privacy (by being tested for drugs) or to sacrifice a certain measure of privacy if doing so presents some perceived benefit.

Although some student athletes have a lowered expectation of privacy, or are at least willing to forsake their privacy to play sports (e.g., Hamilton & Stone, 1990; Issari & Coombs, 1998), these surveys were taken among college athletes, and the results may not extend to younger students. There may be greater support for testing among college athletes because of the superior level of competition and skills required to play at that level and a belief that testing is necessary to protect the integrity and financial interests of college athletics. This support might directly affect expectations for privacy.

Finally, the Court was concerned with whether society would perceive the student athletes' expectations as legitimate. There is no relevant research on this topic, although it too is a question that is amenable to empirical research. Empirical information also would have been helpful regarding the policy provision that only school officials are notified when a test comes back positive. (Parents are told only if a second test is positive.) No one is referred to law enforcement or for criminal prosecution. The Court felt that this safeguard made the test less intrusive, and thus, not a significant breach of privacy. However, the Court's opinion did not address whether the results are safe from a law enforcement search and seizure of the records or a subpoena of them. Could the school protect the child's privacy, for example, if an athlete high on drugs is involved in a lunchtime automobile accident and the victim asks the court to see the test results? Could the school stop a police officer from searching and seizing the records under a valid search warrant while investigating the accident? It would be helpful to know how these considerations would impact the student athlete's expectation of and right to privacy.

Nature of the Search

The Court then determined whether the search (i.e., the drug test) was too intrusive. They looked closely at the test procedures for collecting the specimens from both male and female student athletes and concluded that there was not much difference between the testing conditions proposed by the District and the conditions that might be found when one used an athletic locker room. Thus, the actual method of collecting the test sample could not be viewed as a significant invasion of privacy.

The Court appears to have made the leap from a lowered expectation of privacy when in a locker room to a lowered expectation of privacy when urinating into a bottle and handing it over to a school official. These are two very different kinds of behavior. A student athlete might be comfortable with the former but very uncomfortable doing the latter. The Court's reasoning was based on the safeguards that the program used to preserve some of the participants' dignity: Athletes remained clothed; males kept their backs to the monitor; and females got to go into a stall, all of which is not much different than what happens in a public restroom. Or is it? One does not typically end the session in a restroom with the collection of a urine sample and the requirement that it be handed over to an authority figure standing a few feet away. The Court may have been correct when it equated typical restroom behavior and the amount of privacy that goes along with it to the collection of urine samples under the District's Policy, but there were no behavioral and social science data to prove the accuracy of its assumption.

The Actons had another concern. They were worried that the test procedure and results might invade their son's privacy. Specifically, it would force their son to reveal, at the time of testing, what legal medications he was taking, which would suggest medical conditions he might have. The need to notify the testing laboratory of the medications their son was taking was necessary to avoid a false positive result (an indication of illegal drug use when in fact none had occurred). Female athletes, if required to disclose medications, ran the risk of revealing their sexual activity if they were taking birth control pills or medications related to pregnancy. The Court, however, did not think that there was cause for much concern because only commonly abused drugs were tested for, only a limited group of school officials were told the results, and telling the testers what medications were being taken was not a significant invasion of privacy. Besides, the Court reasoned, there was nothing to stop a student athlete or parent from seeking a more confidential means of notifying the lab directly about prescribed medications without telling the school.

Vernonia's Interest in Conducting the Search

The fact that the Court decided that student athletes had a lowered expectation of privacy than other students and that the testing program was not a significant invasion of privacy was not enough for the Court to say that testing student athletes for drugs was constitutional. The Court still had to determine whether the District had a legitimate and compelling need to administer drug tests to student athletes and if this need outweighed the student athletes' privacy interests.

The Court began its analysis by noting that student athletes are admired in our schools and communities. They then reiterated the District's observations that drug use and disciplinary problems increased dramatically during the mid-1980s, and that student athletes were the leaders of the drug culture. Is this causal chain about student athletes and other students' drug use likely to be accurate? The social science literature is replete with studies demonstrating that athletes serve as important role models for children, particularly among African-American children (e.g., Assibey-Mensah, 1997; Drummond, Senterfitt, & Fountain, 1999). However, the social science literature is devoid of any evidence that students consider *student* athletes as their role models or imitate them. When it comes to using drugs, the most important influence on a child's behavior appears to be the child's peers (National Institute on Drug Abuse, 1991; U.S. Department of Education, 1990). In a study of 2,100 junior high school students, for example, researchers found that students were offered drugs most often by close relations, such as same-sex friends, romantic partners, brothers, and cousins (Trost, Langan, & Kellar-

Guenther, 1999). Other researchers found that the best predictor of an adolescent's drug use was drug use among the adolescent's friends (Pruitt, Kingery, Mirzaee, Heuberger, & Hurley, 1991). Not all researchers, however, share the view that peer influence is the greatest contributing factor to an adolescent's drug use. For example, Bauman and Ennett (1994) argued that researchers have ignored the roles that friendship selection and the psychological phenomena of projection play in drug use. Friendship selection suggests that, rather than non-drug-using adolescents coming under the influence of drug-using peers, drug users seek out other drug users as friends, and non-drug-users seek out other non-drug-users as friends. Projection occurs when a person attributes his or her own behavior to another. In this circumstance, a drug user is likely to report that his or her friends use drugs even if the friends do not use drugs. This would produce a high but misleading correlation between an adolescent's drug use and drug use by his or her friends. Bauman and Ennett (1994) recommended that researchers use the more sophisticated technique of social network analysis (whereby peer groups are identified through a more thorough questioning procedure) rather than simple surveys to determine the real influences of adolescent drug use. Nevertheless, the majority of the research on adolescent drug use suggests that unless nonathletes have athletes as close relations or as friends who offer them drugs, they are unlikely to accept the invitation to use drugs from a substance-abusing athlete.

The District was also concerned that the student athletes would be injured by their drug use. According to the District, this was a particularly dangerous state of affairs. If student athletes were high on drugs while playing a sport, they might injure themselves or others. The Court did not have to make any assumptions regarding the dangers that drug abuse poses for young people, and student athletes in particular. They considered and accepted the scientific evidence that drugs have a deleterious effect on motivation, memory, judgment, reaction time, coordination, and performance.

Researchers have found that marijuana, for example, impairs reasoning in complex situations (Bourassa, 1977) and significantly impairs time perception, reaction time, and memory (Pihl & Sigal, 1978). Many other drugs, including over-the-counter and prescription medications, have deleterious effects on cardiovascular performance and judgment (Schwenk, 1997). Other researchers are developing evidence for the existence of a link between substance abuse and learning disabilities (Brook, Cohen, & Brook, 1998). Although the evidence for this association is not conclusive, researchers believe that the learning disability is a product of a drug's adverse effect on brain metabolism and psychological and emotional functioning (Brook et al., 1998; Brown, Tapert, Granholm, & Delis, 2000). If the drugs are not directly producing the learning disability, their affect on the drug user's judgment in choosing his or her associates might be. That is, students who use drugs tend to hang out with other kids who use drugs, and their behavior is often interpreted as antisocial (Brook et al., 1998). When combined with the declining academic performance that typically accompanies drug use, children are often classified as suffering from a learning disability (Hawkins, Catalano, & Miller, 1992).

All sports to some degree depend on effective, unimpaired psychological and physiological functioning. If either of these functions is adversely affected by drugs, serious injury could result. The trial court also took into account the testimony of Vernonia's high school coaches, teachers, administrators, parents, and students to determine if the link between impaired functioning, injury, and drug use existed. The problem in using these accounts was that, although they may have been accurate reports, they were not supported by objective evidence. They were anecdotal—personal accounts of what a teacher or coach saw a student or group of students say or do in school. The Court had no direct evidence that the students' drug use was the cause for the behavioral problems that the District was experiencing.

Outside of actually witnessing someone take drugs, can a layperson recognize drug use and distinguish it from other types of behavior? The Supreme Court did not seem so sure when it wrote that "spotting and bringing to account drug abuse" was a "diversionary duty" for school teachers and was a task for which they are "ill-prepared." More alarming, physicians have demonstrated that they are ill prepared to diagnose substance abuse in patients. In the most comprehensive survey conducted to date on how doctors diagnose substance-abusing patients, the National Center on Addiction and Substance Abuse (NCASA) reported that 94% of primary-care physicians failed to diagnose substance abuse when presented with an adult showing early signs of alcoholism. When pediatricians were presented with a description of a teenager showing classic symptoms of drug abuse, 41% failed to make the correct diagnosis (NCASA Report, 2000). Another significant finding from the study points to the lack of confidence physicians have in their ability to diagnose either alcoholism or drug abuse. Only 20% felt they were "very prepared" to diagnose alcoholism, and only 17% felt "very prepared" to diagnose illegal drug use. In a survey of about 1,400 drug-addicted patients, 45% reported their physicians were unaware of their drug abuse (Saitz, Mulvey, Plough, & Samet, 1997). Clearly, recognizing drug abuse in others is a specialized skill that even trained health care professionals have difficulty doing. Expecting teachers and school administrators to do likewise may be unreasonable, and relying on their reports may be unreliable.

In another reason for justifying the testing program, the District reported that the number of students who were referred for disciplinary problems had doubled over just a few years. This is actuarial (statistical) evidence. One could go back and confirm this from the school's records. What one does not know is the connection between the increase in referrals and an increase in drug use. Teachers may have been making more referrals because they were told to crack down on disruptive behavior generally. In addition, no mention is made if the students referred for discipline were even the subjects of the testing program (i.e., because they were student athletes). Recall that it was critical to the Court's opinion, to justify the testing of student athletes, that these athletes be identified as the leaders of the drug culture in Vernonia's schools. If, as the District concluded, the increase in disciplinary problems was directly related to student-athlete drug use, then it must logically follow that there was an increase in the number of athletes who were referred for discipline. No evidence suggesting this connection was mentioned in the Court's opinion.

This is not to say that evidence does not exist or could not be gathered. For example, two psychologists (Eccles & Barber, 1999) have followed over 1,200 high school students for 6 years. They found that high school athletes were indeed more likely to abuse drugs and alcohol than were students who participated in other extracurricular activities. However, participation in athletics was not associated with other behavioral problems, such as truancy or dropping out of school. The Court's reasoning for its opinion would have been more accurate had these types of behavioral and social facts been available at the time of its ruling. Unfortunately, justice cannot always wait for relevant research to be conducted (see chap. 10, this volume).

This leads us to what is perhaps the most fundamental question of all: Are drug-testing policies an effective way to reduce drug use and protect schools? These policies are really too new for social scientists to have reached definitive conclusions. On a positive note, scientists have found that requiring drug offenders to adhere to a total abstinence policy, with known consequences if they should be caught using again, is effective for preventing future criminal conduct (Torres, 1997). But a supervision policy designed for convicted drug offenders is a far cry from a drug-testing policy for students. Social scientists will need to collect data concerning the effectiveness and effects of drug testing in schools.

Another interesting point is that the high school personnel who testified about the severity of the drug problem in Vernonia were referring to the behaviors of high school students. James Acton, who made the complaint, was not in high school, but in grade school. The only evidence of a drug problem in the grade school was the principal's contention that the drug problems he witnessed in the high school did not begin there. He testified that the problems began in grade school. As one of the Supreme Court justices acknowledged, there may be a drug problem in the grade school, but "one would not know it from this record." Nevertheless, the majority of the Court ruled that James Acton is subject to drug testing based on the bad behavior of high school students. Regrettably, social and behavioral facts about drug abuse in junior high school and primary school were assumed and not proven.

In finding that the school's interest in the drug-testing policy was compelling, the Court also considered the fact that the drug-testing program was not the first choice of the District as a means for fighting its drug problem. The District tried to intervene by offering special classes, bringing in guest speakers, performing skits, and even using a drug-sniffing dog. These efforts failed and the disciplinary problem got worse. Teachers were observing more drug use and drug glamorization. The trial court described Vernonia's schools as being in a state of rebellion.

Once the drug-testing policy was formally considered, the District gave parents an opportunity to voice their concerns during a special meeting where the testing program was discussed. Parental approval was unanimous, and the Court noted that only the Actons objected to the Policy. The Court used this lack of objection as evidence to indicate that the program had the wide support of the parents. Are comments made at parent–administration meetings really an accurate way to measure parental attitudes? The fact that there were no objections at the meeting cannot be interpreted to mean that there were none. For example, the meeting may have been stacked in favor of the testing proposal because only those parents who were strongly supportive of the drug tests were in attendance. In addition, parents who attended the meeting and did have objections to the proposed Policy may have felt too intimidated to speak out in opposition in front of so many supporters of the program. Some parents may have feared that by publicly opposing a plan to fight drugs they would be perceived by other parents as soft on drugs or not caring about drug use.

A failure to comment or to make an objection under such circumstances is actually consistent with what behavioral and social research has taught us about self-disclosure (Jourard, 1964). That is, people tend to disclose as much, or as little, about themselves as others disclose of themselves. This is known as disclosure reciprocity (Berg, 1987; Reis & Shaver, 1988). When parents who supported the drug-testing program heard other parents speak in favor of it, they may have been prompted to show their support for testing athletes as well. Conversely, parents who were against the Policy, realizing they were apparently part of a small minority at the meeting, may have chosen not to disclose their position or their reasons for holding their position.

Another problem is that there was no scientifically valid survey or poll taken to gauge parental reaction within the District. One does not know if the self-selected group of parents who chose to attend the District's meeting concerning the proposed policy accurately represented the entire population of the school's parents. Only a survey of all parents or a survey of a random sample of all parents would accurately represent parental attitudes toward the Policy. The meeting, therefore, was an inadequate means for gauging parental attitudes toward the Policy, and the response at the meeting did not qualify as a valid indicator of those attitudes.

Finally, even if the parental attitudes were accurately represented at the meeting, they may not have reflected the attitudes of the student athletes. McKinney (1998) asked parents of young children how important they felt privacy was for their child. The parents did not think it very important at all. They were more likely to think of privacy in spatial terms than they were to acknowledge their child's need for body privacy, and they placed little value on mental privacy (McKinney, 1998). When children sought privacy, parents interpreted their child's motivation in largely negative terms (McKinney, 1998). Although these results come from a study of very young children, such parental perceptions of children's privacy needs may persist, which may explain why no parents objected at the school meeting when the testing plan was discussed.

The Court then turned the discussion away from Vernonia's drug problem to the larger drug problem facing all of America. Here it relied on the behavioral and social knowledge regarding the dangers of drugs and the negative effects that drug abuse is having on our society. It noted the importance of our nation's fight against the importation of drugs and referred to scientific research that described the special vulnerability children have to drug abuse. It also was concerned about the effects that drugs had on nonusing students and teachers; they would suffer as well from having to learn and teach in drug-infested schools. Thus, the Court concluded that the District had a legitimate and compelling need to introduce a drug-testing program to its schools.

The Resolution to the Legal Issue

The Court was convinced that the Vernonia School District suffered from severe disciplinary problems fueled by drugs and led by athletes. That drugs are harmful to the physical and psychological well-being of children, particularly student athletes, was reinforced with behavioral and social science facts. The District had proved to the Court's satisfaction that there was a compelling, legitimate interest in testing the student athletes for drugs. Combined with the District's role as a temporary guardian and the Court's belief that student athletes had a lowered expectation of privacy, the Court ruled that the drug tests were reasonable.

Testing of Other Substances

The ruling in this case may suggest that the Court has opened the door for allowing students to be tested for other substances (e.g., excessive fat or sugar consumption). This may be, but remember the Court went to some lengths to satisfy itself that there was adequate behavioral and social knowledge to support its decision. Similar kinds of evidence would be necessary for the Court to allow testing for excess sugar consumption, for example. It may be hard on teeth, but is there behavioral information to show that the adverse effects of eating excessive amounts of sugar provide a compelling justification for state intervention? We doubt that given the present state of scientific knowledge the court would find such a state policy to be based on a compelling state interest.

It is less clear what would happen if the District decided to test for other substances or conditions for which scientific research has proved deleterious effects (e.g., AIDS or other sexually transmitted diseases or the number one killer in America, tobacco). Surely the government's interest in fighting the many diseases caused by tobacco and controlling the enormous economic costs that these diseases inflict is arguably compelling, and the harm that tobacco can do to the developing child is beyond dispute. In fact, some school districts are now screening for tobacco in their drug tests (e.g., *Joy v. Penn-Harris-Madison*, 2000), and students have been suspended for testing positive on tobacco. Like the District's Policy, these testing programs have been upheld by the courts (e.g., *Todd v. Rush*, 1998).

Testing of Other Groups

The District limited its Policy to student athletes because it believed that this group was particularly vulnerable to the adverse effects of drugs and they were the apparent leaders of the local drug culture. Could the Policy be applied to the testing of other groups (e.g., honor students) if they were identified as leaders of the drug culture in some school? There might be a compelling governmental interest to protect our nation's brightest students from the ravages of drug abuse. It might be argued that Merit Scholars have a diminished expectation of privacy because many of them are already singled out for special testing. They may suffer just as serious an injury working in the chemistry lab or working on a science project while high on drugs as a student athlete is likely to suffer on the playing field. Maybe students who take woodworking or automotive repair classes can also be singled out for testing under the Court's rationale. Indeed, the research on drug abuse, as noted earlier, does provide a compelling rationale for stopping its use among all students.

In Rush County, Indiana, this has already happened. School officials there have introduced a random drug-testing policy for all students who wish to participate in any extracurricular activity and for students who drive to school. Using Vernonia as a model, this school district designed a program that would extend drug testing to more students. The Supreme Court declined to hear an appeal of a case that upheld the policy, which left the policy in force (*Todd v. Rush*, 1998). In *Joy v. Penn-Harris-Madison* (2000) a similar policy was upheld by an appellate court. An interesting facet to this case was the admission by school officials that their goal was to have eventually a policy under which all students would be subjected to testing. The school officials informed the Court that they fully expected to appear before them again arguing for such a policy in the near future.

Finally, students who opposed drug testing experienced a temporary victory in *Earls v. Tecumseh* (2001) in Oklahoma. An appellate court ruled that Tecumseh's School District's drug-testing policy was unconstitutional primarily because the school district failed to prove that the district suffered from a real drug problem of the sort experienced in Vernonia. The court in this case criticized the district's evidence of a drug problem as scant and anecdotal, concluding that the school district lacked a compelling interest to test students. The Supreme Court took this case on appeal, however, and overturned the appellate court. The Court ruled that schools are indeed allowed to test any student who wishes to participate in any extracurricular activity. The Court reasoned that the seriousness of the nation's drug problem and the school's responsibility (in its quasi-parental role) for the discipline, health, and safety of the students outweighed the students' expectation of privacy (*Pottawatomie v. Earls*, 2002). Lest students think that school administrators are targeting only them, The Knox County Board of Education in Tennessee requires teachers, principals, and secretaries, among others, to be subject to mandatory drug testing as well. These jobs are considered "safety sensitive" such that if a person holding one of these positions was abusing drugs, that person might pose a danger to the welfare of students and others (*Knox v. Knox*, 1998).

[handwritten margin note: Court overturned Appelate ruling against drug testing]

CHAPTER'S LESSON

The lesson of this chapter, namely that behavioral and social facts are critical to legal decision making, is exemplified every day in our courts, legislatures, and administrative agencies (e.g., chap. 5, this volume). After all, if law is about regulating human behavior, it is only logical that the legal decision makers will have a critical need for accurate information about that behavior.

REFERENCES

Assibey-Mensah, G. O. (1997). Role models and youth development: Evidence and lessons from the perceptions of African-American male youth. *Western Journal of Black Studies, 21*, 242–252.

Bauman, K. E., & Ennett, S. T. (1994). Peer influence on adolescent drug use. *American Psychologist, 49*, 820–822.

Berg, J. H. (1987). Responsiveness and self-disclosure. In V. J. Derlega & J. H. Berg (Eds.), *Self-disclosure: Theory, research, and therapy*. New York: Plenum Press.

Bourassa, M. (1977). The effect of marijuana on judgement and analogical reasoning. *International Review of Applied Psychology, 26*, 21–29.

Brook, J. S., Cohen, P., & Brook, D. W. (1998). Longitudinal study of co-occurring psychiatric disorders and substance use. *Journal of the Academy of Child and Adolescent Psychiatry, 37*, 322–330.

Brown, S. A., Tapert, S. F., Granholm, E., & Delis, D. C. (2000). Neurocognitive functioning of adolescents: Effects of protracted alcohol use. *Alcoholism, Clinical and Experimental Research, 24,* 164–171.

Coombs, R. H., & Coombs, C. J. (1991). The impact of drug testing on the morale and well-being of mandatory participants. *International Journal of the Addictions, 26,* 981–992.

Coombs, R. H., & Ryan, F. J. (1990). Drug testing effectiveness in identifying and preventing drug use. *American Journal of Drug & Alcohol Abuse, 16,* 173–184.

Drummond, R. J., Senterfitt, H., & Fountain, C. (1999). Role models of urban minority students. *Psychological Reports, 84,* 181–182.

Earls v. Tecumseh, 242 F. 3d. 1264 (2001).

Eccles, J. S., & Barber, B. L. (1999). Student council, volunteering, basketball, or marching band: What kind of extracurricular activity involvement matters? *Journal of Adolescent Research, 14,* 10–43.

Hamilton, L. S., & Stone, R. W. (1990). Student attitudes toward drug testing of college athletes. *The Physical Educator, 47,* 33–37.

Hawkins, J. D., Catalano, R. F., & Miller, J. Y. (1992). Risk and protective factors for alcohol and other drug problems in adolescence and early adulthood: Implications for substance abuse prevention. *Psychological Bulletin, 112,* 64–105.

Issari, P., & Coombs, R. H. (1998). Women, drug use, and drug testing: The case of the intercollegiate athlete. *Journal of Sports and Social Issues, 22,* 153–169.

Jourard, S. M. (1964). *The transparent self.* Princeton, NJ: Van Norstrand.

Joy v. Penn-Harris-Madison, 212 F. 3d. 1052 (2000).

Knox v. Knox, 528 U.S. 812 (1998).

Marshall, N. J. (1974). Dimensions of privacy preferences. *Multivariate Behavioral Research, 9,* 255–271.

McKinney, K. D. (1998). Space, body, and mind: Parental perceptions of children's privacy needs. *Journal of Family Issues, 19,* 75–100.

National Center on Addiction and Substance Abuse Report. (2000). *Missed opportunity: The CASA national survey of primary care physicians and patients.* New York: Author.

National Institute on Drug Abuse. (1991). *Drug abuse and drug abuse research: The third triennial report to Congress from the Secretary, Department of Health and Human Services.* Rockville, MD: U.S. Department of Health and Human Services.

O'Reilly, J., & Sales, B. (1987). Privacy for the institutionalized mentally ill: Are court-ordered standards effective? *Law and Human Behavior, 11,* 41–53.

Pedersen, D. M. (1979). Dimensions of privacy. *Perceptual and Motor Skills, 48,* 1291–1297.

Pedersen, D. M. (1982). Personality correlates of privacy. *The Journal of Psychology, 112,* 11–14.

Pedersen, D. M. (1987). Relationship of personality to privacy preferences. *Journal of Social Behavior and Personality, 2,* 267–274.

Pihl, R. O., & Sigal, H. (1978). Motivation levels and the marijuana high. *Journal of Abnormal Psychology, 87,* 280–285.

Pottawatomie v. Earls, 536 U.S. 822 (2002).

Pruitt, B. E., Kingery, P. M., Mirzaee, E., Heuberger, G., & Hurley, R. S. (1991). Peer influence and drug use among adolescents in rural areas. *Journal of Drug Education, 21,* 1–11.

Reis, H. T., & Shaver, P. (1988). Intimacy as an interpersonal process. In S. Duck (Ed.), *Handbook of personal relationships: Theory, relationships, and interventions.* Chichester, England: Wiley.

Saitz, R., Mulvey, K. P., Plough, A., & Samet, J. H. (1997). Physician unawareness of serious substance abuse. *American Journal of Alcohol Abuse, 23,* 343–354.

Schwenk, T. L. (1997). Psychoactive drugs and athletic performance. *Physician & Sports Medicine, 25,* 32–44.

Stewart, W. P., & Cole, D. N. (2001). Number of encounters and experience quality in Grand Canyon backcountry: Consistently negative and weak relationships. *Journal of Leisure Research, 33,* 106–120.

Sujak, D. A., Villanova, P., & Daly, J. P. (1995). The effects of drug-testing program characteristics on applicants' attitudes toward potential employment. *Journal of Psychology, 129,* 401–416.

Todd v. Rush, 133 F. 3d. 984 (1998).

Torres, S. (1997). An effective supervision strategy for substance-abusing offenders. *Federal Probation, 61,* 38–44.

Trost, M. R., Langan, E. J., & Kellar-Guenther, Y. (1999). Not everyone listens when you "just say no": Drug resistance in relational context. *Journal of Applied Communication Research, 27,* 120–138.

U.S. Department of Education. (1990). *A parent's guide to prevention.* Washington, DC: U.S. Government Printing Office.

Vernonia School District v. Acton, 515 U.S. 646 (1995).

Westin, A. (1967). *Privacy and freedom.* New York: Atheneum.

3

MULTIPLE SOURCES OF
FACTUAL KNOWLEDGE

EXAMPLE: ABORTION

In 1973, the U.S. Supreme Court in *Roe v. Wade* granted women the right to have abortions under certain conditions. The Court's decision addressed one of the most divisive issues in our nation today. Americans who feel passionately about protecting the life of the unborn child have worked hard to eliminate the right to an abortion or to at least place restrictions on it. Some of these efforts have been successful at the state level. For example, some states require women who want abortions during the second trimester of their pregnancy to have the procedure performed in an approved clinic or hospital and do not allow public funds to be used to pay for abortions.

In *Planned Parenthood of Southeastern Pennsylvania v. Casey* (1992), several Pennsylvania Planned Parenthood clinics and physicians challenged a Pennsylvania law that imposed restrictive conditions prior to allowing an abortion. The clinics and doctors argued that these requirements unconstitutionally restricted a woman's right to obtain an abortion. To decide this case, the U.S. Supreme Court had to address several very different types of factual concerns. And to do this, the Court relied on a variety of behavioral and social facts coming from a variety of sources (i.e., disciplines and subareas within disciplines) within the behavioral and social sciences. For example, biomedical facts were used to address the trimester framework of *Roe* and the issue of fetal viability. Behavioral and social facts coming from psychology (cognitive, developmental, and clinical psychology), sociology, and criminology were used to understand four other issues: (a) how information given as part of the informed consent process is likely to affect pregnant adult women and minors who seek an abortion, (b) how a 24-hour waiting period affects a woman's decision-making ability and her psychological well-being, (c) how a spousal notification provision affects a pregnant woman's decision making and psychological well-being, and (d) how parents are likely to influence a pregnant minor's abortion decision.

The lesson of this chapter is that behavioral and social facts that are needed in legal decision making will of necessity have to be drawn from the breadth of the behavioral and social sciences. It is the unique issues in each case that dictate which behavioral and social facts will be used in the particular legal decision.

PLANNED PARENTHOOD OF SOUTHEASTERN PENNSYLVANIA V. CASEY

United States Supreme Court

Liberty finds no refuge in a jurisprudence of doubt. Yet 19 years after our holding in *Roe v. Wade* that the U.S. Constitution protects a woman's right to terminate her pregnancy in its early stages, what constitutes a woman's liberty interest is still questioned. At issue in these cases are several provisions of the Pennsylvania Abortion Control Act (henceforth Act) that require that

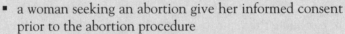

- a woman seeking an abortion give her informed consent prior to the abortion procedure
- a woman wait at least 24 hours between giving her consent and the abortion procedure
- a married woman seeking an abortion sign a statement indicating that she notified her husband of her intended abortion
- a minor obtain the informed consent of one of her parents, or permission of a judge, before she has an abortion

The Act exempts compliance with these requirements in the event of a medical emergency.

Before any of these provisions took effect, five abortion clinics (henceforth Clinics) and one physician representing himself as well as a class of physicians who provide abortion services (henceforth Physicians), brought this suit. They argue that the Act cannot be upheld without overruling *Roe v. Wade*.

The Right to an Abortion

It must be stated at the outset and with clarity that *Roe*'s essential holding, which has three parts, is reaffirmed. First, a woman has the right to choose to have an abortion before viability and to obtain it without undue interference from the state. The concept of viability, as noted in *Roe*, is the time at which there is a realistic possibility of maintaining and nourishing a life outside the womb so that the independent existence of the second life can in reason and all fairness be the object of state protection that now overrides the rights of the woman. Before viability, the state's interests are not strong enough to support a prohibition of abortion or the imposition of a substantial obstacle to the woman's effective right to elect the procedure. Second, the state has the power to restrict abortions after fetal viability if the law contains exceptions for pregnancies that endanger a woman's life or health. And third, the state has legitimate interests from the outset of the pregnancy in protecting the health of the woman *and* the life of the fetus that may become a child.

Protection of the woman's decision to terminate her pregnancy derives from the Due Process Clause of the Fourteenth Amendment to the U.S. Constitution. It declares that no state shall "deprive any person of life, liberty, or property, without due process of law." The controlling word in the case before us is *liberty*, which has been understood to bar certain government actions regardless of the fairness of the procedures used to implement them. It is settled now, as it was when the Court heard arguments in *Roe v. Wade*, that the Constitution places limits on a state's right to interfere with a person's most basic decisions about family and parenthood. The Constitution does not permit a state to forbid a married couple to use contraceptives. That same freedom was later guaranteed, under the Equal Protection Clause, for unmarried couples, and constitutional protection was extended to the sale and distribution of contraceptives.

Men and women of good conscience can disagree, and some always shall disagree, about the profound moral and spiritual implications of terminating a pregnancy, even in its earliest stage. Some of us as individuals find abortion offensive to our most basic principles of morality, but that cannot control this Court's decision. The underlying constitutional issue is whether the state can resolve these philosophic questions in such a definitive way that a woman lacks all choice in the matter, except perhaps in those rare circumstances in which the pregnancy is itself a danger to her own life or health or is the result of rape or incest.

This Court's previous decisions have respected the private realm of family life, which the state cannot enter. These matters, involving the most intimate and personal choices a person may make in a lifetime, choices central to personal dignity and autonomy, are central to the liberty protected by the Fourteenth Amendment. At the heart of liberty is the right to define one's own concept of existence, of meaning, of the universe, and of the mystery of human life. How a person defines these issues is a matter for the person to decide, not the state.

These considerations begin our analysis of the woman's interest in terminating her pregnancy but cannot end it, for this reason: Though the abortion decision may originate within the zone of conscience and belief, it is more than a philosophic exercise. Abortion is a unique act. It is an act fraught with consequences for others: for the woman who must live with the implications of her decision; for the persons who perform and assist in the procedure; for the spouse, family, and society who must confront the knowledge that these procedures exist, procedures some deem nothing short of an act of violence against innocent human life; and depending on one's beliefs, for the life or potential life that is aborted.

Though abortion is conduct, it does not follow that the state is entitled to forbid it in all instances. That is because the liberty of the woman is at stake in a sense unique to the human condition and so unique to the law. The mother who carries a child to full term is subject to anxieties, to physical constraints, to pain that only she must bear. That these sacrifices have from the beginning of the human race been endured by woman with a pride that ennobles her in the eyes of others and gives to the infant a bond of love cannot alone be grounds for the state to insist she make the sacrifice. Her suffering is too intimate and personal for the state to impose, without more justification, its own vision of the woman's role, however dominant that vision has been in the course of our history and our culture. The destiny of the woman must be shaped to a large extent on her own conception of her spiritual imperatives and her place in society.

The Trimester Framework of *Roe*

We have seen how time has overtaken some of *Roe*'s factual assumptions: Advances in maternal health care allow for abortions to be safe to the mother later in pregnancy than was true in 1973, and advances in neonatal care have advanced viability to a point somewhat earlier. But these facts go only to the scheme of time limits on the realization of competing interests, and the divergences from the factual premises of 1973 have no bearing on the validity of *Roe*'s central holding. Viability marks the earliest point at which the state's interest in fetal life is constitutionally adequate to justify a legislative ban on nontherapeutic abortions (i.e., abortions performed for nonmedical reasons). The soundness or unsoundness of that constitutional judgment in no sense turns on whether viability occurs at approximately 28 weeks as was usual at the time of *Roe*, at 23 to 24 weeks as it sometimes does today, or at some moment even slightly earlier in pregnancy as it may if fetal respiratory capacity can somehow be enhanced in the future.

The woman's liberty interest is not so unlimited, however, that from the outset the state cannot show its concern for the life of the unborn and at a later point in fetal development. The line should be drawn at viability so that before that time the woman has a right to choose to terminate her pregnancy.

An Undue Burden Analysis

But even in the earliest stages of pregnancy, the state may enact rules and regulations designed to encourage her to know that there are philosophic and social arguments of great weight that can be brought to bear in favor of continuing the pregnancy to full term and that there are procedures and institutions to allow adoption of unwanted children as well as a certain degree of state assistance if the mother chooses to raise the child herself. The Constitution does not forbid a state, pursuant to democratic processes, from expressing a preference for normal childbirth. It follows that states are free to enact laws to provide a reasonable framework for a woman to make a decision that has such profound and lasting meaning.

Numerous forms of state regulation might have the incidental effect of increasing the cost or decreasing the availability of medical care, whether for abortion or any other medical procedure. The fact that a law that serves a valid purpose, one not designed to strike at the right itself, has the incidental effect of making it more difficult or more expensive to procure an abortion cannot be enough to invalidate it. *Roe v. Wade* recognized the state's important and legitimate interests in preserving and protecting the health of the pregnant woman and in protecting the potentiality of human life. There is a substantial state interest in potential life throughout pregnancy. The very notion that the State has a substantial interest in potential life leads to the conclusion that not all regulations must be deemed unwarranted. Not all burdens on the right to decide whether to terminate a pregnancy will be undue. An undue burden exists, and therefore a provision of law is unconstitutional, if its purpose or effect is to place a substantial obstacle in the path of a woman seeking an abortion before the fetus attains viability.

What is at stake is the woman's right to make the ultimate decision, not a right to be insulated from all others in doing so. Regulations that do no more than create a structural mechanism by which the state, or the parent or guardian of a minor, may express profound respect for the life of the unborn are permitted, if they are not a substantial obstacle to the woman's exercise of the right to choose. Unless it has that effect on her right of choice, a state measure designed to persuade her to choose childbirth over abortion will be upheld if reasonably related to that goal.

The adoption of the undue burden analysis does not disturb the central holding of *Roe v. Wade*. Regardless of whether exceptions are made for particular circumstances, a state may not prohibit any woman from making the ultimate decision to terminate her pregnancy before viability. In promoting its interest in the potentiality of human life, the state may regulate and even forbid abortion subsequent to viability except where it is necessary for the preservation of the life or health of the mother.

The Challenged Provisions in Pennsylvania's Act

Informed Consent

Except in a medical emergency, the Act requires that before performing an abortion a physician inform the woman of the nature of the procedure, the health risks of the abortion and of childbirth, and the probable gestational age of the unborn child. The physician or a qualified nonphysician must inform the woman of the availability of printed materials published by the state describing the fetus and providing information about medical assistance for childbirth, information about child support from the father, and a list of agencies that provide adoption and other services as alternatives to abortion. An abortion may not be performed unless the woman certifies in writing that she has been informed of the availability of these printed materials and has been provided them if she chooses to view them.

As with any medical procedure, the state may require a woman to give her written informed consent to an abortion. In this respect, the Act is unexceptional. But the Clinics and the Physicians challenge the Act's definition of informed consent because it includes the provision of specific information by the doctor. We recognize that there is a substantial government interest in requiring that a woman be apprised of the health risks, including the woman's psychological well-being, of abortion and childbirth. Nor can it be doubted that most women considering an abortion would deem the impact on the fetus relevant, if not dispositive, to the decision. If in attempting to ensure that a woman apprehends the full consequences of her decision, the state may further the legitimate purpose of reducing the risk that a woman may elect an abortion. Not to do so could result in the woman discovering later, with devastating psychological consequences, that her decision was not fully informed. If the information the state requires to be made available to the woman is truthful and not misleading, the requirement may be permissible.

There is no reason why the state may not require doctors to inform a woman seeking an abortion of the availability of materials relating to the consequences to the fetus, even when those consequences have no direct relation to her health. Requiring that the woman be informed of the availability of information relating to fetal development and the assistance available should she decide to carry the pregnancy to full term is a reasonable measure to ensure an informed choice, one that might cause the woman to choose childbirth over abortion. This requirement cannot be considered a substantial obstacle to obtaining an abortion, and it follows, there is no undue burden.

The Act does not require a physician to comply with the informed consent provisions if he or she can demonstrate by a preponderance of the evidence that he or she reasonably believed that furnishing the information would have resulted in a severely adverse effect on the physical or mental health of the patient. Thus, the provision is a reasonable means to ensure that the woman's consent is informed.

The 24-Hour Waiting Period

The Act imposes a 24-hour waiting period between the time when the informed consent information is provided and the abortion is performed. The idea that important decisions will be more informed and deliberate if they follow some period of reflection is not unreasonable, particularly where the Act directs that important information become part of the background of the decision. The Act permits avoidance of the waiting period in the event of a medical emergency, and the evidence shows that in the vast majority of cases, a 24-hour delay does not create any appreciable health risk.

In theory, at least, the waiting period is not an undue burden and is a reasonable measure to implement the state's interest in protecting the life of the unborn. Whether the mandatory 24-hour waiting period is nonetheless invalid because in practice it is a substantial obstacle to a woman's choice to terminate her pregnancy is a closer question. Under the undue burden standard, a state is permitted to enact persuasive measures that favor childbirth over abortion, even if those measures do not further a health interest. And while the waiting period does limit a physician's discretion, that is not, standing alone, a reason to invalidate it. The waiting period does not impose a real health risk, nor is it particularly burdensome. Even the broadest reading of *Roe* has not suggested that there is a constitutional right to abortion on demand. Rather, the right protected by *Roe* is a right to decide to terminate a pregnancy free of undue interference by the state.

Spousal Notification

The Act also provides, except in cases of medical emergency, that no physician shall perform an abortion on a married woman without receiving a signed statement from the woman that she has notified her spouse that she is about to undergo an abortion. The woman has the option of providing an alternative signed statement certifying that her husband is not the man who impregnated her, that her husband could not be located, that the pregnancy is the result of spousal sexual assault that she has reported, or that the woman believes that notifying her husband will cause him or someone else to inflict bodily injury on her. A physician who performs an abortion on a married woman without receiving the appropriate signed statement will have his or her license revoked and is liable to the husband for damages.

The trial court heard the testimony of numerous expert witnesses and made detailed findings of fact, which were supported by studies of domestic violence regarding the effect of this provision.

- The vast majority of women consult their husbands prior to deciding to terminate their pregnancy.
- The bodily injury exception could *not* be invoked by a married woman whose husband, if notified, would, in her

reasonable belief, threaten to (a) publicize her intent to have an abortion to family, friends, or acquaintances; (b) retaliate against her in future child custody or divorce proceedings; (c) inflict psychological intimidation or emotional harm upon her, her children, or other persons; (d) inflict bodily harm on other persons such as children, family members, or other loved ones; or (e) use his control over finances to deprive her of necessary monies for herself or her children.

- Family violence occurs in 2 million families in the United States. This figure, however, is a conservative one that substantially understates the actual number of families affected by domestic violence because battering is usually not reported until it reaches life-threatening proportions. In fact, researchers estimate that one of every two women will be battered at some time in her life.

- A wife may not elect to notify her husband of her intention to have an abortion for a variety of reasons, including the husband's illness, concern about her own health, the imminent failure of the marriage, or the husband's absolute opposition to the abortion.

- Women of all class levels, educational backgrounds, and racial, ethnic, and religious groups are battered.

- Wife battering or abuse can take on many physical and psychological forms. The nature and scope of the battering can cover a broad range of actions and be gruesome and torturous.

- Married women who are victims of battering have been killed by their spouses in Pennsylvania and throughout the United States.

- Battering can often involve a substantial amount of sexual abuse, including marital rape and sexual mutilation.

- In a domestic abuse situation, it is common for the battering husband to also abuse the children in an attempt to coerce the wife.

- Mere notification of pregnancy is frequently a flashpoint for battering and violence within the family. The number of battering incidents is high during the pregnancy and often the worst abuse can be associated with pregnancy. The battering husband may deny parentage and use the pregnancy as an excuse for abuse.

- Secrecy typically shrouds abusive families. Family members are instructed not to tell anyone, especially police or doctors, about the abuse and violence. A battering husband often threatens his wife or her children with further abuse if she tells an outsider of the violence. He will also tell her that nobody will believe her if she tells someone else. A battered woman, therefore, is highly unlikely to disclose the violence against her for fear of retaliation by the abuser.

- Even when confronted directly by medical personnel or other helping professionals, battered women often will not admit to the battering because they have not admitted to themselves that they are battered.
- A woman in a shelter or a "safe house" is not reasonably likely to have bodily harm inflicted upon her by her batterer. However, her attempt to contact her husband could accidentally disclose her whereabouts to him. Her fear of future ramifications would be realistic under the circumstances.
- Marital rape is rarely discussed with others or reported to law enforcement authorities, and of those reported, only a few are prosecuted.
- It is common for battered women to have sexual intercourse with their husbands to avoid being battered. Although this type of coercive sexual activity would be spousal sexual assault as defined by the Act, many women may not consider it to be so and others would fear disbelief.
- The marital rape exception to this Act cannot be claimed by women who are victims of coercive sexual behavior other than penetration.
- The Pennsylvania law, which requires spousal sexual assault to be reported within 90 days, further narrows the class of sexually abused wives who can claim the spousal notification exception because many of these women may have been and may be psychologically unable to discuss or report the rape for several years after the incident.

These findings are supported by studies of domestic violence. Other studies fill in the rest of this troubling picture. Physical violence is only the most visible form of abuse. Psychological abuse, particularly forced social and economic isolation of women, is also common. Many victims of domestic violence remain with their abusers, perhaps because they perceive no superior alternative. Many abused women who find temporary refuge in shelters return to their husbands, in large part because they have no other source of income. Returning to one's abuser can be dangerous. Recent Federal Bureau of Investigation statistics disclose that 8.8% of all homicide victims in the United States are killed by their spouse. Thirty percent of female homicide victims are killed by their male partners.

The limited research that has been conducted with respect to notifying one's husband about an abortion, although involving samples too small to be representative, also supports the trial court's findings of fact. The vast majority of women notify their male partners of their decision to obtain an abortion. In many cases in which married women do not notify their husbands, the pregnancy is the result of an extramarital affair. In cases in which the husband is the father, the primary reason women do not notify their husbands is that the husband and wife are experiencing marital difficulties, often accompanied by incidents of violence.

This information and the trial court's findings reinforce what common sense would suggest. In well-functioning marriages, spouses discuss important intimate decisions such as whether to bear a child. But there are millions of women in this country who are the victims of regular physical and psychological abuse at the hands of their husbands. Should these women become pregnant, they may have very good reasons for not wishing to inform their husbands of their decision to obtain an abortion. Many may have justifiable fears of physical abuse, but may be no less fearful of the consequences of reporting prior abuse to the state.

The spousal notification requirement is thus likely to prevent a significant number of women from obtaining an abortion. It does not merely make abortions a little more difficult or expensive to obtain; for many women, it will impose a substantial obstacle. We must not blind ourselves to the fact that the significant number of women who fear for their safety and the safety of their children are likely to be deterred from procuring an abortion as surely as if Pennsylvania had outlawed abortion in all cases. This requirement is an undue burden, and therefore, invalid.

We recognize that a husband has a deep and proper concern and interest in his wife's pregnancy and in the growth and development of the fetus she is carrying. If this case concerned a state's ability to require the mother to notify the father before taking some action with respect to a living child raised by both, it would be reasonable to conclude that the father's interest in the welfare of the child and the mother's interest are equal. Before birth, however, the issue takes on a very different cast. It is an inescapable biological fact that state regulation with respect to the child a woman is carrying will have a far greater impact on the mother's liberty than on the father's. The effect of state regulation on a woman's protected liberty is doubly deserving of scrutiny in such a case, as the state has touched not only on the private sphere of the family but on the very bodily integrity of the pregnant woman. When the wife and the husband disagree on this decision, the view of only one of the two marriage partners can prevail. Inasmuch as it is the woman who physically bears the child, the balance weighs in her favor. This conclusion rests on the basic nature of marriage and the nature of our Constitution: The marital couple is not an independent entity with a mind and heart of its own but an association of two individuals each with a separate intellectual and emotional makeup. If the right of privacy means anything, it is the right of the individual, married or single, to be free from unwarranted governmental intrusion into matters so fundamentally affecting a person as the decision whether to bear or beget a child. The Constitution protects individuals, men and women alike, from unjustified state interference, even when that interference is enacted into law for the benefit of their spouses.

For the great many women who are victims of abuse inflicted by their husbands, or whose children are the victims of such abuse, a spousal notice requirement enables the husband to wield an effective veto over his wife's decision. Whether the prospect of notification itself deters such women from seeking abortions or whether the husband, through physical force or psychological pressure or economic coercion, prevents his wife from obtaining an abortion until it is too late, the notice requirement will often be tantamount to the veto that is unconstitutional. The women most affected by this law—those who most reasonably fear the consequences of notifying their husbands that they are pregnant—are in the gravest danger. This section of the Pennsylvania Act embodies, therefore, a view of marriage that is repugnant to our present understanding of marriage and of the nature of the rights secured by the Constitution. Women do not lose their constitutionally protected liberty when they marry.

Parental Consent

Except in a medical emergency, an unemancipated young woman under 18 may not obtain an abortion unless she and one of her parents (or guardian) provide informed consent. If neither a parent nor a guardian provides consent, a court may authorize an abortion if it determines that the young woman is mature and capable of giving informed consent, and has in fact given her informed consent, or that the abortion would be in her best interests.

This Court has been over most of this ground before. A state may require a minor seeking an abortion to obtain the consent of a parent or guardian, provided that there is an adequate judicial bypass procedure (e.g., allowing the minor to petition the court for approval). The one-parent consent requirement and judicial bypass procedure in this Act are constitutional. Indeed, some of the provisions regarding informed consent have particular force with respect to minors: The waiting period, for example, may provide the parent or parents of a pregnant young woman the opportunity to consult with her in private and to discuss the consequences of her decision in the context of the values and moral or religious principles of their family.

ANALYSIS AND IMPLICATIONS

The Court was clear in its reaffirmation of *Roe v. Wade's* (1973) "essential holding" that women have the right to terminate their pregnancy before viability and that states may take no action that prevents a woman from doing so. However, once the fetus becomes viable, the state's legitimate interest in protecting life allows it to restrict and even forbid abortions, except in cases in which the woman's health is endangered. Furthermore, because the state's interest in the health of the mother and in protecting fetal life starts at the moment of conception, the state may take such steps that promote life over abortion, so long as those steps do not prevent a woman from exercising her right to an abortion before viability.

Constitutional Right to an Abortion

There were several reasons for the Court's reaffirmation of their *Roe* decision. The first concerns the legal concept of stare decisis. This is the judicial practice of abiding by earlier court decisions, which promotes predictability and confidence in our judicial system. If courts did not practice stare decisis, there could be a new rule of law with every legal decision, even on the same legal matters. Stare decisis is not an unbendable rule, however. Sometimes courts do make wrong decisions. Other times, behavioral and social facts or laws change, making earlier decisions inapplicable in whole or in part to current times. An obvious example is the Dred Scott decision (*Scott v. Sandford*, 1857) in which the Supreme Court ruled that because African Americans were the property of their owners they could not be citizens of the United States, and thus, could not sue for their freedom in federal court. The Civil War effectively overturned this Court opinion (Fehrenbacher, 1978).

Second, although many people believe that *Roe* was wrongly decided and that the Pennsylvania case was an opportunity to overturn it, the Court, in its unexcerpted opinion, pointed out that many Americans had organized the most personal aspects of their lives around the knowledge that the right to choose an abortion was available, should they ever find themselves in a position in which they might need one. The Court also stated that, in effect, the right to abortion expressed in *Roe* was not a haphazard piece of legal reasoning. On the contrary, it was a "reasoned statement, elaborated with great care" that had already been reexamined and reaffirmed two times previously. To overturn it now would simply be to cave in to political pressure and call into question the Court's integrity.

Third, the Court endorsed *Roe*'s analysis of the applicability of the Due Process Clause of the Fourteenth Amendment to the U.S. Constitution. This clause guarantees that the state shall not "deprive any person of life, liberty, or property, without due process of law." A person's liberty interest, which was the basis for providing women with the constitutional right to abortion, has been interpreted to include fundamental rights that are not specifically listed in the Bill of Rights. Among these fundamental rights, according to the Court, is a right to privacy. Marriage, procreation, contraception, family relationships, child rearing, education, and abortion are considered to be private matters into which the state cannot intrude except under very limited and compelling circumstances.

This view comports with our societal desire to keep the government from intruding into our private affairs; Americans are used to their privacy as a matter of tradition. Pregnant women contemplating abortion face a unique, private situation. The state's view of abortion must take second place to the view of the woman because "her suffering is too intimate and personal" and "the mother who carries a child to full term is subject to anxieties, to physical constraints, to pain that only she must bear." Some legal theorists disagree with this view of liberty and privacy. They believe that the only rights to which Americans are entitled are those specifically mentioned in the Bill of Rights. If additional rights are desired, then the Constitution should be amended according to the will of the people, and not by what some judge, or group of judges, decides.

Fourth, the justices were presented with no new medical facts on viability that would justify overruling *Roe*. Even if viability were to occur earlier in a woman's pregnancy because of improvements in medical technology, viability would still be the earliest point at which the state's interest in protecting the fetus and the health of the mother would prevail over the woman's right to an abortion. Thus, a state's interest in protecting life supercedes a woman's right to abortion at the moment life is capable of living outside the womb, unless her life or health is at risk.

In making viability the threshold, the Court discarded the trimester framework outlined in *Roe*. Medical advancements in viability may be modest, but they have been made, and viability does occur "somewhat" sooner in pregnancy than when the trimester framework first was used by the Court. The *Roe* opinion estimated viability at approximately 28 weeks. The Court noted that with improved medical technology viability may occur earlier in pregnancy, but only by about a few weeks. The Court felt that the trimester system was inconsistent with this revised assessment of viability. Thus, the Court hinged its decision, and perhaps its future decisions, on a biomedical fact—when the life of the fetus becomes viable outside of the womb. In 50 or 100 years, it is possible that viability will occur at conception, which would make abortion illegal.

State's Right to Restrict an Abortion

According to the Court, a state has the right to impose regulations on abortion, but only if those regulations do not impose an undue burden on the woman's right to obtain an abortion. If the regulation amounted to an undue burden, which the Court defined as a substantial obstacle in the path of a woman seeking an abortion, then the regulation would be ruled unconstitutional. The fact that a regulation may make an abortion more difficult or expensive to obtain would not be enough to invalidate the regulation. But what does a substantial obstacle mean? The Court decided that Pennsylvania's new regulations were not substantial obstacles for women to overcome if they wanted an abortion, except for the spousal notification requirement. Why? We address this question next.

Pennsylvania's Requirements

Whereas understanding the concepts of trimester and viability involve biomedical facts, understanding and evaluating the Act's regulations involve behavioral and social facts. And as this case illustrates, legal decision makers must sometimes look to multiple sources of behavioral and social information to obtain the needed facts (e.g., psychologists, sociologists, and criminologists). Each of Pennsylvania's restrictions on abortion raised a different set of behavioral and social facts, and assumptions about behavioral and social facts, that required evaluation before the Court could decide whether these restrictions presented a substantial obstacle to a woman's right to an abortion, and hence, were an undue burden.

Informed Consent

As the Court noted, there is a "substantial governmental interest" in making sure that women are aware of the risks of and alternatives to abortion and the facts concerning a particular pregnancy (e.g., the age of the fetus). To advance this interest, a state may require women to sign an informed consent form prior to undergoing an abortion. The purpose of informed consent is to make sure that the woman is fully informed when exercising her right to choose. States may also inform women of the "philosophic and social arguments of great weight" that favor carrying her pregnancy to term. A woman who is made aware by the state of truthful and nonmisleading information concerning her abortion decision, and alternatives to it, is assumed to be making a more rational decision.

The Court was worried that unless a woman was fully informed about her abortion decision (e.g., being told of the abortion's impact on the fetus, the probable age of the fetus, and abortion alternatives) she might suffer "devastating psychological consequence" after an abortion. Do you think the Court was correct in making this psychological assumption? Whether a woman is or will be psychologically devastated is an empirical question.

Although there is no research directly on these questions, there is research on the psychological consequences of abortion on minors and adults. Not surprisingly, minors have been shown to experience more adverse effects than adults, but the effects are much more profound if the minor lacks social support. For example, teens who have had abortions may experience problems concerning sexuality and parenting as they get older if counseling is not provided (Zackus & Wilday, 1987). Different results were found by Zabin, Hirsch, and Emerson (1989) when they compared a group of adolescents who had abortions with a group of adolescents who decided to have their babies. They followed the girls for two years and administered a variety of psychological tests to them every six months. The researchers found that both groups experienced very little negative psychological change over the course of the study. However, minors in the abortion group did do better educationally and economically than the minors who went through with their pregnancies. Finally, recent research has made direct comparisons between minors and adults on their psychological adjustment to abortion (Quinton, Major, & Richards, 2001). One month after their abortion, adolescents reported being both less satisfied and feeling less benefit than adults with their decision to abort, due primarily to less efficient coping strategies and parental conflict. However, when the same women were surveyed again two years later, there were no adjustment differences between adolescents and adults (Quinton et al., 2001). At no time were adolescents found to be more depressed than adults.

The American Psychological Association assembled a panel of experts to look at the effects of abortion on women and concluded that abortion presented no psychological hazards (Adler, David, Major, Roth, Russo, & Wyatt, 1992). However, not all scholars and practitioners agree with this conclusion. For example, some research shows that adult women who have the support of their partners or parents adjust to their abortion very well and fare more favorably than if that support was absent or inadequate (see e.g., Adler, David, Major, Roth, Russo, & Wyatt, 1990; Adler et al., 1992; Bracken, Hachamovitch, & Grossman, 1974; Major, Cozzarelli, Sciacchitano, Cooper, Testa, & Mueller, 1990). In addition, Speckhard and Rue (1992) have proposed that some women may suffer from postabortion syndrome, characterized by, among other things, nightmares, grief, and guilt.

A third perspective is provided by the U.S. Surgeon General. In 1987, when the President of the United States asked the Surgeon General to issue a report on the physical and psychological effects of abortion, the Surgeon General declined, finding that the available research did not permit a conclusion that abortion was either psychologically harmful or harmless (Wilmoth, 1992). An unofficial draft of the report was eventually published (Koop, 1989), and it concluded that although no determination could be made about the psychological consequences of abortion, the medical procedure itself was a safe one.

Another way to judge the informed consent process is to assess its impact on the woman's decision. The Court ruled that the information that states provide to women must be truthful and not misleading. But depending on what information is presented and how it is presented, even truthful information can be misleading. For instance, although the Court did not look to behavioral and social science literature to learn when truthful information may be misleading, the Court could have considered the large psychological literature on the nature of persuasion (for a review, see Wood, 2000). In addition, the psychological literature does indicate that the effects on women of reading antiabortion material is "mild and transient" (Clare & Tyrell, 1994), but that reading antiabortion literature is one of three factors (the decision and coping processes being the other two) that contributed to women's negative responses to their abortion experience (Armsworth, 1996). Further research would be helpful so that we can know whether these negative responses decrease the rationality of one's decision making, and hence, might create an undue burden.

It is also possible that some of the presentation techniques for these antiabortion philosophic and social arguments that states use (i.e., to "persuade the woman to choose childbirth over abortion") might unduly burden the woman's decision process. Do the different presentation approaches (e.g., written materials, verbal presentations, lectures, slides, and video presentations) affect decision making differentially? Does the length or explicitness of the presentation (i.e., showing pictures of aborted fetuses) affect the decision process? Having behavioral and social science answers to questions such as these would improve the Court's ability to assess whether the burden of this particular regulation is undue, and therefore, unconstitutional.

The 24-Hour Waiting Period

Because the Court recognized how difficult the abortion decision is for women and because of a state's profound interest in potential life, the Court held that states may enact regulations to ensure that women make the abortion decision carefully. But how does the Court know that the delay will result in a more thoughtful decision and not unduly chill that decision? For example, if delay is such a good thing for decision making, should we require juries to reach a verdict, wait 24 hours, and then reconsider their verdict before delivering it to the judge? There is little in the psychological literature directly on this point. Cohan, Dunkel-Schetter, and Lydon (1993) interviewed women about their decision to either abort or maintain their pregnancy just before pregnancy testing, 1 day after a positive test, or 4 weeks after. They found that women tended not to change their minds and stuck with their original decision to either abort or carry the pregnancy to term. Of course, the delays associated with this study differ from the waiting period imposed by Pennsylvania because the former were not state-induced delays. It does, however, suggest that the 24-hour delay may have little or no effect on the abortion decision.

Conversely, the psychological literature has consistently shown that the longer the wait, the more stress one is likely to experience (Osuna, 1985). It may not be unreasonable to assume that this is the case with women made to wait 24 hours before they can get their abortion. Whether increased stress resulting from a waiting period is an undue burden was not addressed by the Court. And if it is constitutional for a state to make a woman wait 24 hours before getting an abortion, what is to stop lawmakers from trying to extend the waiting period to 48 hours, 72 hours, or longer? What effects does a longer waiting period have on the decision-making process, and how long is so long that it becomes a constitutionally prohibited undue burden to women seeking an abortion? Research needs to address this issue.

Another potential problem with a waiting period is that it will burden women who live some distance from the clinic or hospital because of increased travel time. They may not be able to explain their prolonged and multiple absences and whereabouts to family members or employers and may thus be prevented from returning to the facility after the 24-hour (or longer) wait. Henshaw (1998) reported data from the Abortion Provider Survey that revealed that 24% of women seeking an abortion at a nonhospital facility must travel at least 50 miles. Eight percent must go more than 100 miles. Multiple trips may also increase their exposure to harassment from antiabortion protestors. For example, 96% of the women entering a New York abortion clinic encountered antiabortion demonstrators with 54% reporting that these protestors attempted to prevent their entrance into the clinic (Cozzarelli & Major, 1998). Research is needed to understand how the burdens of the waiting period will affect a woman's decision-making process under the circumstance noted above.

Finally, should the Court have considered the economic impact of Pennsylvania's measures as a potential undue burden? Although the Court said that a regulation that makes obtaining an abortion more expensive is not an undue burden, there must be a point at which a new regulation could make an abortion prohibitively expensive and thus would be an undue burden. How much extra expense is too much? For a poor woman, an extra day missed from work (while she waits for the 24-hour waiting period to elapse) might prove to be a substantial obstacle. Does the Court's decision have the potential for creating two classes of women, those who can and cannot afford an abortion? A majority of women pay for their abortions themselves because they either have no health insurance, or if they have insurance, they find that their policy does not cover abortion (Henshaw, 1998). In 1993, the average cost of an abortion at an abortion clinic was $296. In a doctor's office it was $410, and in a hospital it was over $1700 (Henshaw, 1998). Once again, behavioral and social research is needed to inform legal decision making in this area.

Spousal Notification

The Court concluded that requiring a woman to notify her spouse of her intention to have an abortion is an undue burden. The Court knew that notification would not be an issue for women in a stable and understanding relationship with their partners. But what about those women who are fearful of their husbands and are in danger of being abused? Spousal notification would give husbands control over their wives' liberty and privacy, which the Court had already decided resides only with the woman. A husband may exercise his parental responsibilities on an equal footing with that of his wife after the birth of their child, but not before.

The court had ample behavioral and social research to conclude that requiring a woman to notify her spouse of her intention to have an abortion is an undue burden. The Court cited empirical studies showing that some women may be in danger of being either physically or psychologically battered by husbands who are either angry about the pregnancy or angry about the decision to abort. Research on male battering of pregnant partners reveals some disturbing statistics. In surveys conducted by Helton (1986) and McCauley (1995), roughly 15% of all pregnant women suffer physical abuse at the hands of their partners. This figure reaches 17% during the last four months of pregnancy (McCauley, 1995). For women whose pregnancy was planned, 7% were likely to experience violence, but if the pregnancy was unplanned, the chances of physical abuse could increase to as much as 20% (Gazmararian, Lazorick, Spitz, Ballard, Saltzman, & Marks, 1996). Moreover, pregnant women are at greater risk for violence than they are for high blood pressure, diabetes, or any other condition for which pregnant women are routinely screened (Gazmararian et al., 1996).

Why men batter, or feel the need to do so, is the object of much research. Condon (1987) has reported that 4% of men feel an urge to "hurt or punish" the fetus (although it must be noted that women feel this urge at twice the rate as men). Some men, particularly in unplanned pregnancies, may feel that a new child will threaten their control over the woman (McCauley, 1995). In relationships characterized by mutual trust and caring, however, abortion decisions do not appear to reach crisis proportions but become part of the "ongoing relational process" between partners (Cotroneo & Krasner, 1997).

In striking down this provision, the Court relied heavily on the behavioral and social research on domestic violence for their facts but also said that this part of their decision represented "commonsense." It certainly appears that the Court supplemented their commonsense understanding from the extensive and conclusive scientific literature.

Parental Consent

Unemancipated minors do not have the same rights as adults under the law. The law presumes that the judgment of these minors is too immature to allow them to make decisions without parental consent. Thus, a minor may be prevented from obtaining an abortion if she cannot obtain the permission of one of her parents (or guardian). But the Court made clear that in those instances in which a minor cannot or does not want to seek the consent of a parent, or believes that the parent will not provide it, the minor must have the opportunity to request a judicial bypass. Here the minor can go before a judge and argue that she should be allowed to obtain an abortion without her parent's consent. If the state provides this opportunity, a parental consent rule is not an undue burden.

Should the Court have considered the effect that parental consent would have on a minor's right to an abortion in the same way they examined the effect of spousal notification on an adult woman's decision making? Might not a minor who lives in an abusive household be at a similar risk as an adult woman who is married to an abusive husband? Is a minor in fear of being beaten any different than a woman who is in fear of being battered? Berenson, San Miguel, and Wilkinson (1992) found that 25% of pregnant teens under 18 years of age had been sexually or physically abused. Worse numbers have been reported by Boyer and Fine (1992). They found that 44% of the adolescent mothers in their study had been raped, and 66% had been sexually abused. These numbers are worse than those reported for pregnant woman, which suggests that the Court ought to reconsider its conclusion that this regulation does not constitute an undue burden.

Is the "judicial bypass" procedure a reasonable solution for minors? It may sound reasonable to legislators and judges, but is it reasonable to expect minors to be aware of the opportunity to seek a judge's approval rather than a parent's or to be able to understand how to navigate through the judicial system to obtain the approval? For example, in states in which parental *notification* (i.e., a minor must notify a parent of her intention to get an abortion) and consent are required, research has shown an increase in births among adolescents. Tomal (1999) examined the effects that parental notification and consent laws had on birth rates for minor (15–17 years old) and nonminor (18–19 years old) teens. She found that both notification and consent laws were significantly related to higher birth rates for both groups of teens. These data suggest that the judicial bypass procedure may not have been realistically usable for teenagers.

The Court focused on at least three behavioral and social fact issues in permitting parental consent. First, the law and the Court assumed that *all* minors lack the necessary cognitive and emotional maturity to make such a momentous decision without consulting with at least one of their parents. Social science research does not support this view. All states have what are called "medical emancipation" statutes (Crosby & English, 1991). These laws allow adolescents to seek and consent to medical services for things like treatment of sexually transmitted diseases without notifying or consulting with a parent. The idea behind these laws is to encourage adolescents to seek care for problems they might otherwise avoid if they had to involve their parents. The states must have believed that adolescents had the ability to make these important decisions or the laws would not have been enacted. Here the social science research backs up the states. In a review of empirical studies that examined the competence of adolescents to make these kinds of decisions, Gittler, Quigley-Rick, and Saks (1990) concluded there is no scientific support for the legal assumption that minors do not have the capacity to make their own health care decisions. In looking at the abortion decision directly, Ambuel and Rappaport (1992) compared the competence of minors and adults (younger than 15 years old to over 21) in thinking about, among other things, either ending or carrying on with their pregnancy. They found that adolescents who were considering abortion in any of the age groups were just as competent as the adults. Their finding supports Lewis's (1987) review of the psychological literature on minors' competence to consent to abortion, which concluded that competence alone was an insufficient justification to restrict a minor's decision to have an abortion.

The second assumption the law makes in requiring parental consent is that parents will act in the minor's best interest. As it turns out, the vast majority of pregnant teens consult with their parents. Zabin, Hirsch, Emerson, and Raymond (1992) reported 91% consulted with a parent or guardian, and 75% of the adolescents in a study by Henshaw and Kost (1992) did the same. More importantly, one study reported that at least 94% of the parents supported their daughter's decision to have an abortion (Henshaw & Kost, 1992). And a review of the research on parental involvement in abortion decisions revealed that 66% to 80% of parents, after adjusting to the news that their child was pregnant, were quite supportive of their daughters (Worthington, Larson, Lyons, Brubaker, Colecchi, Berry, & Morrow, 1991). Involving parents may improve the quality of the adolescent's decision making and may provide important support for the adolescent in coping with her pregnancy, but this research does not address the consequences to those pregnant minors whose parents are nonsupportive.

The third and final assumption is that judges will be capable of deciding (a) whether the minor's decision is informed and whether she has the requisite decision-making capacity to rationally make the abortion decision and understand its consequences—at least to the same extent as an adult or

(b) whether the abortion is in her best interests. The first criterion presents factual issues that require behavioral and social science expertise. The Court cited no research to support their opinions on these points, which is unfortunate because the psychological literature could have presented them with a wealth of information that may have produced a more informed decision. For example, in reviews of a variety of parental involvement laws, it has been found that judges rarely deny a minor's judicial bypass petition to have an abortion (Crosby & English, 1991; Pliner & Yates, 1992). Judges viewed themselves as rubber stamps who felt ill equipped to counsel the minors who appear before them (e.g., hearings in Minnesota last about 10 minutes; 12 minutes in Massachusetts). Even in so brief an encounter, judges have described the minors as agitated, and the whole bypass procedure was seen as burdensome, humiliating, and stressful (Crosby & English, 1991). So do judges have the ability to determine if a minor is mature enough to make an abortion decision on her own? Gathering data on the ability of judges to gauge a minor's competence is not easy because the bypass procedure is closed to the public and the records are confidential. Still, on the basis of the overwhelming rate at which minors' requests are approved and the brevity with which judges conduct the hearings, Pliner and Yates (1992) have argued that this is evidence that judges do not possess the ability to accurately assess a minor's competence.

CHAPTER'S LESSON

To resolve the different issues in this case, the U.S. Supreme Court had to look to facts from multiple sources of expert information. This is a logical result because, as noted in chapter 1, the behavioral and social sciences represent many different disciplines and specialties within disciplines. Although the distinctions between disciplines and specialties are critical for the development of science, they are not so critical for the conduct of legal decision making. The only concern is that the decision maker access the relevant behavioral and social science, and usually this means acquiring it from the multiple scientific sources from which it is derived.

REFERENCES

Adler, N. E., David, H. P., Major, B. N., Roth, S. H., Russo, N. F., & Wyatt, G. E. (1990). Psychological responses after abortion. *Science, 248,* 41–44.

Adler, N. E., David, H. P., Major, B. N., Roth, S. H., Russo, N. F., & Wyatt, G. E. (1992). Psychological factors in abortion: A review. *American Psychologist, 47,* 1194–1204.

Ambuel, B., & Rappaport, J. (1992). Developmental trends in adolescents' psychological and legal competence to consent to abortion. *Law and Human Behavior, 16,* 129–153.

Armsworth, M. W. (1996). Psychological responses to abortion. *Journal of Counseling and Development, 69,* 377–379.

Berenson, A. B., San Miguel, V. V., & Wilkinson, G. S. (1992). Prevalence of physical and sexual assault in pregnant adolescents. *Journal of Adolescent Health, 13,* 466–469.

Boyer, D., & Fine, D. (1992). Sexual abuse as a factor in adolescent pregnancy and child maltreatment. *Family Planning Perspectives, 24,* 4–11, 19.

Bracken, M. B., Hachamovitch, M., & Grossman, G. (1974). The decision to abort and psychological sequelae. *Journal of Nervous and Mental Disease, 158,* 154–162.

Clare, A. W., & Tyrell, J. (1994). Psychiatric aspects of abortion. *Irish Journal of Psychological Medicine, 11,* 92–98.

Cohan, C. L., Dunkel-Schetter, C., & Lydon, J. (1993). Pregnancy decision making: Predictors of early stress and adjustment. *Psychology of Women Quarterly, 17,* 223–239.

Condon, J. T. (1987). "The battered fetus syndrome": Preliminary data on the incidence of the urge to physically abuse the unborn child. *Journal of Nervous and Mental Disease, 175,* 722–725.

Cotroneo, M., & Krasner, B. R. (1997). A study of abortion and problems in decision making. *Journal of Marriage and Family Counseling, 3,* 69–76.

Cozzarelli, C., & Major, B. (1998). The impact of antiabortion activities on women seeking abortions. In L. J Beckman & S. M. Harvey (Eds.), *The new civil war: The psychology, culture, and politics of abortion.* Washington, DC: American Psychological Association.

Crosby, M. C., & English, A. (1991). Mandatory parental involvement/judicial bypass laws: Do they promote adolescents' health? *Journal of Adolescent Health, 12,* 143–147.

Fehrenbacher, D. E. (1978). *The Dred Scott case: Its significance in American law and politics.* New York: Oxford University Press.

Gazmararian, J. A., Lazorick, S., Spitz, A. M., Ballard, T. J., Saltzman, L. E., & Marks, J. S. (1996). Prevalence of violence against pregnant women. *Journal of the American Medical Association, 275,* 1915–1920.

Gittler, J., Quigley-Rick, M., & Saks, M. J. (1990). *Adolescent health care decision making: The law and public policy.* Washington, DC: Carnegie Council on Adolescent Development.

Helton, A. M. (1986). The pregnant battered woman. *Response to the Victimization of Women and Children, 9,* 22–23.

Henshaw, S. K. (1998). Barriers to abortion services. In L. J Beckman & S. M. Harvey (Eds.), *The new civil war: The psychology, culture, and politics of abortion.* Washington, DC: American Psychological Association.

Henshaw, S. K., & Kost, K. (1992). Parental involvement in minors' abortion decisions. *Family Planning Perspectives, 24,* 196–207, 213.

Koop, C. E. (1989). Surgeon General's report: The public health effects of abortion. *Congressional Record,* pp. E906–E909.

Lewis, C. C. (1987). Minors' competence to consent to abortion. *American Psychologist, 42,* 84–88.

Major, B., Cozzarelli, C., Sciacchitano, A. M., Cooper, M. L., Testa, M., & Mueller, P. M. (1990). Perceived social support, self-efficacy, and adjustment to abortion. *Journal of Personality and Social Psychology, 59,* 452–463.

McCauley, J. (1995). The battering syndrome: Prevalence and clinical characteristics of domestic violence. *Annals of Internal Medicine, 123,* 737–746.

Osuna, E. E. (1985). The psychological cost of waiting. *Journal of Mathematical Psychology, 29,* 82–105.

Pliner, A. J., & Yates, S. (1992). Psychological and legal issues in minor's rights to abortion. *Journal of Social Issues, 48,* 203–216.

Planned Parenthood of Southeastern Pennsylvania v. Casey, 505 U.S. 833 (1992).

Quinton, W. J., Major, B., & Richards, C. (2001). Adolescents and adjustment to abortion: Are minors at greater risk? *Psychology, Public Policy, and Law, 7,* 491–514.

Roe v. Wade, 410 U.S. 113 (1973).

Scott v. Sandford, 60 U.S. 393 (1857).

Speckhard, A. C., & Rue, V. M. (1992). Postabortion syndrome: An emerging public health concern. *Journal of Social Issues, 48,* 95–119.

Tomal, A. (1999). Parental involvement laws and minor and non-minor teen abortion and birth rates. *Journal of Family and Economic Issues, 20,* 149–162.

Wilmoth, G. H. (1992). Abortion, public policy, and informed consent legislation. *Journal of Social Issues, 48,* 1–17.

Wood, W. (2000). Attitude change: Persuasion and social influence. *Annual Review of Psychology, 51,* 539–570.

Worthington, E. L., Larson, D. B., Lyons, J. S., Brubaker, M. W., Colecchi, C. A., Berry, J. T., & Morrow, D. (1991). Mandatory parental involvement prior to adolescent abortion. *Journal of Adolescent Health, 12,* 138–142.

Zabin, L. S., Hirsch, M. B., Emerson, M. R. (1989). When urban adolescents choose abortion: Effects on education, psychological status and subsequent pregnancy. *Family Planning Perspectives, 21,* 248–255.

Zabin, L. S., Hirsch, M. B., Emerson, M. R., & Raymond, E. (1992). To whom do inner-city minors talk about their pregnancies? Adolescents' communication with parents and parent surrogates. *Family Planning Perspectives, 24,* 148–154, 173.

Zackus, G., & Wilday, S. (1987). Adolescent abortion option. *Social Work in Health Care, 12,* 77–91.

II

WHY BEHAVIORAL AND SOCIAL FACTUAL KNOWLEDGE IS USED

4

IDENTIFYING AND EVALUATING THE FACTUAL ASSUMPTIONS UNDERLYING LAW

EXAMPLE: SUGGESTIBILITY OF CHILD WITNESSES

Sexual abuse of minors, a horrific crime, seems to be in our national media on a regular basis. We learn of allegations against people who we would immediately classify as criminals, but there are also allegations against clergy and preschool teachers. The case that we present in this chapter is based on an investigation and prosecution of a preschool teacher at a day-care center in New Jersey.

What makes this case so legally interesting is that the prime evidence against the teacher, Margaret Kelly Michaels, was the testimony of the preschool children. The law presumes that children are competent, unbiased witnesses, but this presumption is rebuttable (i.e., refutable). When the New Jersey Supreme Court confronted the testimony of the children against Ms. Michaels, the court gave the defendant a chance to show if there was "some evidence" of the use of suggestive or coercive interview techniques that would make the children's testimony unreliable. If a defendant could meet this relatively low standard, then the prosecution would have to show, by clear and convincing evidence, that the reliability of the children's statements out-weighs the adverse effects of the improper interview techniques.

Behaviorally, this case is also interesting. The law's presumption about the capability of children as witnesses is based on assumptions about children's cognitive abilities and responses to interrogation. How are the legal decision makers to know whether these assumptions are accurate? It is through research by behavioral and social scientists that we learn the facts about behavior and are able to prove the validity or invalidity of the assumptions (Sales, 1983).

That is what occurred in this case. Fifty concerned social scientists filed an amicus brief, a "friend of the court" brief, informing the court about the invalidity of assumptions that law enforcement and the prosecution made in building and prosecuting this case. This research convinced the court that there was a strong likelihood that the testimony of the children was false. The lesson to draw from reading this chapter is that the identification of behavioral and social assumptions, and empirical research to test the validity of these assumptions, is one of the important ways in which behavioral and social science and behavioral and social facts are and should be used by the law.

NEW JERSEY V. MICHAELS

New Jersey Supreme Court

A nursery school teacher was convicted of bizarre acts of sexual abuse against many of the children who had been entrusted to her care. She was sentenced to a long prison term with a substantial period of parole ineligibility. The appellate court reversed the conviction, and ordered that if the state decided to retry the case, a pretrial hearing would be necessary. Its purpose would be to determine whether the testimony of the alleged victims' testimony must be excluded because improper questioning by state investigators had irremediably compromised its reliability.

Facts Leading to Michaels's Arrest and Trial

In September 1984, Margaret Kelly Michaels was hired by Wee Care Day Nursery as a teacher's aide for preschoolers. Located in St. George's Episcopal Church, in Maplewood, New Jersey, Wee Care served approximately 50 families with an enrollment of about 60 children ages 3 to 5.

Michaels, a college senior from Pittsburgh, Pennsylvania, came to New Jersey to pursue an acting career. She responded to an advertisement and was hired by Wee Care, initially as a teacher's aide for preschoolers, then, at the beginning of October, as a teacher. Michaels had no prior experience as a teacher at any level.

Wee Care had staff consisting of eight teachers, numerous aides, and two administrators. The nursery classes for the 3-year-old children were housed in the basement, and the kindergarten class was located on the third floor. During nap time, Michaels, under the supervision of the head teacher and the director, was responsible for about 12 children in one of the basement classrooms. The classroom assigned to Michaels was separated from an adjacent occupied classroom by a vinyl curtain.

During the 7-month period that Michaels worked at Wee Care, she apparently performed satisfactorily. Wee Care never received a complaint about her from staff, children, or parents. According to the state, however, between October 8, 1984, and the date of Michaels's resignation on April 26, 1985, parents and teachers began observing behavioral changes in the children.

On April 26, 1985, the mother of M.P., a 4-year-old in Michaels's nap class, noticed while awakening him for school that he was covered with spots. She took the child to his pediatrician and had him examined. During the examination, a pediatric nurse took M.P.'s temperature rectally. In the presence of the nurse and his mother, M.P. stated, "this is what my teacher does to me at nap time at school." M.P. indicated to the nurse that his teacher, Kelly (the name by which Michaels was known to the children), was the one who took his temperature. M.P. added that Kelly undressed him and took his temperature daily. On further questioning by his mother, M.P. said that Kelly did the same thing to S.R.

The pediatrician then examined M.P. and informed Mrs. P. that the spots were caused by a rash. Mrs. P. did not tell the pediatrician about M.P.'s remarks; consequently, he did not examine M.P.'s rectum. In response to further questioning from his mother after they had returned home, M.P., while rubbing his genitals, stated that "[Kelly] uses the white jean stuff." Although M.P. was unable to tell his mother what the "white jean stuff" was, investigators later found Vaseline in Wee Care's bathroom and white cream in the first-aid kit. During the same conversation, M.P. indicated that Kelly had "hurt" two of his classmates, S.R. and E.N.

M.P.'s mother contacted the New Jersey Division of Youth and Family Services (DYFS) and the director of Wee Care to inform them of her son's disclosures. On May 1, 1985, the Essex County Prosecutor's office received information from DYFS about the alleged sexual abuse at Wee Care. The prosecutor's office assumed investigation of the complaint.

The prosecutor's office interviewed several Wee Care children and their parents, concluding their initial investigation on May 8, 1985. During that period of investigation, Michaels submitted to approximately nine hours of questioning. In addition, Michaels consented to take a lie detector test, which she passed. Extensive additional interviews and examinations of the Wee Care children by the prosecutor's office and DYFS then followed.

Michaels was charged on June 6, 1985, in a three-count indictment involving the alleged sexual abuse of three Wee Care boys. After further investigation, a second indictment was returned July 30, 1985, containing 174 counts of various charges involving 20 Wee Care boys and girls.

After several pretrial hearings, the trial commenced on June 22, 1987, with the bulk of the state's evidence consisting of the children's testimony. That testimony referred extensively to the pretrial statements that had been elicited from the children during the course of the state's investigations. The state introduced limited physical evidence to support the contention that the Wee Care children had been molested.

On April 15, 1988, after 12 days of deliberation, the jury returned guilty verdicts on aggravated sexual assault, sexual assault, endangering the welfare of children, and terroristic threats. The trial court sentenced Michaels to an aggregate term of 47 years of imprisonment with 14 years of parole ineligibility.

The Child Witnesses' Reliability

The focus of this case is on the manner in which the state conducted its investigatory interviews of the children. In particular, this court is asked to consider whether the interview techniques employed by the state could have undermined the reliability of the children's statements and subsequent testimony to the point that a hearing should be held to determine whether either form of evidence should be admitted at retrial.

The question of whether the interviews of the child victims of alleged sexual abuse were unduly suggestive and coercive requires a highly nuanced inquiry into the totality of circumstances surrounding those interviews. The appellate court, which carefully examined the record concerning the investigatory interviews, was concerned over the capacity of the interviewer and the interview process to distort a child's recollection through unduly slanted interrogation techniques. It concluded that certain interview practices are sufficiently coercive or suggestive to alter irremediably the perceptions of the child victims. The appellate court also determined that the children's accusations were founded "upon unreliable perceptions, or memory caused by improper investigative procedures," and that testimony reflecting those accusations could lead to an unfair trial. Accordingly, it held that in the event of a retrial, a pretrial hearing would be required to assess the reliability of the statements and testimony to be presented by those children to determine their admissibility. The state appealed that determination.

Suggestibility of Child Witnesses

Children, as a class, are not to be viewed as inherently suspect witnesses. Age per se cannot render a witness incompetent, and absent a strong showing of abnormality, psychological testing of alleged child victims of sexual abuse is not required or even allowed to determine the credibility of the child-victim witnesses. But under certain circumstances, children's accounts of sexual abuse can be highly reliable. Common experience teaches that children generate special concerns because of their vulnerability, immaturity, and impressionability, and our laws have recognized and attempted to accommodate those concerns, particularly in the area of child sexual abuse.

The broad question of whether children as a class are more or less susceptible to suggestion than adults is one that need not be definitively answered in order to resolve the central issue in this case. The issue is whether the interview techniques used by the state in this case were so coercive or suggestive that they had a capacity to distort substantially the children's recollections of actual events and thus compromise the reliability of the children's statements and testimony based on their recollections.

The investigative interview is a crucial, perhaps determinative, moment in a child-sex-abuse case. A decision to prosecute a case of child sexual abuse often hinges on the information elicited in the initial investigatory interviews with alleged victims that is carried out by social workers or police investigators. That an investigatory interview of a young child can be coercive or suggestive and thus shape the child's responses is generally accepted. If a child's recollection of events has been molded by an interrogation, that influence undermines the reliability of the child's responses as an accurate recollection of actual events.

A variety of factors bear on the kinds of interrogation that can affect the reliability of a child's statements concerning sexual abuse. A fairly wide consensus exists among experts, scholars, and practitioners concerning improper interrogation techniques. They argue that among the factors that can undermine the neutrality of an interview and create undue suggestiveness are a lack of investigatory independence, the pursuit by the interviewer of a preconceived notion of what has happened to the child, the use of leading questions, and a lack of control for outside influences on the child's statements such as previous conversations with parents or peers.

The use of incessantly repeated questions also adds a manipulative element to an interview. When a child is asked a question and gives an answer and the question is immediately asked again, the child's normal reaction is to assume that the first answer was wrong or displeasing to the adult questioner. The insidious effects of repeated questioning are even more pronounced when the questions themselves over time suggest information to the children.

The explicit vilification or criticism of the person charged with wrongdoing is another factor that can induce a child to believe abuse has occurred. Similarly, an interviewer's bias with respect to a suspected person's guilt or innocence can have a marked effect on the accuracy of a child's statements. The transmission of suggestion can also be subtly communicated to children through the interviewer's tone of voice, mild threats, praise, cajoling, bribes and rewards, as well as resort to peer pressure.

The appellate court recognized the considerable authority supporting the deleterious impact improper interrogation can have on a child's memory. Other courts have recognized that once tainted, the distortion of the child's memory is irremediable. The debilitating impact of improper interrogation has an even more pronounced effect among young children.

The critical influence that can be exerted by interview techniques is also supported by the literature that generally addresses the reliability of children's memories. Those studies stress the importance of proper interview techniques as a predicate for eliciting accurate and consistent recollection.

The conclusion that improper interrogations generate a significant risk of corrupting the memories of young children is confirmed by government and law enforcement agencies, which have adopted standards for conducting interviews designed to overcome the dangers stemming from the improper interrogation of young children. The National Center for the Prosecution of Child Abuse, in cooperation with the National District Attorney's Association and the American Prosecutor's Research Institute, has adopted protocols to serve as standards for the proper interrogation of suspected child-abuse victims. Those interview guidelines require that an interviewer remain "open, neutral, and objective"; avoid asking leading questions; never threaten a child or try to force a reluctant child to talk; and refrain from telling a child what others, especially other children, have reported. The New Jersey Governor's Task Force on Child Abuse and Neglect has also promulgated guidelines. It states that the interviewer should attempt to elicit a child's feelings about the alleged offender but that the interviewer should not speak negatively about that person. Further, multiple interviews with various interviewers should be avoided.

We therefore determine that a sufficient consensus exists within the academic, professional, and law enforcement communities, confirmed in varying degrees by courts, to warrant the conclusion that the use of coercive or highly suggestive interrogation techniques can create a significant risk that the interrogation itself will distort the child's recollection of events, thereby undermining the reliability of the statements and subsequent testimony concerning such events.

Interviews Conducted in This Case

Were the interrogations conducted in this case so suggestive or coercive that they created a substantial risk that the statements and testimony thereby elicited lack sufficient reliability to justify their admission at trial? The interrogations undertaken in the course of this case used most, if not all, of the practices that are disfavored or condemned by experts, law enforcement authorities and government agencies.

The initial investigation giving rise to defendant's prosecution was sparked by a child volunteering that his teacher, Kelly, had taken his temperature rectally and that she had done so to other children. However, the overwhelming majority of the interviews and interrogations did not arise from the spontaneous recollections that are generally considered to be most reliable. Few, if any, of the children volunteered information that directly implicated the defendant. Further, none of the child victims related incidents of actual sexual abuse to their interviewers using *free recall* (a technique used in memory research whereby an individual is free to recall material in any order). Additionally, few of the children provided any telltale details of the alleged abuse, although they were repeatedly prompted to do so by the investigators.

The investigators were not trained in interviewing young children. The earliest interviews with children were not recorded and in some instances the original notes were destroyed. As a matter of sound interviewing methodology, nearly all experts agree that initial interviews should be videotaped. In this case, fully one half of the earliest interviews at issue here were not audiotaped or videotaped. The record indicates that the DYFS investigator did not begin taping interviews until June 19, 1985. In addition, only 39 interviews with 34 children, or about one half of those interviewed by DYFS, were transcribed.

Many of the interviewers demonstrated ineptness in dealing with the challenges presented by preschoolers and displayed their frustration with the children. Almost all of the interrogations conducted in the course of the investigation revealed an obvious lack of impartiality on the part of the interviewer. One investigator, who conducted the majority of the interviews with the children, stated that his interview techniques had been based on the premise that the "interview process is in essence the beginning of the healing process." He considered it his "professional and ethical responsibility to alleviate whatever anxiety has arisen as a result of what happened to them." A lack of objectivity was indicated by the interviewer's failure to pursue any alternative hypothesis that might contradict an assumption of the defendant's guilt and a failure to challenge or probe seemingly outlandish statements made by the children.

The record is replete with instances in which children were asked blatantly leading questions that furnished information the children themselves had not mentioned. All but 5 of the 34 children interviewed were asked questions that indicated or strongly suggested that perverse sexual acts had in fact occurred. Seventeen of the children, fully one half of the 34, were asked questions that involved references to urination, defecation, consumption of human wastes, and oral sexual contacts. Twenty-three of the 34 children were asked questions that suggested the occurrence of nudity. In addition, many of the children, some over the course of nearly two years leading up to trial, were subjected to repeated, almost incessant, interrogation. Some children were reinterviewed at the urging of their parents.

The record of the investigative interviews discloses the use of mild threats, cajoling, and bribing. Positive reinforcement was given when children made inculpatory statements, whereas negative reinforcement was expressed when children denied being abused or made exculpatory statements.

Throughout the record, the element of *vilification* appears. Fifteen of the 34 children were told at one time or another that Kelly was in jail because she had done bad things to children, with the children being encouraged to keep Kelly in jail. For example, they were told that the investigators "needed their help" and that they could be "little detectives." Children were also introduced to the police officer who had arrested the defendant and were shown the handcuffs used during her arrest; mock police badges were given to children who cooperated.

In addition, no effort was made to avoid outside information that could influence and affect the recollection of the children. The children were in contact with each other, and more likely than not, exchanged information about the alleged abuses. Seventeen of the 34 children were actually told that other children had told investigators that Kelly had done bad things to children. In sum, the record contains numerous instances of egregious violations of proper interview protocols.

We thus agree with the appellate court that the interviews of the children were highly improper and employed coercive and unduly suggestive methods. As a result, a substantial likelihood exists that the children's recollection of past events was both stimulated and materially influenced by that course of questioning. Accordingly, this court concludes that a hearing must be held to determine whether those clearly improper interrogations so infected the ability of the children to recall the alleged abusive events that their pretrial statements and proposed in-court testimony are unreliable and should not be admitted into evidence.

The basic issue to be addressed at such a pretrial hearing is whether the pretrial events, the investigatory interviews and interrogations, were so suggestive that they give rise to a substantial likelihood of irreparably mistaken or false recollection of material facts bearing on the defendant's guilt. Consonant with the presumption that child victims are to be presumed no more or less reliable than any other class of witnesses, the initial burden to trigger a pretrial taint hearing is on the defendant. The defendant must make a showing of some evidence that the victim's statements were the product of suggestive or coercive interview techniques.

The defendant has met this minimum standard with respect to the investigatory interviews and interrogations that occurred in this case. The kind of practices used here—the absence of spontaneous recall; interviewer bias; repeated leading questions; multiple interviews; incessant questioning; vilification of the defendant; ongoing contact with peers and references to their statements; and the use of threats, bribes, and cajoling, as well as the failure to videotape or otherwise document the initial interview sessions— constitute more than sufficient evidence to support a finding that the interrogations created a substantial risk that the statements and anticipated testimony are unreliable, and therefore, justify a taint hearing.

Once the defendant establishes that sufficient evidence of unreliability exists, the burden shall shift to the state to prove the reliability of the proffered statements and testimony by clear and convincing evidence. Hence, the ultimate determination to be made is whether, despite the presence of some suggestive or coercive interview techniques, when considering the totality of the circumstances surrounding the interviews, the statements or testimony retain a degree of reliability sufficient to outweigh the effects of the improper interview techniques. To make that showing, the state is entitled to call experts to offer testimony with regard to the suggestive capacity of the suspect investigative procedures. The defendant, in countering the state's evidence, may also offer experts on the issue of the suggestiveness of the interrogations.

Finally, if it is determined by the trial court that a child's statements or testimony, or some portion thereof, do retain sufficient reliability for admission at trial, then it is for the jury to determine the probative worth and to assign the weight to be given to such statements or testimony as part of their assessment of credibility. Experts may thus be called to aid the jury by explaining the coercive or suggestive propensities of the interviewing techniques employed, but not of course, to offer opinions as to the issue of a child witness's credibility, which remains strictly a matter for the jury. We add the observation that the jury must make that determination in light of all the surrounding circumstances and without reference to the trial court's determination and ruling on admissibility.

ANALYSIS AND IMPLICATIONS

The trial judge in this case made several important decisions that eventually became the bases for Michaels's appeal of her conviction. The one that concerns us was the decision by the trial court to allow the testimony of the children on the assumption that it was reliable and untainted by the interviewing techniques employed by the investigators. The trial court's decision raises two questions. Were these children subjected to suggestive and coercive interrogations? If they were, did the interviews taint the children's testimony?

In responding, the New Jersey Supreme Court considered the nature of children as witnesses in general, the importance of the initial investigative interviews, factors that can influence child suggestibility, and the interview techniques specific to this case. Although the court emphasized the deficiencies of the interview and interrogation techniques and was very clear in its condemnation of them, its ruling in favor of Michaels was actually quite narrow. Although the court may have thought that the testimony of the children who were subject to these techniques should not be admitted at a retrial, it left this ultimate decision in the hands of the trial judge. The court simply ordered the judge to conduct a taint hearing to assess the reliability of the children's testimony in light of the interviewing techniques employed by the investigators. If the trial judge then decided that the children's testimony could be admitted, it would be up to the jury to decide how credible each child's testimony was.

Children as Witnesses

The prosecution argued that all people are presumed, as a matter of law, to be competent witnesses. Because the law considers children competent, their testimony, if relevant to the case, should be admitted. It would then be up to the jury to decide how credible the child's testimony was. When the New Jersey Supreme Court considered this issue, it said it was not just a matter of the child's competence but of the reliability of the testimony that the children would offer if permitted to testify. Stated another way, although child witnesses are presumed competent, this assumption can be rebutted by the defendant.

The court recognized that child witnesses can be extremely malleable and open to suggestion under certain conditions. If interviews and interrogations are not conducted with care, children's recollections can become hopelessly muddled. The child's resulting unreliable testimony should not be admitted into evidence.

Factors That Affect Children's Testimony

The court understood the problem with assuming the reliability of children's testimony and reviewed factors such as interviewer independence and bias; leading and repetitive questions; repetition of misinformation; emotional tone of the interviewer; peer pressure; interviewer status; vilification of the accused; use of anatomically correct dolls during the interview; and finally, bribes, threats, and rewards. They also noted recommendations made by social scientists for conducting interviews to increase the chances for eliciting complete and accurate recollections from children.

Fundamental to the prosecution of Michaels was a behavioral and social fact assumption: that children were conveying accurate information about Michaels that was not tainted by the methods used to elicit information it. Other related assumptions can also be identified. First, when children understand the gravity of a situation, they will tell the truth; they do not have the complex motives that adults have to lie. Second, interviewers are not biased. This not only includes the police investigators and parents but therapists, social workers, prosecutors, and attorneys. The truth and the child's welfare are what drive the way these legal and social actors conduct themselves with the child. They have no hidden agenda and will not implant stories in children's minds. Third, even if parents are unreliable interviewers, police investigators will obtain reliable information from the children. Unlike parents, police do not have the same emotional attachment to the events under investigation. They are able to maintain a professional, detached attitude that will not taint their investigation or the evidence they gather from witnesses. Most importantly, they are highly trained and experienced in investigative and interviewing techniques, which ensures the elicitation of reliable information. This is the ultimate thread that runs through all of these assumptions. The techniques and methods that investigators use to obtain information from children concerning possible sexual abuse will produce reliable evidence and testimony. Fourth, and finally, repeating the same questions will reconfirm the child's answers. If a child, or anyone for that matter, can answer the same questions consistently, the answers are more likely to be true.

The problem for Michaels was that the validity of the assumptions made during the investigation of her were never questioned. Yet, these assumptions should have been immediately questioned when the investigators realized that some of what the children said about the alleged abuse could not possibly be true. So what evidence can each side present to the court about the validity of the assumptions? The prosecution could present documentation showing how the interviews were conducted (e.g., audiotapes or videotapes of the interviews), which should demonstrate their fairness and appropriateness. Each side (prosecution and defense) could present relevant law enforcement guidelines about how to conduct such investigations, comparing such guidelines to what was actually done in this case. Each side could also present behavioral and social science information about the likely validity of evidence gathered using the techniques employed by the investigators. Finally, the court could grant permission to concerned behavioral and social scientists to submit an amicus brief reviewing the behavioral and social science relevant to the issues raised by the investigators' techniques.

The preparation and presentation of an amicus brief occurred in this case. What follows are edited portions from that brief (Bruck & Ceci, 1995).

Effect of Interviewer Bias on Children's Reports

A review of interviews of children suspected of being sexually abused reveals that some interviewers blindly pursue a single hypothesis that sexual abuse has occurred. In such interviews, the interviewer typically fails to rule out rival hypotheses that might explain the behavior of the child. As a result, the interviewer often concludes that the child was sexually abused.

Some investigative and therapeutic interviewers claim that such techniques are necessary because sexually abused children are so scared or embarrassed that they will never willingly or spontaneously tell any interviewer, including their own parents, of the past abuses. Therefore, they claim, it is necessary to use all available strategies to get the child to reveal sexual abuse. These strategies include the use of repeated leading questions, repeated interviews, bribes or threats, and the induction of stereotypes and expectancies (Ceci & Bruck, 1993b). Such strategies may prove successful when the child has been sexually abused; that is, the interviewer will be successful in drawing out a report of sexual abuse from the child. However, when interviewers have strong preconceived impressions of what happened, these biases can also result in the generation of false confessions from children.

Effect of Repeated Questions

A number of studies have shown that asking children the same question repeatedly within an interview and across interviews, especially a yes or no question (Poole & White, 1991), often results in the child changing his or her original answer. Preschoolers are particularly vulnerable to these effects. Children often do this because they seem to reason: The first answer I gave must be wrong, which is why they are asking me the question again. Therefore, I should change my answer. At other times, children may change their answer to please the adult who is questioning them; they reason that the adult must not have liked the first answer they gave so they will give another answer. At other times, children's answers may change because the interviewer's previous suggestions become incorporated into their memories.

Effect of Repeating Misinformation Across Interviews

A number of studies show that repeatedly giving children misleading information in a series of interviews can have serious effects on the accuracy of their later reports (Poole & White, 1995). Not only can the misinformation become directly incorporated into the children's subsequent reports (they use the interviewers' words in their inaccurate statements) but it can also lead to fabrications or inaccuracies that do not directly mirror the content of the misleading information or questions.

For example, Bruck, Ceci, Francouer, and Barr (1995) found that children will give highly inaccurate reports about a previous visit to a pediatrician's office if they are given multiple suggestions in repeated interviews. The children in this study visited their pediatrician when they were five years old. During that visit, a male pediatrician gave each child a physical examination, an oral polio vaccine, and an inoculation. During that same visit, a female research assistant talked to the child about a poster on the wall, read the child a story, and gave the child some treats.

Approximately one year later, the children were reinterviewed four times over a period of a month. During the first three interviews, some children were falsely reminded that the pediatrician showed them the poster, gave them treats, and read them a story and that the research assistant gave them the inoculation and the oral vaccine. Other children were given no information about the actors of these events. During the final interview, when asked to recall what happened during the original medical visit, children who were not given any misleading information were highly accurate in their final reports. They correctly recalled which events were performed by the pediatrician and by the research assistant. In contrast, the misled children were very inaccurate; not only did they incorporate the misleading suggestions into their reports, with more than half the children falling sway to these suggestions (e.g., claiming that the female assistant inoculated them rather the pediatrician), but 45% of these children also included nonsuggested but inaccurate events in their reports by falsely reporting that the research assistant had checked their ears and nose. None of the control children made such inaccurate reports. Thus, when suggestions are implanted and incorporated, young children use these in highly productive ways to reconstruct and distort reality.

Effect of the Emotional Tone of the Interview

Children are quick to pick up on the emotional tones in an interview and to act accordingly. There is much information that can be conveyed in the emotional tone, including implicit or explicit threats, bribes, and rewards. For example, when an accusatory tone is set by the examiner (e.g., "We know something bad happened"; or "It isn't good to let people kiss you in the bathtub"; "You'll feel better once you tell"; or "Don't be afraid to tell"), children are likely to fabricate reports of past events even in cases when they have no memory of any event occurring. In some cases, these fabrications are sexual in nature (see Ceci & Bruck, 1993a).

There are many other studies in the social science literature to show that reinforcing children for certain behaviors also increases the frequency of these types of behaviors. Telling children "You are a really good boy" is one example of this. In some situations, when used appropriately, these types of supportive statements make children feel at ease and make children more responsive and accurate than when they are provided with no feedback or support (e.g., Goodman, Rudy, Bottoms, & Aman, 1990). If used inappropriately, however, these types of statements can also produce inaccurate statements. Thus it has also been found that when interviewers are overly supportive of children, the children tend to produce many inaccurate as well as many accurate details (e.g., Geiselman, Saywitz, & Bornstein, 1990). Certainly, there appears to be some trade-off in the effect of positive and neutral support on the accuracy of children's reports.

Effect of Peer Pressure or Interaction on Children's Reports

Suggestions or misleading information may also be planted by peers. As early as 1900, it was found that children will change their answers to be consistent with those of their peer group even when it is clear that the answer is inaccurate (Binet, 1900). Importantly, the peer group's actual experiences in an event can contaminate nonparticipants' reports or fabricated memories of the event. For example, Pynoos and Nader (1989) studied people's recollections of a sniper attack. On February 24, 1984, from a second story window across the street, a sniper fired repeated rounds of ammunition at children on an elementary school playground. Scores of children were pinned under gunfire, many were injured, and one child and a passerby were killed. Roughly 10% of the student body, 113 children, were interviewed 6 to 16 weeks later. Each child was asked to freely recall the experience and then to respond to specific questions. Some of those children who were interviewed were not at the school during the shooting, including those already on the way home and those on vacation. Yet, even the nonwitnesses had memories: One girl initially said that she was at the school gate nearest the sniper when the shooting began. In truth she was not only out of the line of fire, she was half a block away. A boy who had been away on vacation said that he had been on his way to the school, had seen someone lying on the ground, had heard the shots, and then turned back. In actuality, a police barricade prevented anyone from approaching the block around the school. What most likely occurred is that the children heard about the event from their peers who were present during the sniper attack, and they incorporated these reports into their own memories.

Effect of Being Interviewed by Adults With High Status

Young children are sensitive to the status and power of their interviewers. As a result they are especially likely to comply with the implicit and explicit agenda of such interviewers. If their account is questioned for example, children may defer to the challenges of the more senior interviewer. To some extent, it is this power differential and its recognition by the child that is one of the most important explanations for children's increased suggestibility. Children are more likely to believe adults than other children; they are more willing to go along with the wishes of adults and to incorporate adults' beliefs into their reports. This fact has been recognized by researchers since the turn of the century and has been demonstrated in many studies (Ceci & Bruck, 1993b).

Another feature of some interviews is that there is often more than one adult questioner present in the interview. One might argue that this might be a safeguard to ensure that the child tells the truth—especially if one of the adults is the child's parent. However, it also seems that additional adults merely multiply the number of questions and suggestive interview strategies to which the children are subjected. These increased questions may increase children's willingness to defer to the adults' agenda rather than to their own memories of whether an event actually occurred.

Effect of Stereotype Inducement and Suggestive Questions

One component of a suggestive interview involves the induction of stereotypes. That is, if a child is repeatedly told that a person "does bad things," then the child may begin to incorporate this belief into his or her reports.

Consider the following study. A stranger named Sam Stone paid a two-minute visit to preschoolers (aged 3–6 years) in their daycare center (Leichtman & Ceci, 1995). Following Sam Stone's visit, the children were asked for details about the visit on four different occasions over a 10-week period. During these four occasions, the interviewer refrained from using suggestive questions. She simply encouraged children to describe Sam Stone's visit in as much detail as possible. One month following the fourth interview, the children were interviewed a fifth time by a new interviewer who asked about two *nonevents* that involved Sam doing something to a teddy bear and a book. In reality, Sam Stone never touched either one. When asked in the fifth interview, "Did Sam Stone do anything to a book or a teddy bear?" most children rightfully replied *no*. Only 10% of the youngest (three–four-year-old) children's answers contained claims that Sam Stone did anything to a book or teddy bear. When asked if they actually saw him do anything to the book or teddy bear, as opposed to "thinking they saw him do something" or "hearing he did something," only 5% of their answers contained claims that anything occurred. Finally, when these 5% were gently challenged ("You didn't really see him do anything to the book or the teddy bear, did you?"), only 2.5% still insisted on the reality of the fictional event. None of the older (5–6-year-old) children claimed to have actually seen Sam Stone do either of the fictional events.

A second group of preschoolers were presented with a stereotype of Sam Stone before he ever visited their school. Each week, beginning a month prior to Sam Stone's visit, these children were told a new Sam Stone story in which he was depicted as very clumsy. For example:

> You'll never guess who visited me last night. [pause] That's right. Sam Stone! And guess what he did this time? He asked to borrow my Barbie, and when he was carrying her down the stairs, he tripped and fell and broke her arm. That Sam Stone is always getting into accidents and breaking things!

Following Sam Stone's visit, these children were given four suggestive interviews over a 10-week period. Each suggestive interview contained two erroneous suggestions, one having to do with ripping a book and the other with soiling a teddy bear (e.g., "Remember that time Sam Stone visited your classroom and spilled chocolate on that white teddy bear? Did he do it on purpose or was it an accident?" and "When Sam Stone ripped that book, was he being silly or was he angry?").

Ten weeks later, when a new interviewer probed about these events ("Did anything happen to a book?" "Did anything happen to a teddy bear?"),

72% of the youngest preschoolers claimed that Sam Stone did one or both misdeeds, a figure that dropped to 44% when asked if they actually saw him do these things. Importantly, 21% continued to insist that they saw him do these things, even when gently challenged. The older preschoolers, though more accurate, still included some children (11%) who insisted they saw him do the misdeeds.

Effect of Using Anatomically Detailed Dolls

Anatomically detailed dolls are frequently used by professionals, including child therapists, police, child protection workers, and attorneys, when interviewing children about suspected sexual abuse. One rationale for the use of anatomical dolls is that they allow children to manipulate objects reminiscent of a critical event, thereby cuing recall and overcoming language and memory problems. Another rationale is that their use is thought to overcome motivational problems of embarrassment and shyness. The dolls have also been used as projective tests. Some professionals claim that if a child actively avoids these dolls, shows distress if they are undressed, or shows unusual preoccupation with their genitalia, this is consistent with the hypothesis that the child has been abused (see Mason, 1991).

The use of anatomically detailed dolls has raised skepticism, however, among researchers and professionals alike. Two related arguments are frequently invoked against their use. The first is that the dolls are suggestive, that they encourage the child to engage in sexual play even if the child has not been sexually abused (e.g., Gardner, 1989; Terr, 1988). A child, for instance, may insert a finger into a doll's genitalia simply because of its novelty or "affordance," much the way a child may insert a finger into the hole of a doughnut. Another criticism is that it is impossible to make firm judgments about children's abuse status on the basis of their doll play because there are no normative data on nonabused children's doll play. Generally very young children may not have the cognitive sophistication to use a doll to represent their own experiences. Hence, the use of dolls may actually impede or distort, rather than facilitate and clarify, their ability to provide accurate testimony. (This concludes the excerpted amicus brief.)

Techniques Used in the Michaels Investigation

After reviewing the conditions under which interviews can adversely affect children's memories, the court looked for parallels with the techniques used in this case. The overlap was remarkable and conclusive. Indeed, besides the factors already mentioned, the court found other problems: the children's retelling of the alleged sexual abuse was not spontaneous or freely recalled; their memories lacked the detail one might expect from a victim; the interviewers lacked training in acceptable interview techniques; many of the interviews (particularly the early ones) were not recorded; investigators failed to challenge the more incredible claims that some of the children made; and finally, the investigators failed to consider alternative explanations for the children's statements. Because of these abuses, the New Jersey Supreme Court ordered the lower court to hold a taint hearing if the prosecution decided to retry Michaels. They wanted to make it very clear that a taint hearing was necessary because of "egregious prosecutorial abuses."

The New Jersey Supreme Court was skeptical that the interviews could survive such scrutiny and be admitted in a subsequent trial. The behavioral and social facts provided to the court by the behavioral and social scientists helped the court realize that the assumptions made by the investigators and the trial judge regarding the reliability of child witnesses were incorrect. That is, children who are subjected to the kinds of interrogation methods used in the Michaels case often become, through no fault of their own, unreliable witnesses.

Science Versus Prosecutorial Needs

The research described in the amicus brief, and the conclusions drawn from it, have not escaped criticism however. Lyon (1995, 1999) and Myers (1995), for example, have accused the authors of the brief of making a seriously flawed assumption, namely that the people who conducted interviews of child abuse victims used the suggestive interview techniques described in the brief. On the contrary, there is little empirical evidence that interviewers used these methods (Myers, 1995), and that even if they did, the negative effects on children's memory would not be as bad as some of the research suggests (Lyon, 1995, 1999; Myers, 1995).

Moreover, Lyon (1995) decried the fact that the amicus brief failed to balance two important but sometimes competing interests: the need for accurate testimony and the need to detect and convict offenders. The brief makes the first interest clear: False allegations of abuse are dangerous and must be avoided. According to the New Jersey Supreme Court, there was a good chance that Michaels was wrongly convicted because children falsely accused her of sexually abusing them. Scientists call this kind of mistake a *false positive* or a Type I error (e.g., claiming Michaels was guilty when she was not).

But the second interest is also critical. No one wants a person who really did abuse children to get away with the crime. Scientists call this kind of mistake a *false negative* or a Type II error (e.g., claiming Michaels was innocent when she was not). It is the Type II error that Lyon (1995) believes gets short shrift in the amicus brief. Although our legal tradition believes that committing a Type I error (convicting a person who is really innocent) is a far more serious mistake than committing a Type II error (letting a guilty person go free), Lyon (1995) argues that abandoning these interviewing techniques may make detection of real abuse impossible and that that is a risk that many social scientists have failed to consider.

Ironically, research has shown that without *significant prompting*, children are reluctant to disclose that they have been sexually abused (Ceci & Friedman, 2000). Children who are simply asked to tell what happened to them (free recall) just do not say much. Although what they do say may be accurate, they often leave out critical details that could be important to an investigation (Ceci & Friedman, 2000). Sometimes leading and direct questions must be asked to get to the truth (Ceci & Friedman, 2000; Lyon, 1995, 1999). It should not be surprising then that investigators may purposely, or perhaps unwittingly, employ some of the more egregious techniques that the amicus brief said can produce tainted memories. The dilemma, as the amicus brief demonstrated, is that these methods may result in false memories, which in turn become incorrect accusations that can have catastrophic results.

There are several reasons why children have a hard time disclosing that they have been abused. According to Lyon (1995), children are embarrassed by the sexual activity and are embarrassed by having to talk about it. In a study in which five- and seven-year-old girls were asked to freely recall the details of a physical examination, most failed to disclose the more intimate aspects of the exam unless they were asked directly (e.g., "Did the doctor touch you here?"). Even so, many of the girls continued to maintain that they had not been touched by the doctor in their private parts, although it was in fact part of their examination (Saywitz, Goodman, Nicholas, & Moan, 1991). Other research has studied children whose sexual abuse had been confirmed by physical evidence (e.g., the presence of a sexually transmitted disease or signs of damage to the genitals) but who did not report that they had been abused. When questioned, only about 50% disclosed the abuse (Lawson & Chaffin, 1992; Muram, Speck, & Gold, 1991). Another reason children may not talk about their abuse is that they want to protect the perpetrator. Most abusers are either a member of the child's family or a person they know and do not want to get into trouble (Lyon, 1995). Finally, unless asked directly, young children may not reveal their abuse because their cognitive development makes it difficult for them to do so. A direct question (e.g., "Did the man touch you here?") taps into a child's recognition memory, as opposed to an open-ended question (e.g., "Tell me what happened"), which elicits recall memory. Research has shown that younger children have an easier time describing events from their recognition memory than they do if asked to rely on their recall memory (Lyon, 1995).

It would be wrong to view this as an *all-or-nothing* debate. Ceci and Friedman (2000) advocate the use of leading questions in the investigative process but only as a last resort. Furthermore, they argue that a child who is subjected to suggestive interview methods should not be automatically precluded from testifying in court. Most children who say they have been abused are usually accurate in their accusations (Ceci & Friedman, 2000), and the methods that elicited the fact should not be reason enough to discount the charge. However, based on their review of the child suggestibility literature,

Ceci and Friedman (2000) concluded that there is a broad consensus among researchers that children are susceptible to suggestion "to a significant degree," and in some instances, children are in error more than half of the time. They recommend that courts take advantage of experts in child suggestibility, just as the New Jersey Supreme Court did, to help them decide if the child's memory was corrupted.

CHAPTER'S LESSON

The behavioral and social assumptions made by the trial court in *New Jersey v. Michaels* (1994) typifies the assumptions that courts, legislators, and administrative policy makers make every day in this country. This is partly caused by lawmakers not having training in the behavioral and social sciences and either believing that their assumptions are correct or not realizing that they are making assumptions about human behavior. And partly it results from a lack of relevant behavioral and social science information (see chapter 10, this volume) being available at the time of the legal decision. But when behavioral and social science facts are available, it is clear from this chapter that they can dramatically improve the accuracy and fairness of legal decision making.

REFERENCES

Binet, A. (1900). *La suggestibilitie*. Paris: Schleicher Freres.

Bruck, M., Ceci, S. J., Francoeur, E., & Barr, R. J. (1995). "I hardly cried when I got my shot!": Influencing children's reports about a visit to their pediatrician. *Child Development, 66*, 193–208.

Bruck, M., & Ceci, S. J. (1995). Amicus Brief for the case of State of New Jersey v. Margaret Kelly Michaels presented by the Committee of Concerned Social Scientists. *Psychology, Public Policy, and Law, 1*, 272–322.

Ceci, S. J., & Bruck, M. (1993a). Children's recollections: Translating research into policy. *SRCD Social Policy Reports, 7*, No. 3.

Ceci, S. J., & Bruck, M. (1993b). The suggestibility of the child witness: A historical review and synthesis. *Psychological Bulletin, 113*, 403–439.

Ceci, S. J., & Friedman, R. D. (2000). The suggestibility of children: Scientific research and legal implications. *Cornell Law Review, 86*, 33–108.

Gardner, R. (1989). *Sex abuse hysteria: Salem witch trials revisited*. Longwood, NJ: Creative Therapeutics Press.

Geiselman, R., Saywitz, K., & Bornstein, G. (1990). *Effects of cognitive interviewing, practice, and interview style on children's recall performance*. Unpublished manuscript.

Goodman, G. S., Rudy, L., Bottoms, B., & Aman, C. (1990). Children's concerns and memory: Issues of ecological validity in the study of children's eyewitness testimony. In R. Fivush & J. Hudson (Eds.), *Knowing and remembering in young children* (pp. 249–284). New York: Cambridge University Press.

Lawson, L., & Chaffin, M. (1992). False negatives in sexual abuse disclosure interviews: Incidence and influence of caretaker's belief in abuse in cases of accidental abuse discovery by diagnosis of STD. *Journal of Interpersonal Violence, 7,* 532–542.

Leichtman, M. D., & Ceci, S. J. (1995). The effects of stereotypes and suggestions on preschooler's reports. *Developmental Psychology, 31,* 568–578.

Lyon, T. D. (1995). False allegations and false denials in child sexual abuse. *Psychology, Public Policy, and Law, 1,* 429–437.

Lyon, T. D. (1999). The new wave in children's suggestibility research: A critique. *Cornell Law Review, 84,* 1004–1087.

Mason, M. A. (1991). A judicial dilemma: Expert witness testimony in child sex abuse cases. *Journal of Psychiatry and Law, 19,* 185–219.

Muram, D., Speck, P. M., & Gold, S. S. (1991). Genital abnormalities in female siblings and friends of child victims of sexual abuse. *Child Abuse and Neglect, 15,* 105–110.

Myers, J. E. B. (1995). New era of skepticism regarding children's credibility. *Psychology, Public Policy, and Law, 1,* 387–398.

New Jersey v. Michaels, 136 N.J. 299 (1994).

Poole, D., & White, L. (1991). Effects of question repetition on the eyewitness testimony of children and adults. *Developmental Psychology, 27,* 975–986.

Poole, D., & White, L. (1995). Tell me again and again: Stability and change in the repeated testimonies of children and adults. In M. S. Zaragoza, J. R. Graham, C. N. Gordon, R. Hirschman, & Y. Ben-Yorath (Eds.), *Memory and testimony in the child witness* (pp. 24–43). Newbury Park, CA: Sage.

Pynoos, R. S., & Nader, K. (1989). Children's memory and proximity to violence. *Journal of American Academy of Child and Adolescent Psychiatry, 28,* 236–241.

Sales, B. D. (1983). The legal regulation of psychology: Professional and scientific interactions. In C. J. Scheirer & B. L. Hammonds (Eds.), *The master lecture series. Volume II: Psychology and the law.* (pp. 5–36). Washington, DC: American Psychological Association.

Saywitz, K. J., Goodman, G. S., Nicholas, E., & Moan, S. F. (1991). Children's memories of a physical examination involving genital touch: Implications for reports of child sexual abuse. *Journal of Consulting and Clinical Psychology, 59,* 682–691.

Terr, L. (1988). Anatomically correct dolls: Should they be used as a basis for expert testimony? *Journal of American Academy of Child and Adolescent Psychiatry, 27,* 254–257.

5

PROVIDING THE LAW WITH FACTUAL KNOWLEDGE TO HELP SET LEGAL GOALS

EXAMPLE: WORKPLACE ACCOMMODATION FOR PERSONS WITH DISABILITIES

The Civil Rights Act of 1964 was enacted by Congress in response to the laws of some states that discriminated against minority groups. For example, some states had laws that prevented people from voting unless certain requirements were met, like home ownership or minimum reading skills. Many minorities had difficulty satisfying these requirements and were often denied their right to vote. When these restrictions failed to prevent the affected groups from *attempting* to vote, physical intimidation and beatings often ensued, sometimes right on the steps of the polling place. The Civil Rights Act sought to remedy these injustices by empowering the federal courts and the U.S. Attorney General to force states to comply with the fundamental rights guaranteed by the U.S. Constitution. The Act also banned discrimination in public accommodations, public facilities, public education, and employment on the basis of race, color, religion, sex, or national origin.

Congress has passed other legislation banning discrimination in employment and in employment compensation based on gender (Equal Pay Act of 1963), age (Age Discrimination in Employment Act of 1967), and disability (Title I of the Americans With Disabilities Act of 1990; henceforth, ADA). It is the responsibility of the U.S. Equal Employment Opportunity Commission (EEOC) to make sure that these laws are enforced. Besides these enforcement activities, the EEOC also issues regulations and guidelines that interpret current employment discrimination laws. One such guideline is the one presented in this chapter, the EEOC Enforcement Guidance: The Americans With Disabilities Act and Psychiatric Disabilities (1997). We have been slow as a society to accept that persons with mental disabilities can be productive in the workplace.

The lesson of this chapter is that behavioral and social knowledge can provide legislators, judges, and administrative agency personnel with the necessary facts to set and achieve legal goals. In this instance, the legal goal was and is to integrate persons with mental disabilities into the labor force so that they may enjoy the rights, privileges, and rewards of full membership in society. Once the legal goal is set, behavioral and social scientists and practitioners can also help those responsible for implementing the law. These scientists and practitioners have acquired vast amounts of knowledge on the abilities and capabilities of persons with mental disabilities and how they can most successfully be integrated into the workforce while respecting the needs of employers. Not surprisingly, our lawmakers seek out and rely on this type of information when setting goals for new laws.

ENFORCEMENT GUIDANCE: THE AMERICANS WITH DISABILITIES ACT AND PSYCHIATRIC DISABILITIES

United States Equal Employment Opportunity Commission

This guidance sets forth the EEOC's position on the application of Title I of the ADA to individuals in the workforce with psychiatric disabilities. The workforce includes many individuals with psychiatric disabilities who face employment discrimination because of stigma or misunderstanding. Congress intended Title I of the ADA to combat this discrimination as well as the myths, fears, and stereotypes on which it is based.

What Is a Psychiatric Disability Under the Americans With Disabilities Act?

Under the ADA, the term disability means (a) having a physical or mental impairment that substantially limits one or more of the major life activities of an individual; (b) having a record of such an impairment; or (c) being regarded as having such an impairment.

Impairment

The ADA defines mental impairment to include any mental or psychological disorder, such as emotional or mental illness. Examples of emotional or mental illness include major depression, bipolar disorder, anxiety disorders (which include panic disorder, obsessive compulsive disorder, and posttraumatic stress disorder), schizophrenia, and personality disorders. The current edition of the American Psychiatric Association's *Diagnostic and Statistical Manual of Mental Disorders* (*DSM–IV*) is relevant for identifying these disorders. The *DSM–IV* has been recognized as an important reference by courts and is widely used by American mental health professionals for diagnostic and insurance reimbursement purposes.

Not all conditions listed in the *DSM–IV*, however, are disabilities, or even impairments, for purposes of the ADA. For example, the *DSM–IV* lists several conditions that Congress expressly excluded from the ADA's definition of disability (e.g., various sexual behavior disorders, compulsive gambling, kleptomania, pyromania, and psychoactive substance use disorders resulting from current illegal use of drugs).

Traits or behaviors are not mental impairments. For example, stress is not automatically a mental impairment. Stress, however, may be shown to be related to a mental or physical impairment. Similarly, traits like irritability, chronic lateness, and poor judgment are not mental impairments, although they may be linked to mental impairments.

Major Life Activities

An impairment must substantially limit one or more major life activities to rise to the level of a disability under the ADA. The major life activities limited by mental impairments differ from person to person. There is no exhaustive list of major life activities. For some people, mental impairments restrict major life activities such as learning, thinking, concentrating, interacting with others, caring for oneself, speaking, performing manual tasks, or working. Sleeping is also a major life activity that may be limited by mental impairments. Moreover, the first question is whether an individual is substantially limited in a major life activity other than working (e.g., sleeping, concentrating, caring for oneself). Working should be analyzed only if no other major life activity is substantially limited by an impairment.

Substantial Limitation

Under the ADA, an impairment rises to the level of a disability if it substantially limits a major life activity. Substantial limitation is evaluated in terms of the severity of the limitation and the length of time it restricts a major life activity. The determination that a particular individual has a substantially limiting impairment should be based on information about how the impairment affects that individual and not on generalizations about the condition. Relevant evidence for EEOC investigators includes descriptions of an individual's typical level of functioning at home, at work, and in other settings as well as evidence showing that the individual's functional limitations are linked to his or her impairment. Expert testimony about substantial limitation is not necessarily required. Credible testimony from the individual with a disability and his or her family members, friends, or coworkers may suffice.

An impairment is sufficiently severe to substantially limit a major life activity if it prevents an individual from performing a major life activity or significantly restricts the condition, manner, or duration under which an individual can perform a major life activity as compared to the average person in the general population. An impairment does not significantly restrict major life activities if it results in only mild limitations.

An impairment is substantially limiting if it lasts for more than several months and significantly restricts the performance of one or more major life activities during that time. It is not substantially limiting if it lasts for only a brief time or does not significantly restrict an individual's ability to perform a major life activity.

> *Example*: An employee has had major depression for almost a year. He has been intensely sad and socially withdrawn (except for going to work), has developed serious insomnia, and has had severe problems concentrating. This employee has an impairment (major depression) that significantly restricts his ability to interact with others, sleep, and concentrate. The effects of this impairment are severe and have lasted long enough to be substantially limiting.

In addition, some conditions may be long-term, or potentially long-term, in that their duration is indefinite and unknowable or is expected to be at least several months. Such conditions, if severe, may constitute disabilities. However, conditions that are temporary and have no permanent or long-term effects on an individual's major life activities are not substantially limiting.

Example: An employee was distressed by the end of a romantic relationship. Although he continued his daily routine, he sometimes became agitated at work. He was most distressed for about a month during and immediately after the breakup. He sought counseling and his mood improved within weeks. His counselor gave him a diagnosis of "adjustment disorder" and stated that he was not expected to experience any long-term problems associated with this event. Although he has an impairment (adjustment disorder), his impairment was short-term, did not significantly restrict major life activities during that time, and was not expected to have permanent or long-term effects. This employee does not have a disability for purposes of the ADA.

Chronic, episodic conditions may constitute substantially limiting impairments if they are substantially limiting when active or have a high likelihood of recurrence in substantially limiting forms. For some individuals, psychiatric impairments such as bipolar disorder, major depression, and schizophrenia may remit and intensify, sometimes repeatedly, over the course of several months or several years.

An impairment substantially limits an individual's ability to interact with others if, as a result of the impairment, he or she is significantly restricted as compared with the average person in the general population. Some unfriendliness with coworkers or a supervisor would not, standing alone, be sufficient to establish a substantial limitation in interacting with others. An individual would be substantially limited, however, if his or her relations with others were characterized on a regular basis by severe problems, for example, consistently high levels of hostility, social withdrawal, or failure to communicate when necessary. These limitations must be long-term or potentially long-term, as opposed to temporary, to justify a finding of ADA disability.

An impairment substantially limits an individual's ability to concentrate if, because of the impairment, he or she is significantly restricted as compared with the average person in the general population. For example, an individual would be substantially limited if he or she was easily and frequently distracted, meaning that his or her attention was frequently drawn to irrelevant sights or sounds or to intrusive thoughts, or if he or she experienced his or her "mind going blank" on a frequent basis. Such limitations must be long-term or potentially long-term, as opposed to temporary, to justify a finding of ADA disability.

Example: An employee who has an anxiety disorder says that his mind wanders frequently and that he is often distracted by irrelevant thoughts. As a result, he makes repeated errors at work on detailed or complex tasks, even after being reprimanded. His doctor says that the errors are caused by his anxiety disorder and may last indefinitely. This individual has a disability because, as a result of an anxiety disorder, his ability to concentrate is significantly restricted as compared with the average person in the general population.

Example: An employee states that he has trouble concentrating when he is tired or during long meetings. He attributes this to his chronic depression. Although his ability to concentrate may be slightly limited as a result of depression (a mental impairment), it is not significantly restricted as compared with the average person in the general population. Many people in the general population have difficulty concentrating when they are tired or during long meetings.

An impairment substantially limits an individual's ability to sleep if, as a result of the impairment, his or her sleep is significantly restricted as compared with the average person in the general population. These limitations must be long-term or potentially long-term as opposed to temporary to justify a finding of ADA disability. For example, an individual who sleeps only a negligible amount for many months because of posttraumatic stress disorder would be significantly restricted as compared with the average person in the general population and therefore would be substantially limited in sleeping. Similarly, an individual who for several months typically slept about two to three hours per night as a result of depression also would be substantially limited in sleeping. By contrast, an individual would not be substantially limited in sleeping if he or she had some trouble getting to sleep or sometimes slept fitfully because of a mental impairment. Although this individual may be slightly restricted in sleeping, he or she is not significantly restricted as compared with the average person in the general population.

Finally, an impairment substantially limits an individual's ability to care for him- or herself if, because of the impairment, an individual is significantly restricted as compared with the average person in the general population in performing basic activities such as getting up in the morning, bathing, dressing, and preparing or obtaining food. These limitations must be long-term or potentially long-term as opposed to temporary to justify a finding of ADA disability. Some psychiatric impairments, for example, major depression, may result in an individual's sleeping too much. In such cases, an individual may be substantially limited if, as a result of the impairment, he or she sleeps so much that he or she does not effectively care for him- or herself.

Requesting Reasonable Accommodation

An employer must provide a reasonable accommodation to the known physical or mental limitations of a qualified individual with a disability unless it can show that the accommodation would impose an undue hardship. An employee's decision about requesting reasonable accommodation may be influenced by his or her concerns about the potential negative consequences of disclosing a psychiatric disability at work.

When an individual decides to request accommodation, the individual or his or her representative must let the employer know that he or she needs an adjustment or change at work for a reason related to a medical condition. To request accommodation, an individual may use plain English and need not mention the ADA or use the phrase reasonable accommodation.

> *Example*: An employee asks for time off because he is depressed and stressed. The employee has communicated a request for a change at work (time off) for a reason related to a medical condition (being depressed and stressed may be "plain English" for a medical condition). This statement is sufficient to put the employer on notice that the employee is requesting reasonable accommodation.
>
> *Example*: An employee submits a note from a health professional stating that he is having a stress reaction and needs one week off. Subsequently, his wife telephones the human resources department to say that the employee is disoriented and mentally falling apart and that the family is having him hospitalized. The wife asks about procedures for extending the employee's leave and states that she will provide the necessary information as soon as possible but that she may need a little extra time. The wife's statement is sufficient to constitute a request for reasonable accommodation. The wife has asked for changes at work (an exception to the procedures for requesting leave and more time off) for a reason related to a medical condition (her husband had a stress reaction and is so mentally disoriented that he is being hospitalized).
>
> *Example*: An employee asks to take a few days off to rest after the completion of a major project. The employee does not link her need for a few days off to a medical condition. Thus, even though she has requested a change at work (time

off), her statement is not sufficient to put the employer on notice that she is requesting reasonable accommodation.

A family member, friend, health professional, or other representative may request a reasonable accommodation on behalf of an individual with a disability. Of course, an employee may refuse to accept an accommodation that is not needed.

Requests for reasonable accommodation do not need to be in writing. Employees may request accommodations in conversation or may use any other mode of communication. Nor is an individual with a disability required to request a reasonable accommodation at the beginning of employment. He or she may request a reasonable accommodation at any time during employment. As a practical matter, it may be in the employee's interest to request a reasonable accommodation before performance suffers or conduct problems occur.

When the need for accommodation is not obvious, an employer may ask an employee for reasonable documentation about his or her disability and functional limitations. The employer is entitled to know that the employee has a covered disability for which he or she needs a reasonable accommodation. A variety of health professionals may provide such documentation with regard to psychiatric disabilities.

> *Example*: An employee asks for time off because he is depressed and stressed. Although this statement is sufficient to put the employer on notice that he is requesting accommodation, the employee's need for accommodation is not obvious based on this statement alone. Accordingly, the employer may require reasonable documentation that the employee has a disability within the meaning of the ADA, and if he has such a disability, that the functional limitations of the disability necessitate time off.
>
> *Example*: This situation is the same as in the previous example, except that the employer requires the employee to submit all of the records from his health professional regarding his mental health history, including materials that are not relevant to disability and reasonable accommodation under the ADA. This is not a request for reasonable documentation. All of these records are not required to determine if the employee has a disability as defined by the ADA and needs the requested reasonable accommodation because of his disability-related functional limitations. As one alternative, in order to determine the scope of its ADA obligations, the employer may ask the employee to sign a limited release allowing the employer to submit a list of specific ques-

tions to the employee's health care professional about his condition and need for reasonable accommodation.

The ADA does not prevent an employer from requiring an employee to go to an appropriate health professional of the employer's choice if the employee initially provides insufficient information to substantiate that he or she has an ADA disability and needs a reasonable accommodation. Of course, any examination must be job related and consistent with business necessity. If an employer requires an employee to go to a health professional of the employer's choice, the employer must pay all costs associated with the visit(s).

Selected Types of Reasonable Accommodation

Reasonable accommodations for individuals with disabilities must be determined on a case-by-case basis because workplaces and jobs vary, as do people with disabilities. Accommodations for individuals with psychiatric disabilities may involve changes to workplace policies, procedures, or practices. Physical changes to the workplace or extra equipment also may be effective reasonable accommodations for some people.

In some instances, the precise nature of an effective accommodation for an individual may not be immediately apparent. Mental health professionals, including psychiatric rehabilitation counselors, may be able to make suggestions about particular accommodations, and of equal importance, help employers and employees communicate effectively about reasonable accommodation. The Job Accommodation Network (JAN, 1999) also provides advice free of charge to employers and employees contemplating reasonable accommodation. JAN is a service of the President's Committee on Employment of People With Disabilities, which is funded by the U.S. Department of Labor.

Possible Reasonable Accommodations

Time Off From Work or a Modified Work Schedule

Permitting the use of accrued paid leave or providing additional unpaid leave for treatment or recovery related to a disability is a reasonable accommodation, unless (or until) the employee's absence imposes an undue hardship on the operation of the employer's business. This includes leaves of absence, occasional leave (e.g., a few hours at a time), and part-time scheduling.

A related reasonable accommodation is to allow an individual with a disability to change his or her regularly scheduled working hours, for example, to work 10 a.m. to 6 p.m. rather than 9 a.m. to 5 p.m., barring undue hardship. Some medications taken for psychiatric disabilities cause extreme grogginess and lack of concentration in the morning. Depending on the job, a later schedule can enable the employee to perform essential job functions.

Physical Changes to the Workplace or Equipment

Simple physical changes to the workplace may be effective accommodations for some individuals with psychiatric disabilities. For example, room dividers, partitions, or other soundproofing or visual barriers between work spaces may accommodate individuals who have disability-related limitations in concentration. Moving an individual away from noisy machinery or reducing other workplace noise that can be adjusted (e.g., lowering the volume or pitch of telephones) is a similar reasonable accommodation. Permitting an individual to wear headphones to block out noisy distractions also may be effective. Some individuals who have disability-related limitations in concentration may benefit from access to equipment like a tape recorder for reviewing events such as training sessions or meetings.

Modifying a Workplace Policy

It is a reasonable accommodation to modify a workplace policy when necessitated by an individual's disability-related limitations, barring undue hardship. For example, it would be a reasonable accommodation to allow an individual who has difficulty concentrating as a result of a disability to take detailed notes during client presentations even though company policy discourages employees from taking extensive notes during such sessions.

> *Example*: A retail employer does not allow individuals working as cashiers to drink beverages at checkout stations. The retailer also limits cashiers to two 15-minute breaks during an 8-hour shift in addition to a meal break. An individual with a psychiatric disability needs to drink beverages approximately once an hour in order to combat dry mouth, a side effect of his psychiatric medication. This individual requests reasonable accommodation. In this example, the employer should consider either modifying its policy against drinking beverages at checkout stations or modifying its policy limiting cashiers to two 15-minute breaks each day plus a meal break, barring undue hardship.

Granting an employee time off from work or an adjusted work schedule as a reasonable accommodation may involve modifying leave or attendance procedures or policies. As an example, it would be a reasonable accommodation to modify a policy requiring employees to schedule vacation time in advance if an otherwise qualified individual with a disability needed to use accrued vacation time on an unscheduled basis because of disability-related medical problems, barring undue hardship. In addition, an employer, in spite of a *no-leave* policy, may, in appropriate circumstances, be required to provide leave to an employee with a disability as a reasonable accommodation, unless the provision of leave would impose an undue hardship.

Adjusting Supervisory Methods

Supervisors play a central role in achieving effective reasonable accommodations for their employees. In some circumstances, supervisors may be able to adjust their methods as a reasonable accommodation, for example, by communicating assignments, instructions, or training by the medium that is most effective for a particular individual (e.g., in writing, in conversation, or by electronic mail). Supervisors also may provide or arrange additional training or modified training materials.

Adjusting the level of supervision or structure sometimes may enable an otherwise qualified individual with a disability to perform essential job functions. For example, an otherwise qualified individual with a disability who experiences limitations in concentration may request more detailed day-to-day guidance, feedback, or structure in order to perform his or her job.

> *Example*: An employee requests more daily guidance and feedback as a reasonable accommodation for limitations associated with a psychiatric disability. In response to his request, the employer consults with the employee, his health care professional, and his supervisor about how his limitations are manifested in the office (the employee is unable to stay focused on the steps necessary to complete large projects) and how to make effective and practical changes to provide the structure he needs. As a result of these consultations, the supervisor and employee work out a long-term plan to initiate weekly meetings to review the status of large projects and identify which steps need to be taken next.

Reasonable accommodation, however, does not require lowering standards or removing essential functions of the job. For example, an attorney with chronic depression and severe personality disturbance was not a qualified individual with a disability because his requested accommodations of more supervision, less complex assignments, and the exclusion of appellate work would free him of the very duties that justified his grade.

Providing a Job Coach

An employer may be required to provide a temporary job coach to assist in the training of a qualified individual with a disability as a reasonable accommodation, barring undue hardship. An employer also may be required to allow a job coach paid by a public or private social service agency to accompany the employee at the job site as a reasonable accommodation.

Making Sure That an Individual Takes Prescribed Medication

Medication monitoring is not a reasonable accommodation. Employers have no obligation to monitor medication because doing so does not remove a barrier that is unique to the workplace. When people do not take medication as prescribed, it affects them on and off the job.

Reassignment to a Different Position

In general, reassignment must be considered as a reasonable accommodation when accommodation in the present job would cause undue hardship. For example, it may be an undue hardship to provide extra supervision as a reasonable accommodation in the present job if the employee's current supervisor is already very busy supervising several other individuals and providing direct service to the public. In addition, reassignment must be considered as a reasonable accommodation when accommodation in the present job would not be possible. For example, it may not be possible to accommodate an employee in his or her present position if he or she works as a salesperson on the busy first floor of a major department store and needs a reduction in visual distractions and ambient noise as a reasonable accommodation. Finally, reassignment may be considered if there are circumstances under which both the employer and employee voluntarily agree that it is preferable to accommodation in the present position.

Reassignment should be made to an equivalent position that is vacant or will become vacant within a reasonable amount of time. If an equivalent position is not available, the employer must look for a vacant position at a lower level for which the employee is qualified. Reassignment is not required if a vacant position at a lower level is also unavailable.

ANALYSIS AND IMPLICATIONS

According to the U.S. Census Bureau, there were 53 million Americans (19.7% of the population) with some level of disability in 1997 (McNeil, 2001). Within this group, 33 million were considered severely disabled (McNeil, 2001).

The most common mental illness in the United States is depression. It afflicts 19 million Americans each year, followed by anxiety disorders (16 million), social phobias (5.3 million), posttraumatic stress disorder (5.2 million), obsessive–compulsive disorder (3.3 million), panic disorder (2.4 million), manic-depressive illness (2.3 million), and schizophrenia (2 million), according to the National Institutes of Health (1999). Psychiatric disorders are the number one cause for hospital admissions with 21% of our nation's hospital beds occupied by people with mental illness at any given time (National Alliance for the Mentally Ill, 2004). Although this may seem to be a high percentage, the number of people who are in hospitals with psychiatric problems has actually fallen quite dramatically in the last 40 years. When adjusted for the growth of the total population, the number of people institutionalized in psychiatric hospitals between 1955 and 1994 fell 92% (Torrey, 1997). Overall, however, these numbers are still staggering.

Attitudes Toward and Myths About the Mentally Ill

Perhaps the most difficult barriers for people with disabilities to overcome are those that reside in the minds of those who do not have a disability. The greatest challenges that people with disabilities face are to dispel the myths and fears that many people possess that prevents the full integration of people with disabilities into society. Government agencies like the EEOC, the President's Committee on Employment of People With Disabilities, and JAN and private organizations like the National Alliance on Mental Illness and the Association of Persons in Supported Employment expend substantial efforts in educating the public on what persons with disabilities can do and what a usually simple process it is to provide them with accommodations at work.

Minton (1999), in an educational kit prepared for employers by the President's Committee on Employment of People With Disabilities, said focusing on the person's disability rather than on the person's abilities was the most pervasive negative attitude that people without disabilities have about people with disabilities. It is the person's ability to get the job done and do it right that matters, not whether the person has some disability that might require the task to be completed a little differently than would be the case if a person without a disability were doing it (Minton, 1999). A more troubling attitude, according to Minton (1999), is that persons with disabilities are not expected to perform up to the same standards as the nondisabled. This leads to patronization of people with disabilities that causes people to say and think things like, for example, "She's so brave for getting a job in her condition." This has the effect of keeping people with disabilities in lower tier jobs (jobs that, it is believed, their disability only permits them to do), lowering performance standards, and alienating fellow employees (Minton, 1999). Other attitudinal barriers described by Minton (1999) are beliefs about inferiority of disabled persons, pity, hero worship of disabled persons because they are overcoming their disability, ignorance of disability, the *spread effect* (i.e., the belief that a disability affects the nondisabled parts of one's behaviors and personality), stereotypes about disabled persons, backlash (i.e., people with disabilities are given an unfair advantage), denial (i.e., disabilities are somehow not "real" disabilities), and fear of persons with a disability.

People with psychiatric disabilities also have to battle myths specific to their condition. For example, it is widely believed that persons with psychiatric disabilities are, or can be, violent (Mancuso, 2000), a stereotype often fed by the way people with psychiatric problems are typically portrayed in the media. For example, Hyler, Grabbard, and Schneider (1991) found that persons with mental illness were often portrayed in movies as homicidal maniacs, even though there is little resemblance between these portrayals and the actual behavior of people with psychiatric disabilities (Monahan, 1992). Additional myths about people with mental illness include the following: Mental illness is uncommon; people with mental illness are also mentally retarded; all mental illness is incurable; and people with mental illness cannot handle stress (Mancuso, 2000).

Acknowledging the existence of these negative attitudes and myths is the first step in the process of overcoming them. Organizations that work on the behalf of people with disabilities try to educate people that it is a normal reaction at first to be nervous or uncomfortable around persons with disabilities (Minton, 1999). We fear most what we do not understand, and acceptance of people with disabilities begins when we make the effort to emphasize the person and not the disability.

Evidence suggests that overcoming these attitudes and myths is not easy. Wahl (1997) reported that psychiatric labels were responsible for 33% of job applicants with severe mental illness being turned down for jobs for which they were qualified and that more than 20% have been denied the opportunity to do even volunteer work. Once hired, 70% of the mentally ill reported being treated less appropriately when their illness became known. In addition, 50% reported that friends and coworkers *often* or *very often* made disparaging or offensive comments about mental illness. Perhaps in anticipation of this kind of treatment, 75% of the respondents said they do not tell anyone of their mental illness beyond their immediate families (Wahl, 1997).

It is a responsibility of social and behavioral scientists to provide policymakers with the necessary facts to dispel these beliefs; such facts can then lead to better public policy. For example, here are some interesting facts about treating mental illness: About 70% of people with schizophrenia show a significant improvement of their symptoms with conventional antipsychotics (Surgeon General's Report, 1999); 50% to 70% of people with mood disorders, which include bipolar disorder (formerly known as manic depression) and major depression, show significant improvement with combined pharmacological and psychosocial treatments (Surgeon General's Report, 1999). In a study conducted by the DuPont Corporation (1993), 90% of persons with disabilities were rated as performing their jobs at average or above average levels. This compares favorably with the 95% of workers without disabilities who were rated at the same job performance levels. One major fast food corporation has made special efforts at hiring persons who are mentally retarded. They found that the job turnover rate for these persons was only 20%, compared to almost 100% for their employees without mental retardation. Finally, in a study on ways to keep people with mental illness employed, Blankertz and Keller (1997) found that persons with mental illness were highly motivated, displayed high levels of job mastery, and possessed moderate self-esteem.

Helping to Influence Public Policy

The guidelines excerpted in this chapter were a result of Congress's recognizing the extent to which workers with psychiatric disabilities were discriminated against in the workplace. In response, Congress passed the ADA. Almost 50 million people were either disabled or severely disabled at the time of the ADA's passage. The unemployment rate for all disabled is about 70% (McNeil, 2001). Of these, 67% want to work (National Organization on Disability, 2002). Behavioral and social scientists and disability rights groups educated Congress about the myths and stigma that are often attached to people with mental disabilities and how prejudicial attitudes and beliefs affect the ability of these persons to improve the quality of their lives. Thus, behavioral and social science facts directly affected the creation of the ADA and the subsequent EEOC guideline considered in this chapter.

Although the ADA applied to workers with physical or mental disabilities, the EEOC feared that many employers were neither aware of this fact nor of how the law should guide their behavior as employers in interacting with these persons. The overall goal of this particular EEOC guideline is to educate employers about the requirements of the ADA when applied to persons with psychiatric disabilities who are seeking employment or who are already employed. The guideline addresses two questions. First, how should it be determined that an individual is psychiatrically disabled? Second, how should workers with psychiatric disabilities be accommodated in the workplace?

Defining Psychiatric Disability

The EEOC tried to define important terms carefully and clearly. They also tried to show how terms were related to one another. For example, they defined disability in terms of a physical or mental impairment that substantially limits one or more major life activities. They then defined mental impairment in terms of emotional or mental illness. Rather than leave employers and employees wondering what is meant by mental illness, the EEOC provided examples. They even referred readers to the *DSM–IV* (American Psychiatric Association, 1994), which classifies mental and emotional disorders. Finally, the EEOC explained what impairment of one of life's major activities is considered to be, lest there be any doubt.

It is not enough just to have some impairment to be considered disabled. The impairment must be of a degree that a major life activity is substantially limited. Note the qualification of the word *limited*. The life activity must be *substantially* limited, not merely affected by the impairment. Whether a major life activity is substantially limited has to be determined in the context of the individual's life experience. Thus, whether a disability exists will depend on functioning when taking medication (*Murphy v. United Parcel Service*, 1999). When the EEOC investigates a complaint, they gather and evaluate social and behavioral facts on the individual's "typical functioning at home, work and other settings."

Reasonable Accommodation

Once qualified, the guidelines do not require an employer to make every possible accommodation for persons who seek protection through the ADA. The guidelines describe the kinds of accommodations that a worker with disabilities might seek. All of the recommendations were made in terms of two very important factors. First, what might be considered reasonable? The EEOC relied on social and behavioral facts to help it determine what is and is not reasonable. The EEOC described and gave examples of different kinds of behavioral and social interventions that might be made by an employer that would allow a person with disabilities to function effectively at work. The guidelines do not hand a person with disabilities a blank check to force an employer to make any accommodation he or she may demand, nor are the accommodations that the ADA requires drastic. They may include such relatively minor things as changing a work schedule, making simple physical changes to a work setting, modifying a workplace policy, changing supervisory methods, providing a job coach, or reassigning a person to a different job if possible.

Second, the EEOC considered the effects that accommodations might have on a business and determined that an accommodation is not reasonable if it results in an *undue hardship* for the employer. This is not to say that an employer would never be expected to make an accommodation that might result in *some* hardship to the business in order to achieve the goals set forth in the guidelines. This is the cost that our society, through its elected representatives, has determined is a reasonable one for the business to incur to achieve integration and inclusion of people with disabilities in our nation's workforce.

The guidelines are very flexible both in their consideration of the employer and the worker. Indeed, the fact that these are called guidelines should give us a significant clue as to how the EEOC intends these to be understood by employers and workers. They are not hard and fast rules. The EEOC realizes that different working environments and different standards of work behavior will interact to produce a situation unique to each worker with disabilities who seeks accommodation. The guidelines state that reasonable accommodations are to be made on a case-by-case basis because workplaces and jobs vary, as do people with disabilities. They also seek cooperation and a partnership among the business, the person with the disability, and if necessary, experts, in accommodating people with disabilities. For example, the JAN, created by the President's Committee on Employment of People With Disabilities (1994), offers free consultation over the phone to employers where they can talk with job accommodation experts and human factor specialists.

Some of the most creative accommodations have come from the world of high technology. Some of these *assistive technologies* include talking watches and alarm systems, novel keyboard layouts (some with larger keys), telephone and computer head-sets, computer software and *mouses* that incorporate zoom features, closed captioning, audio or text messaging and e-mails, voice synthesizers, and voice-activated commands and instructions (International Association, 1999; President's Committee on Employment of People With Disabilities, 1999). But many of the accommodations, particularly for persons with psychiatric disabilities, are remarkably low-tech. These may include simply speaking more slowly and clearly, clarifying and simplifying instructions, providing a quiet work area, granting additional breaks and time off, creating a reliable routine, including the employee in social and company events, and allowing access to the appropriate support groups. Most important, however, is fostering an open relationship based on trust and respect in which problems and their solutions can be discussed honestly (Bruyere & Golden, 1994).

Whatever the nature of the accommodation, the basic procedure for making accommodations is to first determine the tasks or activities that the job requires, their sequence and relationship to one another, the characteristics of the setting where the job is done, the qualifications one must have to do the job, the limitations of people with disabilities in performing those tasks, and whether the resulting proposed accommodation will cause an employer an undue hardship (President's Committee on Employment of People With Disabilities, 1994).

Violations of the Guidelines

Unfortunately, businesses generally believe that complying with the ADA is burdensome and expensive (U.S. Department of Justice, 2004). Among the commonly held misperceptions are the following: The ADA has resulted in a deluge of lawsuits; the government wants all accommodations made; the accommodations have to be made *now*; large fines are levied for noncompliance; and finally, the ADA requires businesses to hire unqualified workers. But perhaps the biggest myth about the ADA is that it is too expensive. In fact, research has shown that the costs to businesses of making reasonable accommodations are generally inexpensive (JAN, 1997). In handling over 100,000 cases in 10 years, the JAN has found that 20% of all accommodations do not cost a company anything, 51% cost less than $500, and 82% cost less than $1,000 (JAN, 1997). In a review of the accommodations made by a major department store chain, 69% cost nothing, and only 3% cost more than $1,000 (U.S. Department of Justice, 2004).

The cost to employers for not making reasonable accommodations is potentially much greater. The EEOC obtained $111 million in benefits for workers when it took employers to court in 1997 (EEOC, 1998). Settlements and conciliation produced another $176.7 million (EEOC, 1998). In November 1999, a jury in Wisconsin awarded the largest amount to date in a case brought by the EEOC. In this case, an employee with mental retardation of a pizza parlor was fired because, according to an executive with the company, they do not hire "those kind of people" (EEOC, 1999). The company argued that because of the employee's mental retardation, he was highly unlikely to have experienced humiliation at having been fired. The jury disagreed and awarded the employee $13 million—enough to buy his own pizza parlor!

Savings also may be realized in a different manner. Hall and Wise (1995) reported that the United States economy lost $44 billion in 1990 as a result of depressive disorders. American businesses could obviously cut these loses significantly by cooperating with the EEOC and adhering to the ADA.

CHAPTER'S LESSON

The goals of both the ADA and the EEOC guidance are laudable, which is the intent of all lawmakers when they design and enact laws on behalf of society. But how can they know what these laws should cover? To some extent their common sense and information provided from their constituents will suffice. But in our increasingly scientific and technological world, we have learned that often what we think is correct can be wrong or only partially correct. We need to know the scientific facts to ensure that our beliefs are accurate and our goals are the most appropriate ones. Thus, there is a need for behavioral and social scientists to make their information available to legal decision makers and for legal decision makers to seek out the expertise of behavioral and social scientists.

REFERENCES

Age Discrimination in Employment Act of 1967, Pub. L. 90-202.

Americans With Disabilities Act, 42 U.S.C.S. 12101 *et seq.* (1990).

American Psychiatric Association. (1994). *Diagnostic and statistical manual of mental disorders* (4th ed.). Washington, DC: Author.

Blankertz, L. E., & Keller, C. (1997). *The provision of long-term vocational supports for individuals with severe mental illness.* Association Paper. Washington, DC: American Sociological Association.

Bruyere, S. M., & Golden, T. P. (1994). *Working effectively with persons who have cognitive disabilities.* Program on Employment and Disability, Cornell University. Retrieved June 18, 2004, from http://www.ilr.cornell.edu/extension/files/download/Cognitive_Disabilities.pdf

Civil Rights Act of 1964, Pub. L. 88-352.

DuPont Corporation. (1993). *Equal to the task II: 1990 DuPont survey of employment of people with disabilities.* Wilmington, DE: Author.

Equal Employment Opportunity Commission. (1998). *EEOC enforcement activities.* Retrieved August 19, 1998, from http://www.eeoc.gov/enforce.html

Equal Employment Opportunity Commission. (1999). *Jury awards $13 million in disability discrimination case.* Retrieved November 15, 1999, from http://www.eeoc.gov/press/11-06-99.html

Equal Employment Opportunity Commission Enforcement Guidance: The Americans With Disabilities Act and Psychiatric Disabilities, 8 FEP Manual (BNA) 915:002 (1997).

Equal Pay Act of 1963, Pub. L. 88-38.

Hall, R. C., & Wise, M. G. (1995). The clinical and financial burden of mood disorders: Cost and outcome. *Psychosomatics, 36,* 11–18.

Hyler, S. E., Gabbard, G. D., & Schneider, I. (1991). Homicidal maniacs and narcissistic parasites: Stigmatization of mentally ill persons in the movies. *Hospital and Community Psychiatry, 42,* 1044–1048.

International Association. (1999). *Complying with the Americans With Disabilities Act: A guide to selected forms of accommodation—modified and specialized equipment.* International Association of Machinists and Aerospace Workers, Center for Administering Rehabilitation and Employment Services. Retrieved May 11, 1998, from http://www.iamcaresdc.org/ADA%20Guides/Equipment.htm

Job Accommodation Network. (1999). *Accommodation benefit/cost data.* Job Accommodation Network, Office of Disability Employment Policy, U. S. Department of Labor. Retrieved June 18, 2004, from http://www.jan.wvu.edu/media/Stats/BenCosts0799.html

Mancuso, L. L. (2000). *Employing and accommodating workers with psychiatric disabilities.* Program on Employment and Disability, Cornell University. Retrieved June 18, 2004, from http://www.ilr.cornell.edu/extension/files/download/Psychiatric_Disabilities.pdf

McNeil, J. (2001). *Americans with disabilities—1997.* U.S. Census Bureau. Retrieved June 18, 2004, from http://www.census.gov/prod/2001pubs/p70-73.pdf

Minton, E. (1999). *Attitudinal barriers.* President's Committee on Employment of People With Disabilities Communications Subcommittee. Retrieved November 15, 1999, from http://www50.pcepd.gov/pcepd/ztextver/pubs/ek99/barriers.htm

Monahan, J. (1992). Mental disorder and violent behavior: Perceptions and evidence. *American Psychologist, 47,* 511–521.

Murphy v. United Parcel Service, 527 U.S. 516 (1999).

National Alliance for the Mentally Ill. (1993). *Facts about mental illness.* Retrieved December 21, 2004, from http://miaw.nami.org/mifact.html

National Institutes of Health. (1999). *The numbers count: Mental illness in America.* NIH Publication No. NIH 99-4584.

National Organization on Disability. (2002). *2000 N. O. D./Harris survey of Americans with disability.* Washington, DC: Author.

President's Committee on Employment of People With Disabilities. (1994). *Accommodations get the job done.* Retrieved November 15, 1999, from http://www50.pcepd.gov/pcepd/ztextver/pubs/fact/accomod.htm

President's Committee on Employment of People With Disabilities. (1999). *Technology and people with disabilities.* Retrieved November 15, 1999, from http://www50.pcepd.gov/pcepd/ztextver/pubs/ek99/tech.htm

Surgeon General's Report. (1999). *Mental health: A report of the Surgeon General.* Rockville, MD: U.S. Department of Health and Human Services.

Torrey, E. F. (1997). *Out of the shadows: Confronting America's mental illness crisis.* New York: Wiley.

United States Department of Justice. (2004). *Myths and facts about the Americans With Disabilities Act.* Retrieved December 21, 2004, from http://www.usdoj.gov/crt/ada/pubs/mythfct.txt

Wahl, O. F. (1997). *Consumers and stigma: Study finds discrimination still pervasive.* National Alliance for the Mentally Ill. Retrieved November 13, 1999, from http://nami.org/research/970913201441.html

6

AIDING IN THE RESOLUTION
OF FACTUAL DISPUTES

EXAMPLE: TRADEMARK INFRINGEMENT

As consumers, we expect certain things. We expect to be treated fairly at the point of purchase. We expect value for our money; the more we spend the better the product should be. We expect reputable companies to stand behind their products by offering a warranty if a product should fail or break after limited use. We expect to be subjected to persuasive advertising or promotion, but we do not expect to be lied to in an advertisement.

As producers, we also expect certain things. We expect to be compensated fairly for what we make. We expect to be paid in a timely fashion if we extend a loan to a consumer so that our product may be used immediately. We expect that we will be allowed to freely market and advertise our products. We expect that other companies will not use our company name and logo (or ones very similar) on their product to try and fool consumers into thinking that their product is made by us.

The consumer's expectation that the name and logo (i.e., an identifying symbol, drawing, or statement) that adorn a product are an accurate reflection of that product's origin and the producer's expectation that a name and logo will not be impermissibly used by another producer are the bases for the law dealing with trademark infringement. In this chapter, we present a classic story about this problem. Everyone is familiar with Volkswagen (VW) and Audi automobiles, and if you owned one and needed it repaired, you might choose an authorized VW or Audi repair shop. If you were in New York City and checked the yellow pages, you would have come across an advertisement for Uptown Motors. To catch your attention, Uptown used the VW and Audi logos in its advertisement, even though these automobile manufacturers had not given Uptown permission to do so. Not surprisingly, VW and Audi sued Uptown for trademark infringement.

Disputes between individuals or businesses usually revolve around specific questions of fact. Although many of these facts can be resolved by the testimony of laypersons (e.g., "I saw the light turn green"), behavioral and social science can often aid in the resolution of more complex factual disputes. In this case, the law wants the trier of fact (the jury when there is one and the judge in other cases) to answer the question about whether consumers are likely to be confused by Uptown's use of the VW and Audi trademarks, by assuming that Uptown is an authorized service center for these automobiles. This is a factual question that behavioral and social scientists can help the legal decision maker answer.

VOLKSWAGEN AND AUDI V. UPTOWN MOTORS

United States District Court for the Southern District of New York

Volkswagen and Audi are makers and importers of automobiles. Volkswagen and Audi allege that Uptown Motors used the VW and Audi logos (also known as *trademarks* or *marks*) in its yellow pages advertisement in a way that violated the federal Lanham Act (Trademark Act of 1946), which prohibits trademark infringement. In order to prevail, VW and Audi must demonstrate that Uptown's use of the logos created a likelihood of confusion. This means that VW and Audi must show that an appreciable number of ordinarily prudent purchasers are likely to be misled or confused as to the source of the services in question. If VW and Audi can prove likelihood of confusion, they can stop Uptown from using their logos in the future. If VW and Audi can prove actual confusion, VW and Audi are entitled to receive (a) Uptown's profits from Uptown's use of VW's and Audi's trademarks, (b) any financial damages sustained by VW and Audi because of Uptown's actions, and (c) the costs of this court action. In assessing damages, the court may enter a judgment for any sum above the amount of actual damages if the facts warrant it, but not exceeding three times the amount of actual damages.

In deciding trademark infringement cases, courts turn to the multifactor test that includes the following:

- the strength of VW's and Audi's trademarks
- the degree of similarity between VW's and Audi's trademarks and Uptown's mark
- the proximity of the products and services (i.e., were VW and Audi in the same business as Uptown)
- the quality of Uptown's product and services
- Uptown's good faith in adopting VW's and Audi's marks
- actual confusion by consumers as to the source of the products and services offered by Uptown

The proper approach is to weigh each factor in the context of the others to determine if, on balance, a likelihood of confusion exists.

Strength of Volkwagen's and Audi's Trademarks

It is undisputed that the VW and Audi logos (henceforth VW) are registered trademarks, distinctive and strong. There have been years of substantial investment in advertising and promoting them, resulting in years of sales, indeed millions of them. And the trademarks at issue here are fanciful (i.e., unrelated to the product or service in any way), which by their very nature make them strong marks.

Degree of Similarity Between Volkswagen's Trademark and Uptown's Mark

There is no issue in dispute here. Uptown was using VW's trademarks in its advertising.

Proximity of the Products and Services

Uptown services and repairs automobiles. It does not sell them. Thus, Uptown claims that their product is very different from VW's. Indeed, Uptown contends that VW's trademark is not strong in the area of servicing and repair of automobiles. However, the undisputed evidence reflects significant expenditures by VW in the promotion and management of its servicing and repair businesses, which belies Uptown's claim.

Quality of Volkswagen's and Uptown's Services

The high quality of VW's service work remains undisputed in this case. There have been substantial investments by VW to make sure that the quality of their services remained high. Volkswagen monitors service quality through a customer satisfaction telephone follow-up system. Whenever dealerships service an automobile covered under VW's service plans, including routine maintenance, the customer is contacted within a week by an agency that conducts a service satisfaction survey. The agency then provides VW with daily service alerts if any customer is dissatisfied with the service received. The agency also reviews those daily alerts each day and then contacts the dealership to make sure that the customer complaint is promptly addressed.

Uptown has been in the business of car repair and service for decades. It specializes in the service and repair of what it calls 12 different high-tech foreign cars. Whenever it does repairs to VW automobiles, it uses genuine VW parts. However, the president, CEO, and manager of Uptown, did not, either at their depositions or at trial, know the names of the four or six mechanics they employ to do the repair and servicing work. They did not know the mechanics' employment background or prior training. They had no formal training program but merely put each employee on probation for a week or two when they were first hired to see if they were capable of performing the work. Management's testimony raises a serious question as to the quality of the repair and service provided at Uptown and certainly indicates that it is not of the same level as that provided by VW. However, the more important point is that VW has no control over the quality of the work done at Uptown today or in the future.

Uptown's Good Faith in Using Volkswagen's Trademark

This factor considers whether Uptown adopted its mark with the intention of capitalizing on VW's reputation and good will and on any confusion between its and VW's products or services. Uptown knew that the VW logo was a trademark. It knew as long as 20 years ago that VW vigorously enforced its trademark rights against car dealers because Uptown's owner heard from a dealer who stopped using the logo because of VW's efforts. And Uptown knew years ago that VW had prevailed in 47 cases of infringement by unauthorized service centers. Uptown also knew that it was not authorized to use the VW logo and never sought permission to do so. Finally, Uptown received a letter from VW demanding that it cease and desist using the VW logo. Over the course of two years that followed from the first letter, Uptown received four separate letters from VW and its attorneys before this lawsuit was filed, and all that while Uptown continued to use VW's logo.

Therefore, there is no question that Uptown made knowing, intentional, and willful use of VW's trademark and that the action it took in doing so was not taken in good faith. Uptown explains its decision, in effect, as a way to advertise its services in a most effective way. Of course it is effective; it reflects the power of trademarks and that is why they are protected. If someone stole Uptown's name or logo to set up a competing business, Uptown would be rightly outraged. Yet Uptown saw no problem in capitalizing unfairly on the good will that VW and its licensees had worked for years to create.

Confusion as to the Source of the Services

Although actual confusion is a factor in determining the likelihood of confusion, VW is not required to prove actual confusion in order to prevail and stop Uptown from using VW's logo in its advertising. It must prove actual confusion, however, to obtain monetary compensation. The confusion asserted here is that some VW owners will read Uptown's ads and mistakenly believe that Uptown is an authorized service center for VW automobiles.

Typically, confusion is proven either through anecdotal evidence or surveys. Here VW primarily presented evidence of confusion through a survey. The survey measured the effect of the VW logo in combination with its name in Uptown's ads on consumers' belief that the advertiser was an authorized VW service center (hereafter logo condition). The impact of the logo was compared to the effect that the use of the VW name without the logo in the same ad had on that belief (hereafter name condition), with both groups receiving the same questions. The exact questions used in the New York study were not reported in the court's opinion. However, from the court's discussion of the case, it appears that two questions were asked: (a) Look at this advertisement and tell me if the repair shop is an authorized VW service center? (b) How confident are you in your decision?

Because the study was done with a control group (i.e., the name condition), using standard scientific and experimental methodologies, many of the criticisms that Uptown made of the survey were irrelevant. For example, because the same questions were asked of both groups, any distorting effect from the questions was canceled out. This was brought home forcefully by a follow-up experiment conducted at the investigator's university in Canada. This study duplicated the original study in New York, but the groups were asked a different question, in effect, is the dealer authorized or independent, in your judgment? The results showed that the percentage difference between the logo and name groups was almost identical in the New York and Canadian studies. Thus, the question asked in the original survey was reasonable and not overly leading, particularly in the context of the entire study and its many controls.

Uptown challenged the study for its having been conducted on the premises of the three New York City VW dealers. Uptown's expert admitted that he did not know how much of an effect the location had or in what direction this impact would be. To eliminate the question of whether the environment had an impact, Uptown's expert recommended that the experiment be replicated in every detail at a neutral location. But something close to this was actually done in the follow-up study, which used undergraduate students from the Canadian university as the respondents. Whereas the original study had a logo effect of 17.3%, the follow-up study had a logo effect of 17.2%. Both of these results were statistically significant and obviously nonsignificantly different from each other. This is a strong indication that the logo effect is not restricted to New York City or VW owners.

It also is important to note that Uptown's expert approved of the use of the logo and name conditions in the overall design of the survey. He also approved the use of the number of respondents as an accepted number for the kind of study that was done to yield statistically significant results. Uptown's expert proposed, however, that an effort be made to get the names and telephone numbers of VW owners on the east side of Manhattan, which is where Uptown is located. He was not clear how these names and telephone numbers would be obtained, and he made no effort to be clear. Next he proposed that he would call individuals from this group and ask them enough questions to camouflage the fact that they were being screened during the telephone call. Among the series of questions that they would be asked were whether they owned a VW, whether they used the yellow pages, and whether they were the person in the family who made the decision as to where servicing of their automobile would be done. Inquiry would also be made as to whether they were an Uptown customer. Uptown's expert proposed that after a sufficient number of questions are asked over the telephone to identify the proper sample for the survey, that he would then entice them to a neutral location to participate in a face-to-face survey by paying them $20 to $25 for their time and effort. Then at that neutral location he would use the same experiment included in the survey, except he would use the question with the alternative phrasing and use trained interviewers only. And following that, he would do a validation study by calling the respondents another time some days later.

Although no study is perfect, Uptown's expert readily admitted that it is difficult to conceive of how his proposed study could work. One must consider the real world and the practicalities of surveys when designing a study. It is inconceivable to this court that Uptown's expert would get participation from a large enough random sample to constitute a valid study. There are two insurmountable barriers after you obtain the names and phone numbers, assuming that you could do so. One would be the willingness of east side VW owners who make repair decisions and read the yellow pages to participate in a telephone screening interview. As Uptown admits, these are busy professionals for whom time is precious. If you could get them to participate in the entire telephone screening process and identify enough participants through that process, you then have the second insurmountable hurdle of convincing them to travel to a neutral site, even with the incentive of $20 to $25. The fact that Uptown's proposal is unworkable perhaps explains why the defendant chose not to conduct a survey. Although the burden remains on VW to prove the likelihood of confusion and actual confusion, the failure of Uptown to provide any meaningful critique of the plaintiffs' survey or alternative survey results is significant.

Uptown also contends that VW's survey was faulty because it was conducted among those who had already made a purchase decision instead of among potential customers. This criticism is made because the survey was conducted at repair sites and of customers who were getting their cars repaired at the three VW locations. This criticism might be valid if a purchase decision is one that is made rarely. But here, when it comes to servicing and repairing a car, it is a decision that is made repeatedly. There was particular advantage, in fact, in asking consumers who are seeking repair service at the moment to answer the questions on the survey because their minds are very focused on the issue. They are, so to speak, in a buying (i.e., servicing and repairing) frame of mind. Moreover, for all the consumers whose cars are still under warranty, there is a strong financial incentive to get the repair and service work done with the dealer until the end of the warranty. Therefore, this is the only place at which you are going to find this potential group of Uptown customers, people who will, at the end of the warranty period, consider going somewhere else. It is interesting to note that in connection with the New York survey results, the logo effect was as strong among those whose cars were still under warranty as among those whose warranties had expired.

The survey is an elegant way of measuring the effect of the defendant's use of the VW logo in its ads as opposed to solely using the VW name. In effect, it answers the question, what extra benefit did the defendant receive from its decision to use the visually effective logo as opposed to using the VW name in advertising his services? Of course, to be relevant and probative, the experiment has to be fairly conducted and relate directly to the issues at hand. The study was directed to the relevant issues and measured the relevant universe, that is, potential customers of Uptown Motors and owners of VWs in the New York City area. The survey was fairly designed and conducted.

The survey used classic scientific methods to measure the effect of the use of the logo against the use of the VW name in Uptown's ad. The survey gathered data on certainty and measured five different levels of certainty. The confidence level was the same between the two conditions, the logo (with the name) and name only conditions, and therefore, the difference in confidence levels cannot explain the logo effect. The survey invited respondents to give open-ended responses that allowed for review of their understanding and the rationality of their reasoning process in answering the survey and that further allowed for measurement of the significance of the logo effect. An analysis of the open-ended responses to the survey reveals that almost two thirds of the respondents who responded yes to the logo condition questionnaire (i.e., "Look at this advertisement and tell me if the repair shop is an authorized VW service center") believed Uptown Motors was authorized because of the presence of the logo. Furthermore, the survey asked questions to evaluate whether there were other possible explanations for the logo effect, for instance, the age of the respondent or whether the car was under warranty. With respect to each of these additional variables, there was no difference in the logo effect. The logo and name condition surveys were randomly assigned to respondents. Finally, there was no statistically significant difference in the responses between those interviewed by the trained personnel and the relatively untrained personnel. Moreover, the survey required that respondents fill out the questionnaires themselves, which reduced the likelihood that they were reacting to cues, even unintentional cues, from the interviewers.

Volkswagen has established likelihood of confusion and actual confusion. Uptown Motors is hereby stopped from using the registered trademark of VW in any manner whatsoever. Uptown may use the word Volkswagen in its advertisements only to convey the information that it services this type of automobile.

ANALYSIS AND IMPLICATIONS

According to the federal law that regulates trademarks, a trademark includes any word, name, symbol, or device, or any combination, that a company intends to use in commerce for the purposes of identifying its product and differentiating it from those of competitors. As with any law, there are exceptions. Generic words are not eligible for trademark protection. Imagine the uproar if a manufacturer of computer software sought a trademark for *Computer Software* brand computer software and then tried to prevent every other software manufacturer from using the term Computer Software. More familiar examples of terms that courts have ruled are generic include lite (as in lite beer), aspirin (as in Bayer aspirin), and soft soap (as in liquid soap). Some of these terms may have once been considered trademarks, but their use has become so common, in the opinion of the courts, that consumers no longer associate them with particular brands.

Trademark Strength

Trademarks can vary in their strength. The strongest trademarks are arbitrary or fanciful. They are often made-up words or symbols, created solely for the purpose of identifying a product. If considered alone, they do not even describe the product. If the term *Exxon*, for example, had been coined yesterday, one would never guess that it referred to an oil company. The uniqueness of such words and symbols implies that they can be associated only with the goods or services to which they are attached. Exxon is a fanciful term that has no meaning other than it is used to identify a place to buy gas and service your car. The fact that it could not be used to plausibly identify anything else makes it a strong trademark.

The second strongest trademarks are suggestive. Unlike arbitrary trademarks, these do suggest something about the goods and services to which they are attached. For example, manufacturers take advantage of the word's meaning to suggest to consumers that the product shares some of the same qualities that the term implies. When Ford Motor Company named one of their car models *Mustang*, it likely did so in the belief that the term would conjure up a certain image for consumers that they would find appealing (e.g., strong, fast, independent, free spirited, and untamed).

The weakest trademarks are descriptive. These terms unambiguously describe a characteristic of the product, such as its color or ingredients. For example, *honey-baked ham* might be used by a manufacturer to suggest to consumers that its hams are baked in honey. The manufacturer may have a hard time trying to convince a court that the term is a trademark unless the term acquired what the law calls *secondary meaning*. A term acquires secondary meaning when it becomes associated in the minds of consumers with the specific brand to which it is attached. Thus, the term honey-baked ham might acquire secondary meaning and become a trademark if it came to be understood as an identifier of a specific brand of baked ham made by a specific manufacturer.

Volkswagen's Interest in Protecting Its Trademark

It may not be obvious why a large company like VW would go after a small player like Uptown. After all, Uptown may just have been using the logo to help potential customers identify the types of cars that it repaired. This seems to be both a reasonable advertising tactic and consumer friendly. But what if you took your VW to Uptown for repairs believing, on the basis of the ad, that it was an authorized VW repair shop, and you were not satisfied with the work? Taking your complaint to VW would not do any good because VW is not associated with Uptown, could not get your money back from Uptown, and could not get Uptown to fix your car properly. In addition, VW was fearful that the reputation it had spent millions of dollars to develop would be harmed by repair practices it had no control over. To protect its reputation and to prevent its potential customers from being deceived by Uptown's use of the VW logo, VW sued Uptown.

There is another reason why companies like VW pursue these suits. Under trademark law, if you do not seek to protect your trademark when it is being used without your permission, you run the risk of actually losing it. At the very least, you run the risk of your trademark becoming weakened. In the minds of consumers, your trademark is no longer exclusively associated with your product and service (the strength of a trademark). This is called dilution (Bible, 1998), and courts are less inclined to protect diluted marks.

Resolving the Likelihood of Confusion Issue

Judges and juries have several issues to resolve in trademark cases, but the one of interest here is the issue of *likelihood of confusion*. It refers to whether an appreciable number of reasonably prudent purchasers are likely to confuse the origin of a product or service. That is, are consumers likely to be confused about who really makes the product, provides the services, or authorizes the products or services? If a judge or jury decides that there is likelihood of confusion, then the judge will rule that the infringer (Uptown) has to stop using the trademark. However, if there was *actual* confusion, as opposed to confusion just being likely, then Uptown may be made to pay the holder of the original trademark (VW) for any damages that were incurred. What makes likelihood of confusion so interesting is that it clearly suggests that the courts want to look into the minds of consumers to find out what they think when they see and evaluate a trademark, and evaluate how they behave in response to their cognitions about the trademark. Who better to help the courts peer into the minds of consumers than behavioral and social scientists?

The court, which used what it called the multifactor test to address the confusion issue, considered the strength of a trademark, trademark similarity, marketplace proximity (do they compete in the same market), product quality, the good faith of the alleged infringer in using another's trademark, and whether consumers were likely to be confused by the way the trademark was used. There are several ways that a court can decide each of these issues. One way is called judicial notice. When a judge takes judicial notice it means that he or she knows something to be true and does not need either side to try and prove it. In trademark cases, judges may take judicial notice that a manufacturer of *Eagle* automobiles does not compete in the same market as a manufacturer of *Eagle* birdseed. Archival data, another source of evidence that judges can use, is information that has been previously collected about something. For example, a judge may include the amount of money that a company has spent in promoting and advertising its product or the number of sales a company made each month in the prior five years. Large advertising expenditures over many years presumably mean that a company is trying to influence consumers to uniquely identify and value their product, whereas high sales over many years presumably mean that the trademark is effective because consumers are associating the trademark with that particular product (i.e., the trademark has acquired secondary meaning). Judges may also hear testimony about the behavior of litigants and other relevant individuals (e.g., consumers). Judges may be interested in hearing first hand from potential and actual consumers on what they were thinking and what they decided when they viewed a trademark. This is testimony about behavioral and social facts, although these facts have not been scientifically proven. Finally, judges can receive testimony about the results of behavioral and social scientific research that proves facts about human behavior. The survey presented in this case is one example of such behavioral and social scientific research.

Science Behind the Social Science Survey

A hypothesis is a statement of what a researcher expects the effect of some variable to be on the behavior of a particular group. In a trademark infringement case, for example, it may be hypothesized that there will be no significant difference in the ability of consumers to tell the difference between two companies that use the same logo in their advertisements.

A behavioral or social scientist would then design an experiment to test the hypothesis. To do so, the behavior of two groups is typically compared. One group, called the experimental or treatment group, is exposed to the independent variable (i.e., the variable whose effect the researcher is interested in). In this case, the trademark is the independent variable, and we expect it to have some influence on the level of confusion of consumers (i.e., the dependent variable). Questions designed to detect confusion are called the dependent measures. The control group will be treated exactly the same way as the experimental group with one critical exception: They will not be exposed to the independent variable. If the two groups differ significantly in their performance on the dependent variable (i.e., one group is significantly more confused than the other), we may attribute the difference to the effect of the independent variable (i.e., the presence of the trademark). This is called the treatment effect. Because both groups were treated identically except for the presence of the independent variable in the experimental group and its absence in the control group, we can conclude that the independent variable is responsible for any performance difference.

If researchers were not sure if both the experimental and control groups were treated the same, they would have to consider the possibility that an extraneous (i.e., confounding) variable was responsible for the performance difference. The scientists would then have little faith in either the accuracy or veracity of the experimental results. Thus, behavioral and social scientists strive to ensure that the only difference between the two groups in an experiment is the manipulation of the independent variable.

Surveys, the preferred method for determining likelihood of confusion and actual confusion, differ from experiments in that surveys are better suited to assess various characteristics of a particular population of people (Fowler, 1993; Ray, 1993). Respondents may be asked questions or asked to react to statements to measure their attitudes, beliefs, opinions, or values. When the surveys include the presentation of the trademark for consumers to evaluate, the surveys take on some of the characteristics of an experiment. The use of experimental methodologies in surveys allows the researcher to make causal inferences on the basis of the collected data (Krosnick, 1999); if the treatment and control groups differ in their responses to the survey, it was because of the independent variable. The results of an experiment survey provide compelling evidence for determining whether consumers were likely or actually confused by a company's use of another's trademark.

Sampling

In a trademark case, the population to be surveyed must comprise individuals who are at least potential customers of the product or service in question. Some courts prefer that actual customers be used in a survey rather than consumers who may or may not one day use the product. An entire population of a particular group of people is rarely surveyed. If a trademark case involved a breakfast cereal, for example, the population of potential consumers could number into the tens of millions. Such a large group could never be surveyed. The alternative is to survey a sample of the population, and it is from this sample of the population that we hope to learn about the characteristics of the population. If the sample is chosen carefully, we can conclude that the results of the survey conducted on the sample reflect what the results would have been had the entire population been surveyed. This is called generalizability. It is critical that the characteristics of the population be reflected in the composition of the sample. If they are not, the validity of the generalizations made about the population, based on the sample, cannot be guaranteed. This would be fatal in an infringement case. A judge or jury could make no determination on the degree to which the population of cereal eaters was confused by a trademark if the sample largely comprised people who skipped breakfast.

There are several ways that researchers use to select adequate samples of a population. Probability sampling ensures that every member of the population has an equal and known probability of being selected for the sample. It is similar to raffling off a prize by putting everyone's name into a hat and randomly drawing the winner. Sometimes, people who have a particular characteristic appear in very small numbers in a population and fail to be included in the sample. To ensure that these people are represented in the sample, researchers may separate them into a separate category from which a random sample is drawn. They are then added to the randomly selected members of the other category to form a representative sample of the population. The logical outgrowth of this approach is stratified random sampling, which requires the researcher to identify each subtype in the population that is important to have represented in the sample and then systematically sample from each subtype or stratum (Fink & Kosecoff, 1998).

Other forms of sampling, called nonprobability sampling, are not equally precise (Fink & Kosecoff, 1998) and may carry little weight with courts. For example, convenience sampling refers to individuals who were selected to participate in a survey by virtue of their mere availability, like shoppers in a mall or students in a classroom. Data based on convenience samples must be interpreted with great care (Fink & Kosecoff, 1998).

Sample size is another important issue. A small sample runs the risk of not including all of the kinds of individuals who exist in the population. This will make it more difficult to generalize the results from the sample to the population. An appropriate sample size is determined by the research question, the size of the population, the homogeneity of the population, and the desired accuracy of the answer to the research question. In general, the larger the variation in the population, the larger the sample must be. Formulas exist to determine the appropriate sample size to take into account the factors just mentioned and a variety of statistical considerations, such as confidence levels, standard deviations, and desired precision (Fink & Kosecoff, 1998).

Survey Format

The format of the questions can have a big influence on the way they are answered. Survey questions are usually either open-ended or fixed-alternative format. Open-ended questions can be answered in any way the respondent chooses. This has the advantage of not directing the respondent to an answer. Scoring open-ended questions can be problematic, however, because of the difficulty of quantifying verbal responses and of categorizing responses in which the respondent provided too much or too little information. Fixed-alternative format questions provide respondents with a predetermined set of responses, from which respondents select the alternative they like most. This makes scoring very easy, but it prevents respondents from explaining their answers and limits respondents to choices that they might not want to make (Bishop, Hippler, Schwarz, & Strack, 1988).

The way the questions are worded is another important factor that can influence answers. Developing fair and nonleading questions is more difficult than one might think. Leading questions result in response bias because they implant suggestions into the minds of respondents where there may have been none. For example, fixed-alternative format questions should include a *don't know* response among the alternatives. Without this alternative, respondents are sometimes forced to make wild guesses. The solution to these problems is to thoroughly pretest the survey on a sample of the same population for which it was designed. Pretesting allows the researcher to identify survey methods, phrasing, and questions that create problems for the respondents. For example, a cognitive pretesting technique requires respondents to "think aloud" while they answer the questions in the survey. Such a method presumably allows the researcher an insight into the cognitive processes by which the respondent comprehends the question and develops a response. When a respondent has a problem with either of these tasks, the researcher can go back and revise the question, inadequate alternatives (in the case of fixed-format surveys), scoring method, or task before the survey is presented as evidence in court (DeMaio & Rothgeb, 1996).

Survey Administration

Once the survey has been designed and revised through pretesting, a decision must be made on how to administer it. Alternatives include face-to-face interviews, mailings, and phone calls. Face-to-face interviews allow a respondent's interest and honesty to be gauged and allow the interviewer to explain something that the respondent may not understand about a question or a response alternative; they result in a higher completion rate compared to surveys conducted either by mail or telephone (Brehm, 1993). Drawbacks of face-to-face interviews are their costs and the possibility that interviewers may give subtle cues to the respondent on how to answer questions. Surveys sent through the mail have the advantage of anonymity for the respondent and ease of administration for the researcher, but they have poor return rates. Telephone interviews are cost effective, but they also suffer from low completion rates. People have a tendency to either not participate or to end the interview early. In addition, they suffer because the respondent is not looking at the trademark in question.

Finally, in trademark infringement cases, mailings and phone interviews fail to satisfy one of the qualities that most judges look for when evaluating the efficacy of a survey. That is, surveys should be conducted in the social environment that most closely resembles the environment to which the researcher wishes to generalize. This does not mean that consumers should only be questioned in stores where the product or service is available for purchase. That would be impracticable. It does mean that, insofar as is possible, a respondent should be in the same buying frame of mind as if he or she were really evaluating the product for purchase.

Rigid Interviewing Versus Conversational Interviewing

The conventional wisdom in survey administration is that the researcher must ask the exact same question and conduct the survey in the exact same manner for each respondent. The fear is that any alteration in either questions or methods will produce differing responses and thus degrade the reliability and validity of the survey. However, Schober and Conrad (1997) have challenged this assumption through their research. Imagine yourself in a conversation with a friend. When either of you says something the other does not understand, one of you will probably ask for a clarification. This is part of the normal give and take of everyday social interaction. It is unlikely that one of you will simply repeat the misunderstood statement exactly as it was uttered the first time, and there is little chance that such a conversational tactic would further the comprehension of the misunderstood statement. You can see the problem when this principle is applied to survey research. If a respondent does not understand either the task or a question and asks for help in understanding it, then a regurgitation of the instructions or the question is unlikely to help the respondent suddenly understand what could not be understood a moment before. Schober and Conrad (1997) produced significant increases in survey validity when they permitted interviewers to rephrase or reexplain questions that respondents were having problems understanding.

Cognitive Processes in Answering Questions

What does a person do cognitively to answer a question? The obvious first steps are either to hear or read the question, locate the meanings of the words and concepts in memory, and come to an understanding of the question's meaning (Clark & Clark, 1977). Next, the respondent searches memory for information that can be used to answer the question. The selected information must then be evaluated for its relevance and appropriateness and eventually integrated into an answer that the respondent feels best answers the question. Based on the judgment made, the last step requires the respondent to generate an accurate written or verbal response or match his or her answer with one of the response choices in the question.

Answering questions can require considerable cognitive effort. Why do people try so hard to answers questions accurately sometimes but other times take a cavalier attitude toward them? They might try and do their best if they thought that the task presented an opportunity to be altruistic, intellectually challenged, self-expressive, successful, or cathartic (Warwick & Lininger, 1975). When people do try their best they are said to be *optimizing* (Krosnick, 1999). On the other hand, some may find the task of answering questions just too cognitively demanding. This may be due to a lack of interest or emotional investment, fatigue, or distractions. In addition, some respondents may simply lack the ability to process what they find to be a complex task. When problems like this occur, respondents adopt a different strategy for answering questions. This strategy involves expending fewer cognitive resources on comprehension of the question, retrieval of information from memory, integrating the information into an optimal judgment, and generating an appropriate response or choice selection (Krosnick, 1991). Under these circumstances a respondent is said to be *satisficing*, that is, selecting an answer that merely satisfies the question. In the worst case, a respondent expends no mental energy and simply guesses (Krosnick, 1991).

Demand characteristics of the survey may also influence responding. For example, Krosnick, Li, and Lehman (1990) have shown that people interpret the information contained in the latter part of a question as more important to the task of answering the question than they do to the information contained in the first part of the question. Respondents apparently interpret the information that comes later as more important and thus more reflective of the researcher's beliefs. They then try to answer the question according to how they think the researcher wants the question answered. Psychologists call this phenomenon a *demand characteristic* of the task (i.e., respondents mistakenly believe that the question demands them to answer a certain way; Orne, 1962).

Another potential source of response bias is a respondent's reluctance to disclose information if the subject of the survey is on a sensitive or personal issue like sex or drug use (Gribble, Miller, Rogers, & Turner, 1999). In addition, some respondents may be perfectly willing to disclose their views on a survey they can take by themselves in the privacy of their own home but be unwilling to make the same disclosures to a complete stranger in a face-to-face encounter (Aquilino, Wright, & Supple, 2000).

Some respondents also may not want to be totally honest in a survey if they believe their answer is not the socially acceptable one. Social scientists have found that the need to provide socially desirable answers is a major source of bias in surveys. Conversely, respondents will avoid answering questions in a way they believe is less socially acceptable (Fisher & Katz, 2000). A related concept, known as acquiescence, is the tendency for some people to generally agree to whatever is put before them. This leads to the curious result of people agreeing to statements that are the exact opposite in meaning although they appear in the same survey (Krosnick, 1999). For example, if a person who acquiesces was asked to take a survey in the Uptown case, he might have agreed with the statement that "Uptown is an authorized VW service repair center because the VW logo appears in Uptown's ad" and with the statement that "The presence of the VW logo in Uptown's ad does not necessarily mean that Uptown is an authorized VW service repair center." It is not clear why some people acquiesce, but it might be because being agreeable is the polite thing to do and thus facilitates social interaction (Brown & Levinson, 1987), because it requires less cognitive effort (Krosnick, 1991), or because it is likely to please the researcher (Carr, 1971).

Interviewer Training

Finally, an ill-prepared or unpracticed interviewer can have an adverse effect on the way respondents behave. Poorly trained interviewers may unknowingly guide the direction of a respondent's answers. Unscrupulous interviewers may purposely guide the responses. If possible, interviewers should not be connected with either party involved in the litigation. In addition, interviewers should be trained to be sensitive to a respondent's discomfort or a lack of honesty in answering the questions. These responses can be marked and set aside for later analysis.

Application of Survey Methods to This Case

Morgan (1990) examined court cases in which judges summarized the findings of survey evidence conducted for trial. He found that judges evaluated the sampling method, questions, operational definitions of legal concepts (e.g., likelihood of confusion), display of trademarks to respondents, qualifications and skill of the interviewers and researchers, and the statistical analysis. The court in Uptown used these and other factors to make its decision.

Anecdotal Evidence

The judge noted that one way to prove confusion is through anecdotal evidence. Whether used in a trademark infringement case or in recommending the *best* product to a friend, such evidence is often very persuasive, but it can be inaccurate. Rather than rely on individual testimonials, VW offered a survey designed and conducted by a university professor. Given the importance that the judge attached to this research because of its scientific credibility, VW made a wise decision.

Control Groups

The judge was impressed by the VW expert's use of a control group. According to the judge, the survey showed some consumers the ad with only the VW name (the control group) and another group the same ad but with the logo added to the name (the experimental group). The difference in each group's level of confusion would be attributable to the presence of the logo, as its inclusion was the only difference between the way each group was treated.

Competing Surveys

The court noted that Uptown did not present its own survey on the likelihood of confusion in the minds of consumers as to whether Uptown was an authorized VW repair shop. Although Uptown could have commissioned such a survey and presented it to the court, they focused on trying to prove that the VW survey was fatally flawed.

If Uptown had conducted such a survey, could they have found results that were opposite to those presented by the VW survey? The answer is yes. Because there is no one *right* way to conduct the survey, differences in methodology between the two surveys could create differences in results. The methodological differences could be in the choice of location to conduct the survey, the population studied, the questions asked, or the responses required of the survey participants. This poses dilemmas from several perspectives. For the courts, the dilemma is relying on a single survey and dealing with different results from competing surveys. For researchers, the dilemma is to design a survey that is reliable and valid to answer the behavioral and social fact question(s) that the litigant needs answered. For litigants and their attorneys, the dilemma is ensuring that the research will accurately and persuasively measure what they are attempting to prove. These problems underscore how important it is for behavioral and social scientists to work closely with the attorneys to ensure that only the information the court requires will be presented and that the research relied on validly tests the disputed fact question in issue in the case.

Importance of the Survey

The court concluded that consumers were likely to be confused by Uptown's ad and ordered Uptown to stop using the VW logo in all future advertising. The court also concluded that the survey provided sufficient proof that an appreciable number of ordinarily prudent purchasers were confused about the relationship between Uptown and VW and thus awarded VW damages (i.e., a financial award).

CHAPTER'S LESSON

The behavioral and social science survey was used to resolve the disputed factual issue in this case (i.e., consumer confusion). The resolution of disputed factual issues can be relevant not only for determining civil liability but also for reaching guilt determinations in criminal cases (e.g., chap. 8, this volume), in imposing civil awards or criminal sanctions, and in determining the constitutionality of governmental action (e.g., chap. 7, this volume).

REFERENCES

Aquilino, W. S., Wright, D. L., & Supple, A. J. (2000). Response effects due to bystander presence in CASI and paper-and-pencil surveys of drug use and alcohol use. *Substance Use & Misuse, 35,* 845–867.

Bible, P. M. (1998). Defining and quantifying dilution under the Federal Trademark Dilution Act of 1995: Using survey evidence to show actual dilution. *University of Colorado Law Review, 70,* 295–340.

Bishop, G. F., Hippler, H. J., Schwarz, N., & Strack, F. (1988). A comparison of response effects in self-administered and telephone surveys. In R. M. Groves, P. P. Biemer, L. E. Lyberg, J. T. Massey, W. L. Nichols, & J. Waksberg (Eds.), *Telephone survey methodology* (pp. 321–324). New York: Wiley.

Brehm, J. (1993). *The Phantom respondents: Opinion surveys and political representation.* Ann Arbor: University of Michigan Press.

Brown, P., & Levinson, S. C. (1987). *Politeness: Some universals in language.* New York: Cambridge University Press.

Carr, L. G. (1971). The Srole items and acquiescence. *American Sociological Review, 36,* 287–293.

Clark, H. H., & Clark, E. V. (1977). *Psychology and language: An introduction to psycholinguistics.* New York: Harcourt Brace Jovanovich.

DeMaio, T, J., & Rothgeb, J. M. (1996). Cognitive interviewing techniques: In the lab and in the field. In N. Schwarz & S. Sudman (Eds.), *Answering questions: Methodology for determining cognitive and communicative processes in survey research* (pp. 177–196). San Francisco: Jossey-Bass.

Federal Trademark Act of 1946, Pub. L. 78-489.

Fink, A., & Kosecoff, J. (1998). *How to conduct surveys: A step-by-step guide.* Thousand Oaks, CA: Sage.

Fisher, R. J., & Katz, J. E. (2000). Social-desirability bias and the validity of self-reported values. *Psychology & Marketing, 17,* 105–120.

Fowler, F. J., Jr. (1993). *Survey research methods* (2nd ed.). Thousand Oaks, CA: Sage.

Gribble, J. N., Miller, H. G., Rogers, S. M., & Turner, C. F. (1999). Interview mode and measurement of sexual behaviors: Methodological issues. *Journal of Sex Research, 36,* 16–24.

Krosnick, J. A. (1991). Response strategies for coping with the cognitive demands of attitude measures in surveys. *Applied Cognitive Psychology, 5,* 213–236.

Krosnick, J. A. (1999). Survey research. *Annual Review of Psychology, 50,* 537–567.

Krosnick, J. A., Li, F., & Lehman, D. R. (1990). Conversational conventions, order of information acquisition, and the effect of base rates and individuating information on social judgments. *Journal of Personality and Social Psychology, 59,* 1140–1152.

Morgan, F. W. (1990). Judicial standards for survey research: An update and guidelines. *Journal of Marketing, 54,* 59–70.

Orne, M. T. (1962). On the social psychology of the psychological experiment: With particular reference to demand characteristics and their implications. *American Psychologist, 17*, 776–783.

Ray, W. J. (1993). *Methods toward a science of behavior and experience.* Pacific Grove, CA: Brooks/Cole.

Schober, M. F., & Conrad, F. G. (1997). Does conversational interviewing reduce survey measurement error? *Public Opinion Quarterly, 61*, 576–602.

Volkswagen Aktiengesellschaft; Audi Aktiengesellschaft; and Volkswagen of America v. Uptown Motors, 1995 WL 605605 (S.D.N.Y., 1995).

Warwick, D. P., & Lininger, C. A. (1975). *The sample survey: Theory and practice.* New York: McGraw-Hill.

7

AIDING IN THE RESOLUTION OF FACTUAL DISPUTES RELATING TO THE CONSTITUTIONALITY OF A LAW

EXAMPLE: DENYING FEMALE APPLICANTS ENTRY
INTO STATE-SUPPORTED ALL-MALE SCHOOLS

This chapter has its origin in a personal life decision that millions of high school students must make each year: what to do after graduation. Do you recall the speech at your graduation, the one given by a member of the school board or perhaps the valedictorian, in which your future was described in terms of limitless potential and infinite opportunity? All you needed was a fair chance, and what you could achieve was up to you. In fact, our society holds this belief in fairness so deeply that it was made part of our federal Constitution (e.g., the Equal Protection Clause of the Fourteenth Amendment).

In discussing future goals, some of your classmates may have expressed a desire to go on to college or to learn a trade and embark on a career immediately after graduating. Some may have expressed a desire to travel, deferring major life decisions until they had seen the world. Others may have aspired to a career in the military, or at least to attend a military academy, that would prepare them, like few schools could, for meeting the stresses and challenges of life after college. If one of the schools on your classmate's wish list was the Virginia Military Institute (VMI) and your classmate was a woman, then the potential and opportunity so glowingly portrayed at graduation would have excluded her. So, although your classmate may have been extraordinarily intelligent and highly motivated, her gender would have automatically disqualified her from attending VMI. This bastion of higher education was reserved for men.

On behalf of a handful of women who applied to VMI in 1990, the United States sued the Commonwealth of Virginia in an effort to make good on the high school aspirations and the constitutional guarantee of equal protection of the laws. The U.S. Supreme Court in this case had to decide a fundamental constitutional issue: Does the Equal Protection Clause of the Fourteenth Amendment of the U.S. Constitution guarantee all citizens an equal educational opportunity at a state-supported school? To answer this constitutional question, the Court first looked to its prior decisions that had already determined that states can lawfully make gender-based classifications for some purposes, but the reasons for doing so must be exceedingly persuasive and in furtherance of an important, legitimate government interest. The Court then looked at the behavioral and social facts to help them decide whether Virginia had exceedingly persuasive justification in excluding women from VMI that furthered a legitimate state interest.

Armed with the behavioral and social facts provided by experts from a variety of disciplines (e.g., psychology and sociology), the Court concluded that the equal protection clause was violated when VMI excluded female applicants. The lesson in this case is that behavioral and social knowledge can help resolve factual disputes that are critical in resolving constitutional questions.

UNITED STATES V. VIRGINIA MILITARY INSTITUTE

United States Supreme Court

Founded in 1839, VMI is today the sole single-sex school among Virginia's 15 public institutions of higher learning. VMI's distinctive mission is to produce citizen-soldiers, men prepared for leadership in civilian life and in military service. VMI pursues this mission through pervasive training of a kind not available anywhere else in Virginia. Assigning a prime place to character development, VMI uses an adversative method (discussed below) modeled on English public schools and once characteristic of military instruction. VMI constantly endeavors to instill physical and mental discipline in its cadets and to impart to them a strong moral code. The school's graduates leave VMI with heightened comprehension of their capacity to deal with duress and stress and a large sense of accomplishment for completing the hazardous course.

VMI has notably succeeded in its mission to produce leaders; among its alumni are military generals, members of Congress, and business executives. The school's alumni overwhelmingly perceive that their VMI training helped them realize their personal goals, with VMI's endowment reflecting the loyalty of its graduates. VMI has the largest per-student endowment of all public undergraduate institutions in the nation.

Neither the goal of producing citizen-soldiers nor VMI's implementing methodology is inherently unsuitable to women. And the school's impressive record in producing leaders has made admission desirable to some women. Nevertheless, Virginia has elected to preserve exclusively for men the advantages and opportunities a VMI education affords.

From its establishment in 1839 as one of the nation's first state military colleges, VMI has remained financially supported by Virginia and subject to the control of Virginia's General Assembly. VMI today enrolls about 1,300 men as cadets. Its academic offerings in the liberal arts, sciences, and engineering are also available at other public colleges and universities in Virginia, but VMI's mission is special. It is the mission of the school to produce educated and honorable men, prepared for the varied work of civil life, imbued with love of learning, confident in the functions and attitudes of leadership, possessing a high sense of public service, advocates of the American democracy and free enterprise system, and ready as citizen-soldiers to defend their country in time of national peril. In contrast to the federal service academies, institutions maintained to prepare cadets for career service in the armed forces, VMI's program is directed at preparation for both military and civilian life with only about 15% of VMI cadets entering career military service.

As already noted, VMI produces its citizen-soldiers through an adversative model of education, which features physical rigor, mental stress, absolute equality of treatment, absence of privacy, minute regulation of behavior, and indoctrination in desirable values. The adversative method dissects the young student and makes him aware of his limits and capabilities so that he knows how far he can go with his anger, how much he can take under stress, and exactly what he can do when he is physically exhausted.

VMI cadets live in spartan barracks where surveillance is constant and privacy nonexistent; they wear uniforms, eat together in the mess hall, and regularly participate in drills. Entering students are incessantly exposed to the rat line, an extreme form of the adversative model, comparable in intensity to Marine Corps boot camp. Tormenting and punishing, the rat line bonds new cadets to their fellow sufferers, and when they have completed the 7-month experience, to their former tormentors.

VMI's adversative model is further characterized by a hierarchical class system of privileges and responsibilities: a dyke system in which each incoming student (known as a rat) is assigned a first classman as a mentor (called a dyke) to engender loyalty and cross-class bonding and to provide a model for leadership and support. In addition this system relies on a stringently enforced honor code that prescribes that a cadet does not lie, cheat, steal, or tolerate those who do.

VMI attracts some applicants because of its reputation as an extraordinarily challenging military school and because its alumni are exceptionally close to the school. In 1990, prompted by a complaint filed with the U.S. Attorney General by a female high school student seeking admission to VMI, the United States sued the Commonwealth of Virginia and VMI, alleging that VMI's exclusively male admission policy violated the Equal Protection Clause of the Fourteenth Amendment. This Amendment reads in part:

> No state shall make or enforce any law which shall abridge
> the privileges or immunities of citizens of the United States;
> nor shall any state . . . deny to any person within its jurisdic-
> tion the equal protection of the laws."

The trial of this case involved an array of expert witnesses on each side.

In the two years preceding the lawsuit, the trial court noted, VMI had received inquiries from 347 women but had responded to none of them. Some women would want to attend the school if they had the opportunity. The court further recognized that, with recruitment, VMI could achieve at least 10% female enrollment, a sufficient critical mass to provide the female cadets with a positive educational experience. And it was also established that some women are capable of all of the individual activities required of VMI cadets. In addition, experts agreed that if VMI admitted women, the VMI ROTC experience would become a better training program from the perspective of the armed forces because it would provide training in dealing with a mixed-gender army.

The trial court ruled in favor of VMI, however, and rejected the equal protection challenge pressed by the United States. That court correctly recognized that a party seeking to uphold government action based on sex (such as Virginia's action in this case) must establish an exceedingly persuasive justification for the classification. In addition, it must show at least that the classification serves important governmental objectives and that the discriminatory means employed are substantially related to the achievement of those objectives.

The trial court reasoned that education in a single-gender environment, be it male or female, yields substantial benefits. VMI's school for men brought diversity to an otherwise coeducational Virginia system and that diversity was enhanced by VMI's unique method of instruction. If single-gender education for men ranks as an important governmental objective, it becomes obvious, the trial court concluded, that the *only* means of achieving the objective is to exclude women from the all-male institution (i.e., VMI).

The trial court acknowledged that women are denied a unique educational opportunity that is available only at VMI. But VMI's single-sex status would be lost, and some aspects of the school's distinctive method would be altered if women were admitted. Allowance for personal privacy would have to be made, physical education requirements would have to be altered, at least for the women, and the adversative environment could not survive unmodified. Thus, sufficient constitutional justification had been shown, the trial court held, for continuing VMI's single-sex policy.

The court of appeals disagreed and held that the Commonwealth of Virginia has not advanced any state policy by which it can justify its determination to afford VMI's unique type of program to men and not to women. The appeals court greeted with skepticism Virginia's assertion that it offers single-sex education at VMI as a facet of the commonwealth's policy to advance autonomy and diversity. The appellate court underscored Virginia's nondiscrimination commitment by citing the 1990 Report of the Virginia Commission on the University of the 21st Century, which stated that it is extremely important that Virginia colleges and universities deal with faculty, staff, and students without regard to sex, race, or ethnic origin. That statement, the court of appeals said, is the only explicit one that we have found in the record in which the commonwealth has expressed itself with respect to gender distinctions. Furthermore, the appeals court observed, in urging diversity to justify an all male VMI, Virginia had supplied no explanation for the movement away from single-sex education by its other state-supported colleges and universities. In short, the court concluded that a policy of diversity that aims to provide an array of educational opportunities, including single-gender institutions, must do more than favor one gender.

The parties agreed that some women can meet the physical standards now imposed on men, and the trial court was satisfied that neither the goal of producing citizen-soldiers nor VMI's implementing methodology is inherently unsuitable to women. The court of appeals, however, accepted the trial court's finding that at least these three aspects of VMI's program—physical training, the absence of privacy, and the adversative approach—would be materially affected by coeducation. The appeals court assigned to Virginia, in the first instance, responsibility for selecting a remedial course of action. The court suggested these options for the commonwealth: admit women to VMI; establish parallel institutions or programs; or abandon state support, leaving VMI free to pursue its policies as a private institution.

In response to the appellate court's ruling, Virginia proposed a parallel program for women: Virginia Women's Institute for Leadership (VWIL). The 4-year, state-sponsored undergraduate program would be located at Mary Baldwin College, a private liberal arts school for women, and would be open initially to about 25 to 30 students. Although VWIL would share VMI's mission to produce citizen-soldiers, the VWIL program would differ, as does Mary Baldwin College, from VMI in academic offerings, methods of education, and financial resources.

The average combined Scholastic Aptitude Test (SAT) score of entrants at Mary Baldwin is about 100 points lower than the score for VMI freshmen. Mary Baldwin's faculty hold significantly fewer PhDs than the faculty at VMI and receive significantly lower salaries. Whereas VMI offers degrees in liberal arts, the sciences, and engineering, Mary Baldwin, at the time of trial, offered only bachelor of arts (BA) degrees. A VWIL student seeking to earn an engineering degree could gain one, without public support, by attending Washington University in St. Louis, Missouri, for two years, paying the required private tuition.

VWIL students would participate in ROTC programs and in a newly established, largely ceremonial Virginia Corps of Cadets, but the VWIL House would not have a military format, and VWIL would not require its students to eat meals together or to wear uniforms during the school day. In lieu of VMI's adversative method, VWIL would have a cooperative method that reinforces self-esteem. In addition to the standard bachelor of arts program offered at Mary Baldwin, VWIL students would take courses in leadership, complete an off-campus leadership externship, participate in community service projects, and assist in arranging a speaker series.

Virginia represented that it would provide equal financial support for in-state VWIL students and VMI cadets, and the VMI

Foundation agreed to supply a $5.4 million endowment for the VWIL program. Mary Baldwin's own endowment is about $19 million; VMI's is $131 million. Mary Baldwin would add $35 million to its endowment based on future commitments; VMI would add $220 million. The VMI Alumni Association has developed a network of employers interested in hiring VMI graduates. The association has agreed to open its network to VWIL graduates, but those graduates would not have the advantage afforded by a VMI degree.

Virginia returned to the trial court seeking approval of its proposed remedial plan, and the court decided the plan met the requirements of the Equal Protection Clause. The trial court again acknowledged that the VMI approach to education could be used to educate women, and in fact, some women may prefer the VMI approach to the VWIL approach, but the controlling legal principles, the trial court decided, do not require Virginia to provide a mirror image VMI for women. The trial court anticipated that the two schools would achieve substantially similar outcomes. It concluded that if VMI marches to the beat of a drum, then Mary Baldwin marches to the melody of a fife, and when the march is over, both will have arrived at the same destination.

A divided court of appeals affirmed the trial court's judgment. Respect for the goal that the Virginia legislature was trying to achieve, the court reasoned, meant that the judiciary should take a cautious approach and ask if that goal was a legitimate governmental objective while refusing to approve any goal that may be pernicious. Providing the option of a single-gender college education may be considered a legitimate and important aspect of a public system of higher education, the appeals court observed, and that objective is not pernicious. Moreover, the appellate court continued, the adversative method vital to a VMI education has never been tolerated in a sexually heterogeneous environment. The adversative method was not designed to exclude women, but women could not be accommodated in the VMI program, the appellate court believed, because female participation in VMI's adversative training would destroy any sense of decency that still defines the relationship between the sexes.

Having determined the legitimacy of Virginia's purpose, the appellate court considered the question of means. Exclusion of men at Mary Baldwin College and women at VMI, the court said, was essential to Virginia's purpose, for without such exclusion, the commonwealth could not accomplish its objective of providing single-gender education. The court recognized that means merged into end, and the merger risked bypassing any equal protection scrutiny. The appellate court therefore added another inquiry, a decisive test it called *substantive comparability*. The key question, the court said, was whether men at VMI and women at VWIL would obtain substantively comparable benefits at their institution or through other means offered by the state. Although the appeals court recognized that the VWIL degree lacks the historical benefit and prestige of a VMI degree, it nevertheless found the educational opportunities at the two schools sufficiently comparable.

It is with this history that this case comes to the U.S. Supreme Court. The case presents two ultimate issues. First, does Virginia's exclusion of women from the educational opportunities provided by VMI—extraordinary opportunities for military training and civilian leadership development—deny to women who are capable of all of the individual activities required of VMI cadets the equal protection of the laws guaranteed by the Fourteenth Amendment? Second, if VMI's unique situation as Virginia's sole single-sex public institution of higher education offends the Constitution's equal protection principle, what is the required remediation?

Equal Protection of the Laws

Our nation has had a long and unfortunate history of sex discrimination. Through a century plus three decades and more of that history, women did not count among voters composing "We the People"; not until 1920 did women gain a constitutional right to the franchise. And for a half century thereafter, it remained the prevailing doctrine that government, both federal and state, could withhold from women opportunities accorded men so long as any basis in reason could be conceived for the discrimination.

In 1971, for the first time in our nation's history, this Court ruled in favor of a woman who complained that her state had denied her the equal protection of its laws. In that case, this Court ruled that a state could not show preference for appointing men as the administrator of a decedent's estate (i.e., the estate of someone who has passed away). Since that case, this Court has repeatedly recognized that the federal and state governments do not act compatibly with the equal protection principle when a law or official policy denies to women, simply because they are women, full citizenship stature.

In reviewing this type of governmental action, a court must determine whether the proffered justification is exceedingly persuasive, with the burden of proving the justification resting entirely on the state. The state must show at least that the challenged classification serves important governmental objectives and that the discriminatory means employed are substantially related to the achievement of those objectives. The justification must be genuine, not hypothesized or invented post hoc in response to litigation. And it must not rely on overbroad generalizations about the different talents, capacities, or preferences of men and women.

This standard for review does not make sex a prohibited classification. Physical differences between men and women are enduring; the two sexes are not interchangeable. A community made up exclusively of one sex is different from a community composed of both. Inherent differences between men and women, we have come to appreciate, remain cause for celebration, but not for denigration of the members of either sex or for artificial constraints on an individual's opportunity. Sex classifications may be used to compensate women for particular economic disabilities they have suffered, to promote equal employment opportunity, to advance full development of the talent and capacities of our nation's people. Such classifications may not be used, as they once were, to create or perpetuate the legal, social, and economic inferiority of women.

Measuring the record in this case against the review standard just described, we conclude that Virginia has shown no exceedingly persuasive justification for excluding all women from the citizen-soldier training afforded by VMI. We therefore affirm the appellate court's initial judgment, which held that Virginia had violated the Fourteenth Amendment's Equal Protection Clause. The remedy offered by Virginia—the Mary Baldwin VWIL program—does not cure the constitutional violation (i.e., it does not provide equal opportunity).

The appellate court initially held that Virginia had advanced no state policy by which it could justify, under equal protection principles, its determination to afford VMI's unique type of program to men and not to women. Virginia asserts two justifications in defense of VMI's exclusion of women. First, Virginia contends that single-sex education provides important educational benefits and contributes to diversity in educational approaches. Second, Virginia argues that the unique VMI method of character development and leadership training—the school's adversative approach—would have to be modified were VMI to admit women. The two justifications will be considered in turn.

Single-sex education affords pedagogical benefits to at least some students Virginia emphasizes, and that reality is uncontested in this litigation. Both men and women can benefit from a single-sex education, the trial court recognized, although the beneficial effects of such education, the trial court added, apparently are stronger among women than among men. The United States does not challenge that recognition. Similarly, it is not disputed that diversity among public educational institutions can serve the public good. But, by its categorical exclusion of women, Virginia has not shown that VMI was established or has been maintained with a view to diversifying educational opportunities within the commonwealth.

Neither recent nor distant history bears out Virginia's alleged pursuit of diversity through single-sex educational options. In 1839, when Virginia established VMI, a range of educational opportunities for men and women was scarcely contemplated. Higher education at the time was considered dangerous for women, reflecting widely held views about women's proper place. Dr. Edward H. Clarke of Harvard Medical School, whose influential book, *Sex in Education*, went through 17 editions, was perhaps the most well-known speaker from the medical community opposing higher education for women. He maintained that the physiological effects of hard study and academic competition with boys would interfere with the development of girls' reproductive organs ("identical education of the two sexes is a crime before God and humanity, that physiology protests against, and that experience weeps over"). H. Maudsley, in *Sex in Mind and in Education* (1874), argued that it is not that girls have no ambition nor that they fail generally to run the intellectual race in coeducational settings, it is that they do it at a cost to their strength and health that entails life-long suffering and even incapacitates them for the adequate performance of the natural functions of their sex. C. Meigs, in *Females and Their Diseases* (1848), noted that after five or six weeks of mental and educational discipline, a healthy woman would lose the habit of menstruation and suffer numerous ills as a result of depriving her body for the sake of her mind. Finally, the nation's first universities and colleges—for example, Harvard in Massachusetts, William and Mary in Virginia—admitted only men. VMI was not at all novel in this respect. In admitting no women, VMI followed the lead of the commonwealth's flagship school, the University of Virginia, founded in 1819.

No struggle for the admission of women to a state university, a historian has recounted, was longer drawn out, or developed more bitterness, than that at the University of Virginia. In 1879, the Virginia State Senate resolved to look into the possibility of higher education for women, recognizing that Virginia has never, at any period of her history, provided for the higher education of her daughters, though she has liberally provided for the higher education of her sons. Despite this recognition, no new opportunities were instantly open to women.

Virginia eventually provided for several women's seminaries and colleges. Farmville Female Seminary became a public institution in 1884. Two women's schools, Mary Washington College and James Madison University, were founded in 1908; another, Radford University, was founded in 1910. By the mid-1970s, all four schools had become coeducational.

Debate concerning women's admission as undergraduates at the main university continued well past the century's midpoint. Familiar arguments were rehearsed. If women were admitted, it was feared, they would encroach on the rights of men; there would be new problems of government, perhaps scandals; the old honor system would have to be changed; standards would be lowered to those of other coeducational schools; and the glorious reputation of the university as a school for men would be trailed in the dust.

Ultimately, in 1970, the most prestigious institution of higher education in Virginia, the University of Virginia, introduced coeducation and, in 1972, began to admit women on an equal basis with men. But Virginia describes the current absence of public single-sex higher education for women as a historical anomaly. The historical record indicates action more deliberate than anomalous. First, there was protection of women against higher education; next, schools for women were far from equal in resources and stature when compared with schools for men; finally, there was conversion of the separate schools to coeducation. The state legislature, prior to the advent of this controversy, had repealed all Virginia statutes requiring individual institutions to admit only men or women. And in 1990, an official commission, legislatively established to chart the future goals of higher education in Virginia, reaffirmed the policy of affording broad access while maintaining autonomy and diversity. Significantly, the commission reported that because colleges and universities provide opportunities for students to develop values and learn from role models, it is extremely important that they deal with faculty, staff, and students without regard to sex, race, or ethnic origin. This statement, the court of appeals observed, is the only explicit one that we have found in the record in which Virginia has expressed itself with respect to gender distinctions.

This Court finds no persuasive evidence in this record that VMI's male-only admission policy is in furtherance of a state policy of diversity. No such policy, the court of appeals observed, can be discerned from the movement of all other public colleges and universities in Virginia away from single-sex education. That court also questioned how one institution with autonomy, but with no authority over any other state institution, can give effect to a state policy of diversity among institutions. A purpose genuinely to advance an array of educational options, as the court of appeals recognized, is not served by VMI's historic and constant plan—a plan to afford a unique educational benefit only to men. However liberally this plan serves the commonwealth's sons, it makes no provision whatever for her daughters. That is not *equal* protection.

Virginia next argues that VMI's adversative method of training provides educational benefits that cannot be made available, unmodified, to women. Virginia asserts that alterations to accommodate women would necessarily be so drastic as to transform or destroy VMI's program. Neither sex would be favored by the transformation because men would be deprived of the unique opportunity currently available to them, and women would not gain that opportunity because their participation would eliminate the very aspects of the program that distinguish VMI from other institutions of higher education in Virginia.

The trial court forecast from expert witness testimony, and the court of appeals accepted, that coeducation would materially affect at least three aspects of VMI's program—physical training, the absence of privacy, and the adversative approach. And it is uncontested that women's admission would require accommodations, primarily in arranging housing assignments and physical training programs for female cadets. It is also undisputed, however, that the VMI methodology could be used to educate women. The trial court even allowed that some women may prefer it to the methodology a women's college might pursue, and some women, the expert testimony established, are capable of all of the individual activities required of VMI cadets. The parties, furthermore, agree that some women can meet the physical standards VMI now imposes on men. In sum, as the court of appeals stated, neither the goal of producing citizen-soldiers nor VMI's implementing methodology is inherently unsuitable to women.

In support of its initial judgment for Virginia, the trial court made findings on gender-based developmental differences. These findings restate the opinions of Virginia's expert witnesses, opinions about typically male or typically female tendencies. For example, experts asserted that men tend to need an atmosphere of adversativeness, whereas women tend to thrive in a cooperative atmosphere. Another expert testified that even though some women would do well under the adversative model, educational experiences must be designed around the rule and not around the exception.

The United States does not challenge any expert witness's estimation of average capacities or preferences of men and women. Instead, the United States emphasizes that time and again this Court has cautioned lower courts to take a hard look at generalizations or tendencies of the kind pressed by Virginia and relied upon by the trial court. State actors controlling gates to opportunity may not exclude qualified individuals based on fixed notions concerning the roles and abilities of men and women.

Most women would not choose VMI's adversative method. It is also probable that many men would not want to be educated in such an environment. The question is whether Virginia can constitutionally deny to women who have the will and capacity, the training and attendant opportunities that VMI uniquely affords.

The notion that admission of women would downgrade VMI's stature, destroy the adversative system, and with it even the school, is a judgment hardly proved. One expert witness for Virginia testified, "If VMI were to admit women, it would eventually find it necessary to drop the adversative system altogether and adopt a system that provides more nurturing and support for the students." Such judgments have attended and impeded women's progress toward full citizenship stature throughout our nation's history. When women first sought admission to the practice of law and access to legal education, concerns of the same order were expressed. For example, in 1876, the Court of Hennepin County, Minnesota, explained why women were thought ineligible for the practice of law. Women train and educate the young, the court said, which

> forbids that they shall bestow that time and labor, so essential in attaining to the eminence to which the true lawyer should ever aspire. It cannot therefore be said that the opposition of courts to the admission of females to practice is to any extent the outgrowth of old fogyism. It arises rather from a comprehension of the magnitude of the responsibilities connected with the successful practice of law, and a desire to *grade up* the profession.

A like fear, according to a 1925 report, accounted for Columbia Law School's resistance to women's admission, although

> the faculty never maintained that women could not master legal learning. No, its argument has been more practical. If

women were admitted to the Columbia Law School, the faculty said, then the choicer, more manly and red-blooded graduates of our great universities would go to the Harvard Law School!

Medical faculties similarly resisted men and women as partners in the study of medicine. More recently, women seeking careers in policing encountered resistance based on fears that their presence would undermine male solidarity, deprive male partners of adequate assistance, and lead to sexual misconduct. Field studies did not confirm these fears.

Women's successful entry into the federal military academies (i.e., women cadets have graduated at the top of their class at every federal military academy) and their participation in the nation's military forces indicate that Virginia's fears for the future of VMI may not be solidly grounded. Inclusion of women in settings in which, traditionally, they were not wanted inevitably entails a period of adjustment. As one West Point cadet squad leader recounted, "The classes of '78 and '79 see the women as women, but the classes of '80 and '81 see them as classmates."

Virginia's justification for excluding all women from citizen-soldier training for which some are qualified cannot rank as exceedingly persuasive. Virginia's misunderstanding, and in turn, the trial court's, is apparent from VMI's mission: to produce

> citizen-soldiers, individuals imbued with love of learning, confident in the functions and attitudes of leadership, possessing a high sense of public service, advocates of the American democracy and free enterprise system, and ready to defend their country in time of national peril.

Surely that goal is great enough to accommodate women, who today count as citizens in our American democracy equal in stature to men. Just as surely, Virginia's great goal is not substantially advanced by women's categorical exclusion, in total disregard of their individual merit, from Virginia's premier citizen-soldier corps.

Virginia's Remedial Plan

Virginia's remedial plan, which received the trial court's approval, would maintain VMI as a male-only college and create VWIL as a separate program for women. The court of appeals agreed, deciding that the two single-sex programs directly served Virginia's reasserted purposes: single-gender education and achieving the results of an adversative method in a military environment. Inspecting the VMI and VWIL educational programs to determine whether they afforded to both genders benefits comparable in substance, if not in form and detail, the court of appeals concluded that Virginia had arranged for men and women opportunities sufficiently comparable to survive equal protection evaluation. The United States challenges this remedial ruling as pervasively misguided.

A remedial decree, this Court has said, must closely fit the constitutional violation; it must be shaped to place persons unconstitutionally denied an opportunity or advantage in the position they would have occupied in the absence of discrimination. The constitutional violation in this case is the categorical exclusion of women from an extraordinary educational opportunity afforded men. A proper remedy for an unconstitutional exclusion aims to eliminate so far as possible the discriminatory effects of the past and to bar like discrimination in the future.

Virginia chose not to eliminate but to leave untouched VMI's exclusionary policy. Virginia proposed a separate program for women only, different in kind from VMI and unequal in tangible and intangible facilities. Having violated the Constitution's equal protection requirement, Virginia was obliged to show that its remedial proposal directly addressed and related to the violation (i.e., the equal protection denied to women ready, willing, and able to benefit from educational opportunities of the kind VMI offers). Virginia described VWIL as a parallel program and asserted that VWIL shares VMI's mission of producing citizen-soldiers and VMI's goals of providing education, military training, mental and physical discipline, and character and leadership development. If the VWIL program could not eliminate the discriminatory effects of the past, could it at least bar like discrimination in the future? A comparison of the programs said to be parallel informs our answer. In exposing the character of, and differences in, the VMI and VWIL programs, we recapitulate facts earlier presented.

VWIL affords women no opportunity to experience the rigorous military training for which VMI is famed. No other school in Virginia or in the United States, public or private, offers the same kind of rigorous military training as is available at VMI. Instead, the VWIL program deemphasizes military education and uses a cooperative method of education that reinforces self-esteem.

VWIL students participate in ROTC and a largely ceremonial Virginia Corps of Cadets, but Virginia deliberately did not make VWIL a military institute. The VWIL House is not a military style residence, and VWIL students need not live together throughout the four-year program, eat meals together, or wear uniforms during the school day. VWIL students thus do not experience the barracks life crucial to the VMI experience, the spartan living arrangements designed to foster an egalitarian ethic. The most important aspects of the VMI educational experience occur in the barracks, the district court found, yet Virginia deemed that core experience nonessential, indeed inappropriate, for training its female citizen-soldiers.

VWIL students receive their leadership training in seminars, externships, and speaker series, episodes and encounters lacking the physical rigor, mental stress, minute regulation of behavior, and indoctrination in desirable values made hallmarks of VMI's citizen-soldier training. Kept away from the pressures, hazards, and psychological bonding characteristic of VMI's adversative training, VWIL students would not know the feeling of tremendous accomplishment commonly experienced by VMI's successful cadets.

Virginia maintains that these differences are justified pedagogically, based on important differences between men and women in learning and developmental needs, psychological and sociological differences Virginia describes as real and not stereotypes. The task force charged with developing the leadership program for women, drawn from the staff and faculty at Mary Baldwin College, determined that a military model, and especially VMI's adversative method, would be wholly inappropriate for educating and training most women. Virginia embraced the task force's view, as did expert witnesses who testified for Virginia.

Generalizations about the way women are and estimates of what is appropriate for most women no longer justify denying opportunity to women whose talent and capacity place them outside the average description. Notably, Virginia never asserted that VMI's method of education suits most men. It is also revealing that Virginia accounted for its failure to make the VWIL experience the entirely militaristic experience of VMI on the ground that VWIL is planned for women who do not necessarily expect to pursue military careers. By that reasoning, VMI's entirely militaristic program would be inappropriate for men in general or for men as a group for only about 15% of VMI cadets enter career military service.

In contrast to the generalizations about women on which Virginia rests, we note again these dispositive realities: VMI's implementing methodology is not inherently unsuitable to women; some women do well under the adversative model, would want to attend VMI if they had the opportunity, are capable of all of the individual activities required of VMI cadets, and can meet the physical standards VMI now imposes on men. It is on behalf of these women that the United States has instituted this suit, and it is for them that a remedy must be crafted, a remedy that will end their exclusion from a state-supplied educational opportunity for which they are fit.

In myriad respects other than military training, VWIL does not qualify as VMI's equal. VWIL's student body, faculty, course offerings, and facilities hardly match VMI's. Nor can the VWIL graduate anticipate the benefits associated with VMI's 157-year history, the school's prestige, and its influential alumni network.

Mary Baldwin College, whose degree VWIL students will gain, enrolls first-year women with an average combined SAT score about 100 points lower than the average score for VMI freshmen. The Mary Baldwin faculty hold significantly fewer PhDs, and receive substantially lower salaries than the faculty at VMI.

Mary Baldwin does not offer a VWIL student the range of curricular choices available to a VMI cadet. VMI awards baccalaureate degrees in liberal arts, biology, chemistry, and civil, electrical, computer, and mechanical engineering. VWIL students attend a school that does not have a math and science focus; they cannot take at Mary Baldwin any courses in engineering or the advanced math and physics courses VMI offers.

For physical training, Mary Baldwin has two multipurpose fields and one gymnasium. VMI has an NCAA competition-level indoor track and field facility; a number of multipurpose fields; baseball, soccer and lacrosse fields; an obstacle course; large boxing, wrestling, and martial arts facilities; an 11-laps-to-the mile indoor running course; an indoor pool; indoor and outdoor rifle ranges; and a football stadium that also contains a practice field and outdoor track.

Although Virginia has represented that it will provide equal financial support for in-state VWIL students and VMI cadets, and the VMI Foundation has agreed to endow VWIL with $5.4 million, the difference between the two schools' financial reserves is pronounced. Mary Baldwin's endowment, currently about $19 million, will gain an additional $35 million based on future commitments; VMI's current endowment, $131 million—the largest public college per-student endowment in the nation—will gain $220 million.

The VWIL student does not graduate with the advantage of a VMI degree. Her diploma does not unite her with the legions of VMI graduates who have distinguished themselves in military and civilian life. VMI alumni are exceptionally close to the school and that closeness accounts, in part, for VMI's success in attracting applicants. A VWIL graduate cannot assume that the network of business owners, corporations, VMI graduates, and nongraduate employers interested in hiring VMI graduates will be equally responsive to her search for employment.

Virginia, in sum, while maintaining VMI for men only, has failed to provide any comparable single-gender women's institution. Instead, the commonwealth has created a VWIL program fairly appraised as a pale shadow of VMI in terms of the range of curricular choices and faculty stature, funding, prestige, alumni support, and influence.

Virginia's VWIL solution is reminiscent of the remedy Texas proposed 50 years ago. In response to a trial court's ruling that, given the equal protection guarantee, African Americans could not be denied a legal education at a state facility, Texas set up a separate school for Black law students. As originally opened, the new school had no independent faculty or library, and it lacked accreditation. Nevertheless, the state trial and appellate courts were satisfied that the new school offered these Black students opportunities for the study of law substantially equivalent to those offered by the state to White students at the University of Texas.

Before this Court considered that case, the new school had gained a faculty of five full-time professors, a student body of 23, a library of some 16,500 volumes serviced by a full-time staff, a practice court and legal aid association, and one alumnus who had become a member of the Texas Bar. This Court contrasted resources at the new school with those at the school from which the Black students had been excluded. The University of Texas Law School had a full-time faculty of 16, a student body of 850, a library containing over 65,000 volumes, scholarship funds, a law review (a legal journal edited by law students), and moot (simulated) court facilities.

More important than the tangible features, this Court emphasized, are those qualities that are incapable of objective measurement but that make for greatness in a school, including reputation of the faculty, experience of the administration, position and influence of the alumni, standing in the community, traditions and prestige. Facing the marked differences between the schools, this Court unanimously ruled that Texas had not shown substantial equality in the separate educational opportunities and ruled that the Equal Protection Clause required Texas to admit African Americans to the University of Texas Law School.

Virginia has not shown substantial equality in the separate educational opportunities the commonwealth supports at VWIL and VMI. Valuable as VWIL may prove for students who seek the program offered, Virginia's remedy affords no cure at all for the opportunities and advantages withheld from women who want a VMI education and can make the grade. Virginia's remedy does not match the constitutional violation. The commonwealth has shown no exceedingly persuasive justification for withholding from women, who are qualified for the experience, premier training of the kind VMI affords. There is no reason to believe that the admission of women capable of all the activities required of VMI cadets would destroy the institute rather than enhance its capacity to serve the "more perfect Union."

ANALYSIS AND IMPLICATIONS

When the appeals court ruled that VMI's admission policy violated the Fourteenth Amendment's Equal Protection Clause, VMI was given several options to fix the violation. One of them was to maintain VMI as a male-only college and to create an equivalent program for women elsewhere. Virginia chose this option. Virginia proposed to create VWIL as an institute at Mary Baldwin College that would use the educational techniques that supposedly were best suited to women. The appellate court agreed that VMI and VWIL were substantially comparable and approved the plan.

The U.S. Supreme Court, however, concluded that the solution as implemented was not good enough. There were differences between the two programs in teaching methods, living conditions, course offerings, physical fitness requirements, faculty qualifications, and financing. In addition, even if Virginia wanted to create an identical program at VWIL (which it did not), it could never reproduce the intangibles, like the prestige and influential network of benefactors that VMI enjoyed. Any solution to a constitutional violation of the kind that VMI was found to have made can only be remedied by providing the benefit or advantage that the violation denied in the first place. Placing women in a separate but unequal educational environment was not the appropriate remedy.

Diversity in Educational Opportunity

Virginia tried to justify its separate institutions on a number of grounds, including that it promoted diversity in educational approaches and opportunities. But there was no record of such a history for Virginia. In fact, the history of its educational system suggests the opposite—namely, that Virginia's schools were developed solely for the benefit of male students. When women were permitted to attend college, Virginia created separate schools in the late 1800s that were inferior to their male counterparts. By the mid-1970s, these schools became coeducational, further undermining Virginia's claim to a policy of educational diversity. In addition, if promulgating diversity in education was such an important goal, why was Virginia backpedaling in their words and deeds by allowing women to enter its other schools including the system's flagship university, the University of Virginia, in the 1970s?

The Court needed exceedingly persuasive evidence from Virginia that VMI's men-only admission policy furthered a legitimate state policy. Finding the historical evidence for diversity lacking, the Court recognized the diversity argument for what it was: an attempt by Virginia, in response to the lawsuit, to come up with a plausible excuse for its discriminatory practice.

Women and the Adversative Method

Another of Virginia's key arguments was that women could not handle VMI's adversative educational model that is premised on confrontation. The goal of this method is to confront the cadet so intensely as to get him to doubt and eventually discard the values and attitudes that he brought with him to the school. Once stripped of these attributes, the adversative method is designed to instill those values and qualities that the school believes are most likely to produce a citizen-soldier. The method is unceasing and is physically and emotionally exhausting. One witness testifying for VMI likened it to marine boot camp. It is so difficult that more than 15% of first-year cadets drop out of VMI, a notably high rate given that the students who attend VMI are self-selected (Avery, 1996).

The belief that women could not handle the adversative method was an element of Virginia's argument that if women were admitted to VMI, its adversative method would be fundamentally and unalterably changed, and VMI could not fulfill its mission of graduating citizen-soldiers. Several of Virginia's experts testified that most women resent the adversative method and would not thrive under it. Also, life in the barracks, although essential for men, would be an inappropriate environment for training women. In fact, Virginia's experts believed that very few women would go to VMI even if it were opened to them because of their aversion to its technique and lifestyle.

Perhaps it was time for VMI to change its educational approach. Outside of VMI and the Citadel (a military college in South Carolina that was forced to go coeducational about the same time as VMI), the adversative educational method is rarely used. The U.S. military academies used to possess some adversative characteristics and to some extent still do. However, the more harsh and petty aspects of the system have been largely done away with as military leaders realized that a changing student population neither tolerated nor required these methods for effective military training (Avery, 1996).

But if VMI chose not to change, could women handle its adversative method? The Supreme Court used the experiences of the federal military academies as evidence of the successful transition that VMI could make if it admitted women. Specifically, the Court noted the achievements that women have made since their admission to the nation's military academies, like graduating at the top of their class and attaining high rank both as cadets and in their ensuing military careers. The best evidence, however, was not available at the time of the Supreme Court's opinion. One of the new women admitted to VMI became the first female cadet to be named to the prestigious position of battalion commander in March 2000 (Rosellini & Marcus, 2000). Clearly, within just a few years of her admittance, at least one female cadet excelled at VMI and disproved Virginia's assertion that the adversative method would prevent women from developing as leaders.

Another way to explore the criticism that women would not fare well under the adversative method is to ask if there is research demonstrating that the adversative approach to teaching was beneficial for most men? The Supreme Court found none and concluded that the evidence Virginia was relying on to justify excluding women from VMI was really nothing more than generalizations and estimates that purported to describe most women. But *most* women did not want to go to VMI. Those women who wanted to attend saw themselves as more than average and wanted the physical and mental challenge of VMI's unique citizen-soldier training. The behavioral and social facts that Virginia's experts were presenting were not addressing these women.

Differences Between Men and Women

The early history of excluding women from higher education was supported by the argument that it was necessary to protect a woman's physical health. For example, the Court referred to old medical texts that asserted that higher education adversely affected a woman's ability to have children. A century later, Virginia used assumed psychological and physical differences between men and women to argue that VMI's adversative approach to education was appropriate for men but not for women.

The trial court accepted this argument, drawing certain conclusions with the help of Virginia's experts about the typical tendencies of men and women. The U.S. Supreme Court, however, was dubious of these generalities and so-called tendencies. Even if the generalizations about women were true, they did not justify putting women who exceeded the average at a disadvantage by denying them an equal opportunity at VMI. Neither the Court, Virginia, nor the United States denied that differences existed. But the Court went on to say that such differences could not be used to keep one sex in an inferior position to the other. Lower courts had to examine these generalities closely and not accept them uncritically.

The United States' experts acknowledged that some differences existed, but their analysis of the differences led them to conclude that the differences were negligible. More important was the fact that when it came to psychological factors that affect learning, men and women showed greater within-group variability than between-groups variability. That is, on average, the differences *within* a group of women and *within* a group of men are greater than the differences *between* a group of men and a group of women. After reviewing the psychological literature on the ways that men and women learn, an expert for the United States concluded that there were far more similarities between men and women than there were differences and that what differences existed did not justify Virginia's claims.

Intellectual Differences Between Men and Women

Some of the most important research on sex differences has been conducted by Eleanor Maccoby and Carol Jacklin. In fact, Jacklin testified for the United States against VMI in this case. In their comprehensive review of the research on sex differences, Maccoby and Jacklin (1974) concluded that boys, on average, scored higher than girls on tests of visual-spatial ability and mathematical ability, whereas girls were better at verbal ability. Their review dispelled some of the more common stereotypes about the differences between girls and boys, such as that girls are better at listening, less motivated, and less analytical than boys.

In 1986, Maccoby and Jacklin's earlier review was revisited using a more rigorous statistical analysis (Fausto-Sterling, 1985). This new study concluded that the differences identified by Maccoby and Jacklin were not so compelling as first believed and that the differences in verbal ability were nonexistent. Whatever real or imagined sex differences exist, neither Maccoby and Jacklin nor Fausto-Sterling advocated making educational decisions on the basis of gender (Avery, 1996). The ways that men and women learn are so similar, and there is so much within-group variability, that only an assessment of an individual's strengths and weaknesses can adequately predict how he or she will do in a given educational situation.

This finding is supported by a meta-analysis of research on sex differences that revealed that earlier studies showing girls with stronger verbal abilities than boys and boys with stronger mathematical and spatial abilities than girls were hindered by methodological problems (Hyde, 1990). In addition, these differences were becoming less pronounced over time. Hyde concluded that boys maintained an advantage in math, but differences in verbal abilities had disappeared. Differences in cognitive abilities like spelling, language, mechanical reasoning, spatial relations, verbal reasoning, and abstract reasoning showed a significant decline in a 30-year period (Feingold, 1988). Differences in numerical ability, however, remained relatively constant.

Physical and Emotional Differences Between Men and Women

Virginia's experts also argued that women would fail at VMI because they are physically weaker, less competitive, more emotional, and do not handle stress as well as men. Since physical and emotional strength, competition, and stress are all integral elements of the VMI experience, these experts concluded that women would not be able to keep up with the men if they were admitted. In her testimony, Jacklin acknowledged that girls are less confident than boys in their academic ability and performance on certain tasks and that a competitive learning environment may have an adverse effect on girls' motivation (Avery, 1996). Yet, her research with Maccoby was inconclusive as to whether there were any differences between men and women in regard to fear, anxiety, competitiveness, dominance, and nurturance.

Related to this, Virginia argued that women have lower self-esteem than men and that VMI's use of the adversative method would exacerbate this problem. For example, the adversative method centers on confrontation, inducing stress, denying privacy, treating all people equally, and continually monitoring all behaviors. Virginia assumed that these characteristics would further erode women's already low self-confidence and self-esteem. One expert for Virginia went so far as to opine that if women were admitted to VMI the adversative method could lead to an increased incidence of anorexia among this group of female cadets (Avery, 1996).

The U.S. government's experts disagreed. There was no empirical evidence that the adversative method improved *anyone's* self-confidence or self-esteem or that it would erode qualified female applicants' self-esteem more than that of the male cadets (Avery, 1996). The Supreme Court agreed, but does the research support its conclusion? Although Harper and Marshall (1991) found lower self-esteem scores among teenage girls than teenage boys, other research shows that self-esteem variables are strongly influenced by factors that exist in the individual's life at the time self-esteem is measured. For example, young women who are employed or attending school full time exhibit higher degrees of self-esteem than women who either are not working or are in part-time jobs (Stein, Newcomb, & Bentler, 1990). Higher levels of self-esteem have also been found in young women who aspired to nontraditional careers in science and engineering when compared with young women who wanted to become homemakers (Mau, Domnick, & Ellsworth, 1995). Although women who sought a VMI education were not analyzed, their educational goal suggests that they would be among the women who would have higher self-esteem. In addition, VMI's strong programs in science and engineering would likely attract some of the women who have an interest in those fields, suggesting that they too would have higher self-esteem.

Moreover, whatever differences do exist between men and women in self-esteem appear to be inconsequential. In an analysis of the research on self-esteem covering more than 155,000 participants, it was discovered that although men generally score higher on measures of self-esteem than women, the differences are small (Kling, Hyde, Showers, & Buswell, 1999). More on point, some research has shown that the role of self-esteem in future military leadership may be overstated. Chemers, Watson, and May (2000) had military science professors rate cadets from several universities on future leadership potential. The researchers then measured, among other things, the self-esteem of the cadets and compared it to their leadership ratings and leadership performance at a cadet summer training camp. They found that self-esteem did not predict either how well the cadets were rated by their superiors or their leadership performance at the camp (Chemers et al., 2000). Based on a study of 530 third-year midshipmen at the U.S. Naval Academy, those who possessed characteristics such as ambition, prudence, *intellectance* (an individual's interpersonal style that leads others to think of that person as intelligent), and school success were most likely to attain high class ranking in settings in which class ranking was used as a measure of future leadership success (Lall, Holmes, Brinkmeyer, Johnson, & Yatko, 1999).

This body of research calls into serious question Virginia's claim that women's supposed low self-esteem, and the supposed deleterious effect that the adversative educational method would have on it, would be a critical impediment to a woman's efforts to become a successful citizen-soldier. Thus, the behavioral and social science data do not support the gender-based stereotype that Virginia wanted the Supreme Court to accept.

In regard to confrontation and denying privacy, Virginia argued that these characteristics, when mixed with the later stages of adolescence, would create unavoidable and volatile sexual tensions between male and female students. Referring to reports in the news media describing increases in date rape, violent crime, and drinking in coeducational schools, the appellate court agreed and feared that "female participation (in the adversative method) would destroy . . . any sense of decency that still permeates the relationship between the sexes" (*United States v. Virginia*, 1995). Once again, there was no factual basis for this assumption, and it seemed to contradict VMI's own notion that its male cadets always behave with the utmost decorum.

Conclusion

One researcher criticized Virginia's experts for providing facts to the court on issues they know little about and for relying on "pseudo-scientific arguments and oversimplified interpretations" of the field (Epstein, 1997). The United States' experts argued that one of the dangers in excluding women from VMI was the perpetuation of stereotypes that portray women as requiring special treatment for them to succeed rather than allowing them the freedom and right to compete alongside men (Epstein, 1997). In addition, such an educational policy denies to both men and women the opportunity to learn how to get along with one another and fails to prepare them for life outside of school in jobs and professions that are rapidly becoming gender integrated.

It was the testimony that there are no sex differences relevant to the educational experience that the Supreme Court relied on when they said that VMI's policy of excluding women was based on generalities (Avery, 1996). Virginia might very well have been right when it said that most women would not succeed at VMI, but the same is true for most men. Neither Virginia nor behavioral or social scientists could accurately predict the probabilities of success at VMI based on gender.

The Court concluded that the "facts" that Virginia's experts were relying on were nothing more than the same tired stereotypes that had been used historically to keep women in a subservient role to men. The best behavioral and social facts that the Supreme Court could use to dispel these myths were the achievements of the women who overcame these stereotypical burdens in fields once dominated by men, the success of women at the federal military academies, and the absence of behavioral and social facts indicating that women could not tolerate the adversative method.

Egalitarianism

VMI feared that the admission of women would upset one of its foundations—egalitarianism (i.e., treating all people equally). As has been noted, accommodations would have to be made for privacy, and some rituals that all VMI cadets are expected to endure would have to be either modified or eliminated. For example, it has been reported by Avery (1996) that one of the hazing practices (not approved by the VMI administration), involves forcing first-year cadets to run naked through the communal showers while hot water is being discharged from some showerheads and cold water from others. Clearly this ritual could not be made to include women at the same time as the men. Introducing female students who must be treated differently would upset both the egalitarian principles of VMI and VMI's esprit de corps. Despite Virginia's claim, however, it does not treat all of its cadets uniformly. For example, VMI has a strong intercollegiate athletic program. Its athletes are exempt from some of the physical training that other cadets must participate in, and allowances are made to miss class time while traveling to athletic events (Avery, 1996). In addition, even if all of VMI's cadets wanted to play on one of the athletic teams, they would be prevented from doing so because of insufficient skill, finances, National Collegiate Athletic Association (NCAA) rules, and other reasons. If such exceptions are already being made for the male cadets, then why not make needed exceptions for future female cadets?

Likely Destruction of VMI

Virginia ultimately argued that admitting women to VMI would result in its destruction. Admitting women to VMI would, all agreed, require some changes in housing, physical training requirements, and privacy matters. Virginia argued that such modifications would change VMI unalterably and it would not, indeed could not, ever be the same again. Virginia also contended that admitting women would fundamentally alter the adversative approach to education unique to VMI, which in turn would change the very educational opportunities that women sought to participate in. The VMI that women got into would not be the same VMI that they wanted to get in to. In order to preserve the educational character and special goals of VMI, Virginia argued that women could not be admitted.

The Supreme Court was unconvinced and cited the successful accommodation of women in previously all-male bastions such as exclusive law and medical schools and the military academies. The same fears were raised in these instances regarding the admission of women, and the Court noted that these fears were not realized. Changes in privacy and physical requirements (at least in the case of the service academies) certainly had to be made, but neither resulted in the destruction of these other institutions. On the contrary, they were strengthened for it. If women could succeed in these places, they could certainly succeed at VMI.

Finally, the Court noted that VMI had already faced and overcome significant changes to its admissions practices.

> The school admitted its first African American cadets in 1968. Students no longer sing "Dixie," salute the Confederate flag or the tomb of General Robert E. Lee at ceremonies and sports events. As the trial court noted, VMI established a program on retention of Black cadets designed to offer academic and social cultural support to minority members of a dominantly White and tradition-oriented student body. The school maintains a special recruitment program for Blacks, which, the trial court found, has had little, if any, effect on VMI's method of accomplishing its mission (*United States v. Virginia*, 1996, p. 546, footnote 16).

These changes did not prevent VMI from achieving its goal of graduating citizen-soldiers. Thus, Virginia's concerns over the future integrity of VMI if women were admitted failed to rise to the level of an exceedingly persuasive reason for denying women the right to go to VMI.

CHAPTER'S LESSON

The use of behavioral and social facts in this case aided the legal decision maker in resolving a constitutional question, but it did so by resolving disputes about facts. For example, were some women up to the challenge posed by the adversative method of education at VMI? Having behavioral and social science experts address these disputed facts is no different than having them resolve the disputed facts regarding the likelihood of confusion on the part of consumers that we addressed in chapter 6. What differs is that the disputed facts, which were resolved by the behavioral and social science information, were then used to resolve a constitutional issue.

REFERENCES

Avery, D. (1996). Institutional myths, historical narratives and social science evidence: Reading the "record" in the Virginia Military Institute case. *Southern California Review of Law and Women's Studies, 5*, 189–386.

Chemers, M. M., Watson, C. B., & May, S. T. (2000). Dispositional affect and leadership effectiveness: A comparison of self-esteem, optimism, and efficacy. *Personality and Social Psychology Bulletin, 26*, 267–277.

Epstein, C. F. (1997). The myths and justification of sex segregation in higher education: VMI and The Citadel. *Duke Journal of Gender Law & Policy, 4*, 101–117.

Fausto-Sterling, A. (1985). *Myths of gender: Biological theories about women and men.* New York: Basic Books.

Feingold, A. (1988). Cognitive gender differences are disappearing. *American Psychologist, 43*, 95–103.

Harper, J. F., & Marshall, E. (1991). Adolescents' problems and their relationship to self-esteem. *Adolescence, 26*, 799–808.

Hyde, J. S. (1990). Meta-analysis and the psychology of gender differences. *Signs, 16*, 55–73.

Kling, K. C., Hyde, J. S., Showers, C. J., & Buswell, B. N. (1999). Gender differences in self-esteem: A meta-analysis. *Psychological Bulletin, 125*, 47–500.

Lall, R., Holmes, E. K., Brinkmeyer, K. R., Johnson, W. B., & Yatko, B. R. (1999). Personality characteristics of future military leaders. *Military Medicine, 164*, 906–910.

Maccoby, E. E., & Jacklin, C. N. (1974). *The psychology of sex differences.* Stanford, CA: Stanford University Press.

Mau, C., Domnick, M., & Ellsworth, R. A. (1995). Characteristics of female students who aspire to science and engineering or homemaking occupations. *Career Development Quarterly, 43*, 323–337.

Rosellini, L., & Marcus, D. (2000, April 10). A leader among men. *U. S. News & World Report, 128*, 46–48.

Stein, J. A., Newcomb, M. D., & Bentler, P. M. (1990). The relative influence of vocational behavior and family involvement on self-esteem: Longitudinal analyses of young adult women and men. *Journal of Vocational Behavior, 36*, 320–338.

United States v. Virginia, 44 F. 3d. 1229 (1995).

United States v. Virginia, 518 U.S. 515 (1996).

8

PROVIDING FACTUAL, EDUCATIONAL KNOWLEDGE TO AID LEGAL DECISION MAKING

EXAMPLE: EYEWITNESS IDENTIFICATION

In fictionalized courtroom stories, one of the most dramatic moments comes when a witness identifies the defendant, usually with a proclamation like "That's him. I'll never forget that face as long as I live!" Eyewitness identifications are compelling because they are something we can all relate to. We are all witnesses to life's events, and we each have probably experienced the same kind of assuredness in our memory for events as witnesses do. An eyewitness who gives the appearance of being confident in his or her identification provides one of the most powerful pieces of evidence in a trial.

Cognitive psychologists, however, have long known that not everything is what it appears to be. We are all familiar, for example, with visual illusions. Here, visual processes lead us to believe we see something that in fact is an inaccurate representation of the physical properties of what we are looking at. We are not suggesting that in cases of mistaken identity the witness has experienced a visual illusion (although it is possible). We are suggesting that a set of circumstances can exist that when combined with cognitive processes may cause a witness to make an inaccurate eyewitness identification.

The case that we present in this chapter, *Arizona v. Chapple* (1983), concerns this problem. The Arizona Supreme Court allowed a behavioral expert, a cognitive psychologist, to educate the jury about the fallibility of eyewitness identifications in similar conditions to those that existed in the *Chapple* case. In allowing this educational testimony, the court made the behavioral assumption that the average juror would either not know or fully understand the psychological factors that affect eyewitness identifications. The court concluded that the only way for jurors to understand these factors satisfactorily was to have an expert explain the underlying science to them. The court did not intend for the expert to answer, or even address, the issue of whether the eyewitnesses in this case identified the defendant accurately (see chap. 6, this volume). That would be up to the jury. Rather, it intended for the expert to educate the jury on the factors known to affect such eyewitness identifications. A jury armed with this knowledge would be more likely to make an informed, intelligent decision about the credibility of the identification.

ARIZONA V. CHAPPLE

Arizona Supreme Court

The instigator of this bizarre drama was Mel Coley, a drug dealer who resided in Washington, DC, but who was also connected with dealers in Kansas City. Coley had a history of dealing with a supplier named Bill Varnes, who lived near Phoenix. In fact, Coley, Varnes, and a man named James Logan had been arrested once near Yuma, Arizona, in connection with a heroin transaction. They were released fairly quickly, and this made Coley suspicious that someone had talked to the authorities.

Coley had made a large number of drug deals through Malcolm Scott, a middleman who lived near Phoenix. Scott was also well acquainted with Varnes and had recently returned from Kansas City, where Scott had helped Varnes in a drug transaction involving marijuana and probably some heroin. The trip to Kansas City was not without complications because Varnes had been withholding money from the Kansas City dealers who were purchasing from him. They were unhappy over this and had threatened to take action to collect the money they felt Varnes owed them. Coley evidently was involved in these problems and shared the feelings of his Kansas City colleagues toward Varnes.

In early December 1977, Coley telephoned Scott and told him that he was interested in purchasing approximately 300 pounds of marijuana. He asked Scott to act as middleman in the transaction. Scott was to get $700 for his efforts. Scott testified that he called one or two of the Arizona suppliers with whom he was acquainted and found they could not supply the necessary quantity. He then called his sister, Pamela Buck, who was a good friend of Varnes and had worked with him in some drug deals. Scott asked Buck to contact Varnes and see whether he could handle the sale. Buck talked to Varnes and reported to her brother that Varnes could supply the necessary amount of marijuana at an agreed upon price. Scott relayed this information to Coley. Scott instructed Buck not to tell Varnes that Coley or anyone from Washington, DC, was involved in the deal.

On the evening of December 10 or the early morning of December 11, 1977, Coley arrived at the Phoenix airport from Washington, DC. Scott met him at the airport and found that Coley was accompanied by two strangers who were introduced as Dee and Eric. Scott drove the three men to a trailer located at his parents' farm near Higley, Arizona. Scott had used this trailer in the past as a meeting place to consummate drug transactions. This meeting place was part of the service that Scott provided for his finder's fee.

Coley, Dee, and Eric spent the night at the trailer, and Scott returned to his residence in Mesa, Arizona. The next morning Scott returned to the farm and took Coley to the airport where they picked up a brown leather bag. Back at the trailer, Scott observed Coley, Eric, and Dee take four guns from the bag and clean them. Scott examined and handled one of the guns. Buck had also arrived at the trailer, and she and Dee were dispatched to meet Varnes in order to purchase a sample of the marijuana.

Later that morning, a conversation between Coley, Eric, and Dee suggested to Buck that Coley did not intend to pay for the goods. When Buck told Scott about her fear that Varnes would seek revenge if his goods were stolen, Scott told her not to worry because Varnes might never be seen again.

That evening, Scott and his sister met at the trailer with Coley, Eric, and Dee. Varnes arrived with two companions, Eduardo Ortiz and Carlos Elsy. Ortiz and Elsy began to unload the marijuana and put it in the trailer. Buck was in the trailer with Coley, Eric, and Dee at this time. Scott was some distance away, sitting on the porch of his parents' house. Dee or Coley told Buck that after the marijuana was unloaded she should lock herself in the bathroom.

After Ortiz and Elsy had finished unloading the marijuana and stacking it in the living room of the trailer, Dee suggested to Varnes that they go in the bedroom and count the money. They started toward the bedroom and Buck went into the bathroom. A few moments later, Buck heard several shots, opened the bathroom door and ran out. Scott heard the shots while he was on the porch of his parents' home and saw a door of the trailer open. Elsy ran out, pursued by either Eric or Dee. After seeing Buck run out of the door at the other end of the trailer, Scott went back to the trailer and found Varnes dead in the bedroom of a gunshot wound to the head and Ortiz in the living room dead of a gunshot wound to the body. Subsequent ballistic tests showed they had been shot with different weapons. Elsy was outside, dead from a blow to the back of the head.

Dee and Eric then removed the marijuana from the trailer and loaded it into a car that Coley had directed Scott to buy the previous day. Scott, Eric, and Dee loaded the three bodies into the trunk of Varnes's car. That car was driven out to the desert, doused with gasoline and set on fire. The trailer was cleaned to remove evidence of the crime and the carpet in the trailer was burned. The parties then left the scene of the crime and returned to Scott's house in Mesa. Eric and Dee asked for directions regarding the route to Kansas City and then left in the car containing the marijuana. Coley gave Scott and Buck $500 each. He then called the airport and reserved a seat to leave for Washington, DC, under the name of James Logan. Scott returned to the trailer and completed the cleanup. Fear or remorse, or both, drove Scott to seek the aid of a lawyer. Eventually both Scott and Buck successfully negotiated an immunity deal with the prosecution.

On learning of Mel Coley's participation in the crime, the sheriff's office quickly procured photographs of Coley, which were shown to Scott and Buck in a photographic lineup on December 16, 1977. Both of them identified Coley. The detectives then showed Scott and Buck various photographs and lineups containing pictures of known acquaintances of Coley. At this same session, Scott pointed to a picture of James Logan and stated that it resembled Dee, though he could not be sure. So far as the record shows, no follow-up was made of this tentative identification. One of the photographic lineups displayed to Scott, but not to Buck, contained a picture of the defendant, Dolan Chapple, but Scott did not identify him as Dee. At a time and in a manner not disclosed by the record, both Scott and Buck made a tentative identification of a photograph of Eric. The photograph portrayed Coley's nephew, Eric Perry.

The police continued to show the witnesses photographic lineups in an attempt to obtain an identification of Dee. Police efforts were successful on January 27, 1979, when Scott was shown a nine-picture photo lineup. For the first time, this lineup included photos of both Eric Perry, who had already been tentatively identified by Scott and Buck, and of the defendant Dolan Chapple; however, James Logan's photo was not included. On seeing this lineup, Scott immediately recognized Eric's picture again. About 10 minutes later, Scott identified Chapple's picture as Dee. Scott was then shown the picture of Chapple that he had failed to identify at a previous session and asked to explain why he had not previously identified him. He stated that he had no recollection of having seen it before. After Scott had identified Dee and before he could talk to his sister, the police showed Buck the same lineup. Buck identified the photograph of Chapple as Dee and then re-identified Eric.

Dolan Chapple denied that he was the perpetrator, Dee. At his hearing in Illinois to extradite him from that state to Arizona, seven witnesses placed him in Cairo, Illinois, during the entire month of December 1977, three of them testifying specifically to his presence in that town on December 11, the day of the crime. The same witnesses testified for him in the trial at which he was convicted. No direct or circumstantial evidence of any kind connected Chapple to the crime, other than the testimony of Malcolm Scott and Pamela Buck, neither of whom had ever met Chapple before the crime and neither of whom saw him after the crime except at the trial. Chapple was apprehended and tried only because Scott and Buck picked his photograph out of a lineup more than one year after the date of the crime; he was convicted because they later identified both the photograph and Chapple at the trial.

Chapple argued at trial that the identification was erroneous because

1. The identification by Scott and Buck was a case of mistaken identity. Scott and Buck picked the wrong picture out of the photographic lineup and their subsequent photographic and in-court identifications were part of the *feedback phenomenon* and are simply continuations or repetitions of the same mistake.

2. The time interval between the occurrence of the crime and the lineup and the anxiety and tension inherent in the situation surrounding the entire identification process, made the identification un-

reliable. Buck and Scott both said they were frightened for their lives during the crime. Because they were the only witnesses and because Eric and Dee were both at liberty during the criminal investigation, Scott and Buck were likely frightened and apprehensive during the time period.

3. Scott and Buck had smoked marijuana on the day of the crime. This would have affected their perception, making their identification through photographs less reliable.

4. The January 27, 1979 identification of Dee by Scott and Buck from the photographic lineup was the product of an unconscious transfer. Scott picked his picture and identified it as Dee because he remembered that picture from the previous lineup (when he had not been able to identify Chapple's picture as Dee).

5. The in-court identifications were merely repetitions of the initial error.

6. Eric's picture in the lineup heightened the memory transfer and increased the chance of an incorrect photographic identification.

7. James Logan's picture, which resembled Chapple, was not displayed again to the witnesses.

8. The identification was made on the basis of subsequently acquired information that affected memory.

9. The confidence and certainty that Scott and Buck displayed in making their in-court identification at trial had no relation to the accuracy of that identification and were instead the product of other factors.

Chapple also offered the testimony of an expert on eyewitness identification in order to rebut the testimony of Malcolm Scott and his sister, Pamela Buck. The expert, a cognitive psychologist, specialized in visual perception, memory retention, and recall. The trial court would not admit the expert's testimony, and Chapple contended that the court erred in its decision.

The rule governing the admissibility of expert testimony allows it if it will assist the trier of fact to understand the evidence or to determine a fact in issue. Put conversely, the test is whether the subject of the inquiry is one of such common knowledge that people of ordinary education could reach a conclusion as intelligently as the witness. Furthermore, the test is not whether the jury could reach some conclusion in the absence of the expert evidence but whether the jury is qualified without such testimony to determine intelligently and to the best possible degree the particular issue without enlightenment from those having a specialized understanding of the subject. We have concluded that it was an error to refuse the expert testimony in this case.

The law has long recognized the inherent danger in eyewitness testimony, but it is difficult to tell whether the ordinary juror shares the law's inherent caution of eyewitness identification. Experimental data indicate that many jurors may reach intuitive conclusions about the reliability of such testimony that psychological research would show are misguided. Even assuming that jurors of ordinary education typically need no expert testimony to enlighten them to the danger of eyewitness identifications, Chapple's expert would have informed the jury that there are many specific variables that affect the accuracy of identification and that apply to the facts of this case.

Forgetting Curve

Although most jurors would no doubt realize that memory dims as time passes, the forgetting curve is not uniform. Forgetting occurs very rapidly and then tends to level out; immediate identification is much more trustworthy than long-delayed identification. Thus, Scott's recognition of Logan's features as similar to those of Dee when Logan's picture was shown at the inception of the investigation is probably a more reliable identification than Scott's identification of Chapple's photograph in the photographic lineup 13 months later. By the same token, Scott's failure to identify Chapple's photograph when it was first shown to him on March 26, 1978 (4 months after the crime) and when Scott's ability to identify would have been far greater is of key importance.

Stress and Perception

Research shows that most laymen believe that stressful events cause people to remember better so that what is seen in periods of stress is more accurately related later. However, experimental evidence indicates that stress causes inaccuracy of perception with subsequent distortion of recall.

Unconscious Transfer

The phenomenon of unconscious transfer occurs when the witness confuses a person seen in one situation with a person seen in a different situation. Thus, a witness who takes part in a photo identification session without identifying any of the photographs and who then later sees a photograph of one of those persons may relate his or her familiarity with the picture to the crime rather than to the previous identification session.

Assimilation of Postevent Information

Experimental evidence confirms that witnesses frequently incorporate into their identifications inaccurate information gained subsequent to the event and confused with the event. An additional problem is the feedback factor. We deal here with two witnesses who were related and who purportedly engaged in discussions with each other about the identification of Dee. Such discussions can reinforce the individuals' identifications and often heighten the certainty of the identification. The same may be said of the continual sessions that each witness had with the police in poring over large groups of photographs. We do not suggest that the police attempted to prejudice the identification procedure. The facts show that the police were careful to avoid the possibility of prejudice. However, it is not possible to discuss identification of photographs with witnesses on seven different occasions, looking at over 200 pictures, without giving the witness some feedback with respect to what the officers anticipate or expect the witness to find.

Identification Confidence and Accuracy

There is no relationship between the confidence that a witness has in his or her identification and the actual accuracy of that identification. Again, this factor was specifically tied to the evidence in the case because both Scott and Buck indicated in their testimony that they were absolutely sure of their identification. Evidently their demeanor on the witness stand also showed absolute confidence.

The average juror would not be aware of the variables concerning identification and memory about which the expert witness was qualified to testify. Depriving the jurors of the benefit of scientific research on eyewitness testimony forced them to search for the truth without full knowledge and opportunity to evaluate the strength of the evidence. This deprivation prevented the jurors from having the best possible degree of understanding the subject toward which the law of evidence strives. The expert testimony might assist the jury to resolve the issues raised by the facts, for example:

1. The photographs in evidence show that there is a resemblance between Logan and Chapple. Scott

told the police that Logan's photograph resembled Dee. Scott then failed to identify Chapple's photograph when it was first shown to him. In light of these facts, might Scott's comments regarding the Logan photographs be considered an identification? Should it be considered more accurate than his identification of Chapple from the photographic lineup one year later? Expert testimony regarding the forgetting curve would have assisted the jury in deciding this issue.

2. On the assumption that the jury disregarded, as was its right, Scott's and Buck's denials of having discussed Dee's description prior to the identification of January 27, 1979, did the feedback and postevent information phenomena play a part in Buck's identification of Chapple? We cannot assume that ordinary jurors would necessarily be aware of the impact of these factors.

3. Logan and Chapple bear some resemblance. Logan's picture had been the object of some comment between Scott and the sheriff's deputies shortly after the killing. Although he professed to have no memory of it, Scott had seen a picture of Chapple within a few months of the shooting. Was Scott's identification of Chapple on the January 27, 1979 lineup therefore influenced by an unconscious transfer of memory? Because Dee evidently looked like Logan and Chapple, was this transfer phenomenon with regard to their photographs more pronounced than it was with regard to other photographs that were shown to Scott on more than one occasion?

4. Because a cropped-hair picture of Logan, who bore a resemblance to Chapple and was tentatively identified by Scott soon after the killing, was not included in the lineup of January 1979, were Scott and Buck given a reasonable choice with respect to the photos that they examined on the occasion on which they identified Chapple?

5. Did the witnesses' absolute confidence in the identification bear any relationship to the accuracy of that identification? Contrary to the scientific research, most people might assume that it would.

Each of the factual issues described above is raised by evidentiary facts in the record or on reasonable inferences from those facts. In effect, the trial judge ruled that all of the information necessary to resolve the conflicting factual contentions on these issues was within the common experience of the jurors and could be covered in cross-examination of the identification witnesses.

It is difficult to support this conclusion. For instance, although jurors are aware that lapse of time may make identification less reliable, they are almost certainly unaware of the forgetting-curve phenomenon and the resultant inference that a prompt tentative identification may be much more accurate than later positive identification. Similarly, cross-examination is unlikely to establish any evidentiary support for the argument that eyewitnesses who have given similar nonfactual descriptions of the criminal may have been affected by the feedback phenomenon. Again, experimental data provide evidentiary support to arguments that might otherwise be unpersuasive because they seem contrary to common wisdom.

Although this court has no problem with the usual ruling that a jury needs no assistance from expert testimony on the question of reliability of an eyewitness identification, the unusual facts of this case compel the contrary conclusion. The examples listed above demonstrate that under the facts here, there were a number of substantive issues of fact on which the expert's testimony would have been of significant assistance. Accordingly, we hold that the order precluding the expert testimony was legally incorrect.

ANALYSIS AND IMPLICATIONS

In chapters 6 and 7, we considered how behavioral and social knowledge can be used to resolve a particular fact question in a case. If the expert had been providing case fact information in this trial, the expert would have addressed whether the identifications by Scott and Buck were likely to be accurate. But the expert was not asked to comment on these eyewitnesses. Rather, the expert was asked to *educate* the jury about the factors that create problems for eyewitness identifications in similar conditions. It would then be up to the jury to decide how likely it was that some or all of the factors were operating in this case, and if they were operating, to decide how they affected the accuracy of the eyewitness identifications.

Educational Testimony on Eyewitness Reliability

The indisputable key to Chapple's conviction was the identification of his photograph by Scott and Buck. Chapple made several arguments to the

Arizona Supreme Court disputing the accuracy of his identification by the witnesses. Chapple argued that Scott's and Buck's identifications were faulty because of problems in perception and memory that were partially induced by the identification process. Chapple sought to have an expert testify to help the jury understand how perceptual and memorial factors could affect the accuracy of an identification.

The prosecution argued that the expert's information would not help the jury resolve any of the questions they had to answer concerning the accuracy of the eyewitness identifications. Because the expert was not going to offer a specific opinion about the accuracy of Scott's and Buck's identification, what was the use of the testimony? The court, however, disagreed, noting that it could not be sure how much the average juror knew about the problems with eyewitness identifications, but empirical research indicated that many jurors have misconceptions about it. Thus, the court concluded that educating the jury with information on the relevant scientific knowledge about eyewitness identifications would allow the jury to apply this information when judging the credibility of the witnesses, and thereby, improve juror and jury decision making.

Importance of Educational Testimony

The court's decision could have a significant impact because some studies have shown that jurors find eyewitness testimony very persuasive. Loftus (1974) presented mock jurors with a case in which the evidence was only circumstantial (i.e., did not point directly at the defendant). Under this condition, jurors voted to convict the defendant only 18% of the time. However, when the same circumstantial evidence was paired with the testimony of an eyewitness who identified the defendant, the conviction rate rose to 72%. Other studies have shown that a majority of mock jurors will believe eyewitnesses even when they know that the witnesses observed the crime under poor conditions (Wells, Lindsay, & Ferguson, 1979).

What happens when experts are permitted to testify? After hearing experts testify about such factors as eyewitness accuracy, weapon focus (described below), stress, eyewitness confidence, and lineup procedures, mock jurors tend to view the testimony of eyewitnesses more skeptically (Leippe, 1995). In some instances, mock jurors who are exposed to expert testimony about eyewitness identification problems are less likely to convict than are mock jurors who do not get a chance to hear an expert (Loftus, 1980).

Psychological Factors Clarified by Expert Testimony

Time and the Forgetting Curve

The first factor the court dealt with was the length of time (more than a year) that elapsed between the murders and the eventual identification of

Chapple's photograph. The court cited the forgetting curve, a phenomenon well known to cognitive psychologists (Ebbinghaus, 1913/1964). It does not take long to start forgetting, and once it begins, the drop off is at first rapid and then levels off, although it is always continuous. This is a robust finding and has been found under a variety of experimental conditions (Rose, 1992). One of the more difficult conditions in which to study the forgetting curve, however, is over very long time intervals. The practical limitations of securing research funding to follow research participants for several years and of getting people to stay in the study are significant obstacles for scientists to overcome. One researcher who has had some success in this area is Squire (1989). He tested volunteers' memory of certain television programs for as far back as 15 years and found that forgetting, as lab experiments using shorter intervals have suggested, is gradual and continuous. The court concluded that if the jury was made aware of the nature of the forgetting curve, they might view the identification that Scott made soon after the murders, when he identified Logan's photo as looking like Dee, as more reliable than the identifications he and his sister made a year later.

Stress, Perception, and Memory

The second factor that the expert would tell the jury about has to do with the effects of stress on perception and memory. People tend to think that some amount of stress heightens one's awareness such that memory for events is enhanced. In fact, according to the research presented by the expert, stress distorts memory and makes accurate recall more difficult. Some victims of abuse and witnesses to traumatic events suffer from impaired learning and memory (Bremner & Narayan, 1998; Sapolsky, 1996), as do people who have experienced particularly stressful or emotional events (McEwen, 1998).

People also tend to demonstrate better memory for the central aspects of an event as opposed to those that are more peripheral. For example, participants who saw slides of a gruesome car accident were more likely to remember the central details of the crash (e.g., the condition of the victim) than other less salient details (Christianson & Loftus, 1987). This finding is similar to what happens when people witness a robbery in which a weapon is used by the perpetrator. Here, witnesses can recall very accurately the characteristics of the weapon (called weapon focusing) but may have a difficult time describing anything else associated with the crime, like a description of the robber (Loftus, Loftus, & Messo, 1987). Apparently, weapons cause so much emotional arousal within the witnesses that most of their attentional resources are, quite understandably, devoted to the weapon and not much else. The events surrounding the murders may have been so traumatic that Scott and Buck focused their attention on other elements of the crime (e.g., the weapons or a desire not to be involved in the shootings) rather than on the physical characteristics of the perpetrators.

In addition, because Scott and Buck admitted smoking marijuana on the day the crime was committed, the effect that marijuana may have had on their perception and memory should be considered. The main active ingredient in marijuana is delta-9-tetrahydrocannabinol (THC). When THC finds its way to the brain, it binds to very specific receptors. The greatest concentration of these particular receptors is found in the hippocampus (Hubbard, Franco, & Onaivi, 1999). The hippocampus is central to the encoding of sensory information and to the creation and storage of memory (Pope & Yurgelun-Todd, 1996). Among heavy users, marijuana has been found to impair attention, memory, and learning. These effects are persistent and have also been found among users who had not smoked for at least 24 hours (Pope & Yurgelun-Todd, 1996). One of the most specific memory impairments is an increase in memory intrusions (Adams & Martin, 1996). For example, if a person is asked to memorize a list of items and then to recall the items a short time later, the person will report items that never appeared on the list. Marijuana also produces temporal disintegration (Melges, Tinklenberg, Hollister, & Gillespie, 1970), an inability to remember, coordinate, and index memories that are related to a specific goal that a person is trying to achieve. For example, Melges et al. gave subjects varying doses of THC and asked them to perform a simple mathematical task (e.g., adding and subtracting a series of numbers to reach a predetermined value). Subjects were also asked to recite what they were doing out loud. Subjects who were given THC performed significantly worse on the task than did subjects who were given a placebo, and their ability to recite what they were doing was characterized by disorganized speech and thinking. The effects of marijuana on brain function are broad and are not limited to impairments of memory. Marijuana can impair perception and alter peripheral vision, slow reaction time, impair decision making, reduce locomotor activity, impair spatial memory, sedate and cause drowsiness, adversely affect accuracy in divided attention and sustained attention tasks, and impair concentration (Adams & Martin, 1996; Hubbard et al., 1999; Pope & Yurgelun-Todd, 1996).

Finally, Abel (1970) has established a state-dependent learning effect for marijuana. State-dependent learning means that people tend to remember things better if the conditions under which they are asked to remember resemble the conditions under which they learned the material in the first place. Abel exposed subjects to marijuana and asked them to read and remember a narrative. Some of these subjects were allowed to recall the material while high on marijuana (i.e., the condition under which they learned the narrative); others had to recall the narrative while sober (i.e., not the same condition under which they learned the narrative). Subjects who were allowed to recall the narrative under the influence of marijuana performed better than the subjects who had to recall the narrative while sober. Ironically, Scott and Buck may have been better eyewitnesses if they had been allowed to use marijuana when they were interviewed by the police.

We do not know how much marijuana that either Scott or Buck smoked on the day of the murders. Because some of the effects of marijuana are dose specific, we cannot say to what degree Scott and Buck experienced some or all of the effects we have described. The possibility certainly exists, however, that their use of marijuana, in combination with the obviously stressful events, impaired their ability to make an accurate identification of Dee in the photo lineup.

Unconscious Transfer

The third factor was unconscious transfer in which the witness believes that an individual seen in the second situation is the same individual who was seen in the first situation. The witness unconsciously transfers an individual from one time and place to another in his or her memory. This phenomenon has occasionally led witnesses to identify innocent bystanders as the perpetrators of a crime. Loftus (1976) demonstrated this phenomenon in the laboratory when she showed participants photographs of various characters from a crime scene. Some characters were bystanders, and only one character was the perpetrator. Several days later, the research participants were asked to identify the perpetrator from a photographic lineup. If the perpetrator's picture was included in the lineup, participants were quite accurate in selecting it (84% correct). However, if the perpetrator's photograph was removed and replaced with a photo of an innocent bystander, 84% of the participants mistakenly identified the bystander as the perpetrator. Indeed, of those who made an incorrect identification, 24% selected a person from the lineup who was neither a perpetrator nor a bystander but a new face inserted into the array of photographs. Although we will never know for certain if Scott and Buck experienced unconscious transference, the possibility clearly exists given the facts of this case.

Assimilation of Postevent Information

Assimilation of postevent information occurs when a witness mistakenly believes that information learned after the event was really part of the event. For example, researchers showed participants a series of slides depicting a crime scene, followed by a narrative of the crime that included information that, in some instances, contradicted what they had just seen in the slides (Heath & Erickson, 1998). When participants' memories were tested later, they often identified the incorrect information as being part of what they had witnessed in the slides. Participants were more resistant to the misleading information if they were allowed to freely recall what they had seen (as opposed to being asked to recognize it) and if it concerned a central rather than a more peripheral detail (Heath & Erickson, 1998).

A related factor, known as the feedback phenomenon, comes from social psychological research (Rosenthal, 1966; Wells & Bradfield, 1998). In the *Chapple* case, Scott and Buck may have picked up cues from investigators that subsequently guided them during the identification process. The cues do not have to be intentionally transmitted. We are all very adept at detecting a subtle nod of the head or a slight change in the inflection of a speaker's voice. People exhibiting these behaviors may be unaware of their importance or even if they are doing them at all. Observers may not realize that they are detecting these cues either, but the behaviors can serve as feedback to communicate to the witness what the investigators would like him or her to find. Feedback does not always have to be so subtle. The court noted, for example, that Scott and Buck might have exchanged information with one another about their performance during the identification process.

Identification Confidence and Accuracy

The final factor considered by the court was the relationship between identification confidence and accuracy. The court stated that there was no relationship between the two. This is accurate, but research evidence does show that there is a relationship between confidence and *perceived* accuracy. That is, the more confidently a witness expresses the accuracy of his or her identification, the more likely it is for a juror and the witness to believe that the identification was accurate. This is one of the most enduring findings in the social science literature on jury information processing. Several comprehensive reviews have shown that jurors persistently believe that the witnesses who exude the most confidence are the most accurate and that those witnesses overestimate their own accuracy (Deffenbacher, 1980; Penrod & Cutler, 1995; Sporer, Penrod, Read, & Cutler, 1995). Indeed, the confidence that a witness exhibits is the single most important factor used by jurors to assess the truthfulness of that witness (Cutler, Penrod, & Stuve, 1988). If jurors in the *Chapple* case were aware that confident witnesses were just as likely to be wrong as right, they may have reached a different conclusion in regard to the accuracy of the Scott's and Buck's identifications.

Impact of the Eyewitness Identification Problem

In a review of eyewitness identification experiments using lineups in which the perpetrator was present, Haber and Haber (2000) found that people selected someone from the lineup who was either not at the scene of the crime or was an innocent bystander 25% of the time. In simulations that contained weapons, violence, stress, bystanders, postevent information, and long time delays between witnessing the event and the identification procedure, correct identification of the perpetrator was less than 50%. When conditions surrounding the original event (i.e., the crime) were less than optimal (i.e., containing weapons and violence) and the witness was led to believe that the perpetrator was present in the current lineup (when the perpetrator was really absent from the lineup), an innocent person was selected 90% of the time. Under this condition, the witness should have admitted that he or she was unable to recognize the perpetrator (because, in fact, the perpetrator was not there). Having been told falsely that the perpetrator was present, the witnesses apparently felt compelled to identify someone they could not possibly have seen.

The identification problems are not limited to the witnesses of a crime. Cognitive problems also affect the way jurors evaluate eyewitness identifications. Seltzer, Lopes, and Venuti (1990) questioned real jurors about eyewitness identifications, and their interviews revealed that jurors were not aware of and did not understand the many factors that can affect identification accuracy. Reviewing a number of studies in which potential jurors were asked about memory, Haber and Haber (2000) reported that participants either agreed or strongly agreed that memory is more accurate when a witness is more confident, a weapon is present during the crime, and an event is either personally traumatic or more violent than an everyday event. In addition, potential jurors believed that memory is stable and can be kept separate from postevent information, that faces are easy to remember, that eyewitness reports are accurate evidence of what happened, that retelling the same story improves its reliability, and that memory works like a video recording that can be played back at will (Haber & Haber, 2000).

Response of the United States Department of Justice

Perhaps not surprisingly, according to Lindsay and Pozzulo (1999) the number one cause of wrongful convictions is mistaken eyewitness identifications. Alarmed by the number of convictions that were being overturned as a result of DNA testing, the U.S. Department of Justice (DOJ) ordered a study of those individuals who had been released. The study revealed a frightening statistic: 80% of those who were wrongfully convicted had been positively identified by an eyewitness (Connors, Lundregan, Miller, & McEwan, 1996). In response, the DOJ asked the National Institute of Justice to convene a working group of psychologists, prosecutors, defense attorneys, and members of law enforcement whose task it was to develop national guidelines for conducting lineups (Wells, Malpass, Lindsay, Fisher, Turtle, & Fulero, 2000). Relying heavily on much of the same and similar psychological literature that the Arizona Supreme Court justices in this case used, the panel eventually produced a set of procedures for use by police departments around the country (Technical Working Group for Eyewitness Evidence, 1999). The guidelines called for the following:

1. Law enforcement personnel who come into contact with a witness should try to establish a personal relationship with that witness. Witnesses may be traumatized by the event they have seen and then feel depersonalized by the ensuing investigative process. Investigators who take the time to take the

needs of witnesses into consideration are more likely to find cooperative and helpful witnesses.

2. Investigators should allow witnesses to describe what they saw and heard freely without undue prompting. Typical law enforcement interviews are driven by the investigators. This puts the witness in a passive role and places on the investigator the burden of asking just the right questions in order to extract the relevant information from the witness (Wells et al., 2000).

3. Witnesses should be asked open-ended questions, not leading questions. This recommendation is based on research that showed that what witnesses report can be shaped by the kinds of questions they are asked, often in the most subtle ways. For example, an investigator who asks, "How fast were the cars going when they smashed each other" will get a very different estimate of the cars' speed than the investigator who asks, "How fast were the cars going when they contacted each other" (Loftus & Palmer, 1974). Simply asking the witness to tell what he or she saw is more likely to result in a more accurate recounting of the event.

4. Witnesses should be discouraged from guessing. Some witnesses, in an effort to be a *good* witness, will try to fill in what they do not know or do not recall (Wells et al., 2000).

5. Only one suspect should be placed in a lineup. Placing more than one suspect in a lineup raises the chances of a mistaken identification. If all of the others in a lineup are known by investigators not to have committed the crime (fillers), their selection by the witness is a harmless error.

6. Fillers in a lineup should match the general description of the perpetrator by the witness. Obviously, placing a suspect into a lineup of dissimilar people biases the procedure and unfairly raises the chances that he or she will be selected by the witness.

7. Witnesses should be told that the suspect may or may not be present in the lineup. This relieves witnesses from having to make a choice when they are really unsure of whom to select, and it also protects innocent suspects from being wrongfully selected.

8. Witnesses should be asked how certain they are of their identification before they are told anything about the accuracy of their selection. This prevents witnesses from being more confident in their identification than they would be if they had been provided information about their selection by investigators.

CHAPTER'S LESSON

Future research will tell us if law enforcement agencies that use these guidelines produce fewer erroneous identifications than departments that elect not to adopt them. But the importance of the lesson of this chapter is already proven. Behavioral and social scientists can educate legal decision makers about behavioral and social facts that can be critical for reaching the best decisions.

REFERENCES

Abel, E. L. (1970). Marijuana and memory. *Nature, 227,* 1151–1152.

Adams, I. B., & Martin, B. R. (1996). Cannabis: Pharmacology and toxicology in animals and humans. *Addiction, 91,* 1585–1614.

Arizona v. Chapple, 135 Ariz. 281 (1983).

Bremner, J. D., & Narayan, M. (1998). The effects of stress on memory and the hippocampus throughout the life cycle: Implications for childhood development and aging. *Developmental Psychopathology, 10,* 871–886.

Christianson, S. A., & Loftus, E. F. (1987). Memory for traumatic events. *Applied Cognitive Psychology, 1,* 225–239.

Connors, E., Lundregan, T., Miller, N., & McEwan, T. (1996). *Convicted by juries, exonerated by science: Case studies in the use of DNA evidence to establish innocence after trial.* Alexandria, VA: National Institute of Justice.

Cutler, B. L., Penrod, S. D., & Stuve, T. E. (1988). Juror decision making in eyewitness identification cases. *Law and Human Behavior, 12,* 41–55.

Deffenbacher, K. A. (1980). Eyewitness accuracy and confidence: Can we infer anything about their relationship? *Law and Human Behavior, 4,* 243–260.

Ebbinghaus, H. (1964). *Memory: A contribution to experimental psychology.* New York: Dover. (Original work published 1913)

Haber, R. N., & Haber, L. (2000). Experiencing, remembering, and reporting events. *Psychology, Public Policy, and Law, 6,* 1057–1097.

Heath, W. P., & Erickson, J. R. (1998). Memory for criminal and peripheral actions and props after varied post-event presentation. *Legal and Criminological Psychology, 3,* 321–346.

Hubbard, J. R., Franco, S. E., & Onaivi, E. S. (1999). Marijuana: Medical implications. *American Family Physician, 60,* 2583–2593.

Leippe, M. R. (1995). The case for expert testimony about eyewitness memory. *Psychology, Public Policy, and Law, 1,* 909–959.

Lindsay, R. C., & Pozzulo, J. D. (1999). Sources of eyewitness identification error. *International Journal of Law & Psychiatry, 22,* 347–360.

Loftus, E. F. (1974). Reconstructing memory: The incredible witness. *Psychology Today, 8,* 116–119.

Loftus, E. F. (1976). Unconscious transference in eyewitness identification. *Law and Human Behavior, 2,* 93–98.

Loftus, E. F. (1980). Impact of expert psychological testimony on the unreliability of eyewitness identification. *Journal of Applied Psychology, 65,* 9–15.

Loftus, E. F., Loftus, G., & Messo, J. (1987). Some facts about "weapon focus." *Law and Human Behavior, 11,* 55–62.

Loftus, E. F., & Palmer, J. C. (1974). Reconstruction of automobile destruction: An example of the interaction between language and memory. *Journal of Verbal Learning and Verbal Behavior, 13,* 585–589.

McEwen, B. S. (1998). Protective and damaging effects of stress mediators. *New England Journal of Medicine, 338,* 171–179.

Melges, F. T., Tinklenberg, J. R., Hollister, L. E., & Gillespie, H. K. (1970). Marijuana and temporal disintegration. *Science, 168,* 1118–1120.

Penrod, S., & Cutler, B. (1995). Witness confidence and witness accuracy: Assessing the forensic relation. *Psychology, Public Policy, and Law, 1,* 817–845.

Pope, H. G., & Yurgelun-Todd, D. (1996). The residual cognitive effects of heavy marijuana use in college students. *Journal of the American Medical Association, 272,* 521–527.

Rose, S. P. R. (1992). *The making of memory: From molecules to mind.* New York: Anchor Books.

Rosenthal, R. (1966). *Experimenter effects in behavioral research.* New York: Appleton-Century-Crofts.

Sapolsky, R. M. (1996). Why stress is bad for you. *Science, 273,* 749–750.

Seltzer, R., Lopes, G. M., & Venuti, M. (1990). Juror ability to recognize the limitations of eyewitness identifications. *Forensic Reports, 3,* 121–137.

Sporer, S. L., Penrod, S., Read, D., & Cutler, B. (1995). Choosing, confidence, and accuracy: A meta-analysis of the confidence-accuracy relation in eyewitness identification studies. *Psychological Bulletin, 118,* 315–327.

Squire, L. R. (1989). The course of forgetting in very long-term memory. *Journal of Experimental Psychology: Learning, Memory, and Perception, 15,* 241–245.

Technical Working Group for Eyewitness Evidence. (1999). *Eyewitness evidence: A guide for law enforcement* [Booklet]. Washington, DC: U. S. Department of Justice, Office of Justice Programs.

Wells, G. L., & Bradfield, A. L. (1998). "Good, you identified the suspect": Feedback to eyewitnesses distorts their reports of the witnessing experience. *Journal of Applied Psychology, 83,* 360–376.

Wells, G. L., Lindsay, R. C. L., & Ferguson, T. J. (1979). Accuracy, confidence, and juror perceptions in eyewitness identification. *Journal of Applied Psychology, 64,* 440–448.

Wells, G. L., Malpass, R. S., Lindsay, R. C. L., Fisher, R. P., Turtle, J. W., & Fulero, S. M. (2000). From the lab to the police station: A successful application of eyewitness research. *American Psychologist, 55,* 581–598.

III

PROBLEMS RELATED TO THE USE OF BEHAVIORAL AND SOCIAL FACTUAL KNOWLEDGE

9

LAW REFUSES TO RELY ON
RELEVANT FACTUAL KNOWLEDGE

EXAMPLE: COMPREHENSION OF JURY INSTRUCTIONS

Research on jury decision making shows that the average juror does not know much about the law or how our legal system works. What jurors do understand seems to be based on a notion of law that has been called commonsense justice (Finkel, 1995). Unfortunately, this notion is typically not derived from fact but from what is seen and heard in the popular media, how each individual perceives and remembers information, and how attitudes and biases color interpretation of perceived information.

One way to correct these misperceptions is for the court to instruct the jury about the trial process, the jury's role in it, and the substantive law that is to guide their decision making. The judge reads instructions to the jury at the beginning (i.e., preliminary instructions) and at the end (i.e., substantive instructions) of the trial. The jury is also given a written copy to take with them into the jury room for use during the jury deliberations. The decision by the U.S. Court of Appeals presented in this chapter considered an appeal by a serial sex murderer, John Wayne Gacy, who claimed that his jury did not understand a critical part of those instructions.

The court in this case was presented with a social science study (hereafter Study) that purportedly demonstrated the accuracy of Gacy's claim. The court also was familiar with other behavioral and social science research concluding that jurors only understand about 50% of the jury instructions in most cases. Given that courts throughout this country rely on behavioral and social science to prove relevant facts that will aid the legal decision maker, why might this court have chosen to reject Gacy's claim? Answering this question exemplifies the lesson of this chapter.

GACY V. WELBORN

United States Court of Appeals for the Seventh Circuit[1]

Between 1972 and 1978, John Wayne Gacy enticed young men to his home near Chicago for homosexual liaisons. At least 33 never left. Gacy tied up or handcuffed his partners, then strangled or choked them. Twenty-eight of the bodies were dumped into the crawl space under the Gacy residence; one was entombed under the driveway; the rest were thrown into the river. Gacy, who operated a construction business, had his workers dig trenches and throw lime into the crawl space. Gacy's wife complained about an awful stench, but the slaughter continued until the disappearance of a 15-year-old who vanished after telling his mother that he was going to see a building contractor about a summer job. The presence of Gacy's truck outside the place where the young man was to meet his potential employer led to Gacy's arrest within two days.

The discovery of so many skeletons, several with rags stuffed in their mouths, created a national sensation. Gacy regaled the police with stories about his exploits, which he attributed to Jack, an alternative personality. A jury convicted Gacy of 33 counts of murder, rejecting his defense of insanity. The same jury sentenced Gacy to death for 12 of these killings.

If the jury convicts a defendant of a capital offense, there is a sentencing proceeding. At this proceeding, the prosecution bears the burden of establishing the existence of defined aggravating circumstances (i.e., a factor that increases the degree of blame that should be assigned to a defendant for a criminal act). If the jury unanimously decides that there is at least one aggravating circumstance, the defendant becomes eligible for a death sentence. If the jury determines unanimously that there are no mitigating

[1]This case was first heard in an Illinois trial court but eventually appealed to the Illinois Supreme Court. Gacy then appealed to the U.S District Court and then to the U.S. Court of Appeals.

factors (i.e., a factor that reduces the degree of blame that should be assigned to a defendant for a criminal act) sufficient to preclude the imposition of the death sentence, the court shall sentence the defendant to death. Stated another way, unless the jury unanimously finds that there are no mitigating factors sufficient to preclude the imposition of the death sentence, the court shall sentence the defendant to a term of imprisonment. A single juror's belief that the defendant has demonstrated the existence of a single mitigating factor precludes the death sentence.

At the beginning of the sentencing proceeding, the trial court instructed the jury:

> If, after your deliberations, you unanimously determine that there are no mitigating factors sufficient to preclude the imposition of the death sentence on the defendant, you should sign the verdict form directing a sentence of death. If, after your deliberations, you are not unanimous in concluding that there are no mitigating factors sufficient to preclude imposition of the death sentence, you must sign the verdict form directing a sentence of imprisonment.

This written instruction is completely accurate. The jurors had this instruction during their deliberations, along with all of the other jury instructions that the judge read to them. Unfortunately, the trial court did not read the instruction to the jury as written— or at least the court reporter did not take down the same words that appear in the written instructions. The transcript indicated that the second sentence of this instruction was delivered as, "If, after your deliberations, you unanimously conclude there are mitigating factors sufficient to preclude the imposition of the death penalty, you must sign the verdict form directing a sentence of imprisonment."

The oral version of the instruction is accurate, as far as it goes. But the instruction did not give the jury the whole truth because it did not tell the jurors what to do in the event of disagreement. This court concludes, however, that reasonable jurors would not have been under the misapprehension that they had to reach unanimous agreement. The trial court opened the sentencing phase of Gacy's trial by describing to the jurors the findings they would need to make. The judge said, among other things, "If you cannot unanimously agree that there are no sufficient mitigating factors to preclude the imposition of the death penalty, you will sign that verdict so indicating, and the court will sentence the defendant to imprisonment." Defense counsel emphasized during these arguments what unanimity was unnecessary:

> The only way that you can impose the death penalty on Mr. Gacy, and His Honor will instruct you, it is a unanimous decision, all 12 of you have to agree to give Mr. Gacy the death penalty. If there is just one of you who feels that he was acting under an emotional disturbance, or if there is just one of you who feels it would not be the right thing to do, if there is one of you who feels that he should be studied for any reason at all, if there is one of you, then you must sentence him or direct the court to sentence him to a term of imprisonment.

This argument, an accurate statement of Illinois law, was presented without objection from the prosecutor. For his part, the prosecutor did not urge the jury to seek unanimity on mitigating factors. The final (substantive) instructions came close on the heels of the preliminary instructions because the jury did not receive fresh evidence; instead the lawyers presented arguments based on the evidence at the five-week trial.

What we have, in sum, is a slip of the judicial tongue. No one noticed at the time; defense counsel did not object to the misreading of the written instruction. The complete, and completely accurate, instructions were available to the jurors during their deliberations. The text was short; vital information did not drown in a sea of words. If the jurors wondered about the consequences of disagreement, they had correct answers at their elbows. Within two hours, the jurors brought back death verdicts on all 12 counts.

This is too little time to reach unanimous agreement on aggravating factors and beat down even a single holdout on mitigating factors. So the question at hand probably did not arise in the jury's deliberations; they must have been in agreement from the outset. These circumstances rule out any substantial possibility that the jury may have rested its verdict on the improper ground. Jurors do not sit in solitary isolation booths parsing instructions for subtle shades of meaning in the same way lawyers might. Differences among them in interpretation of instructions may be thrashed out in the deliberative process with commonsense understanding of the instructions in the light of all that has taken place at the trial likely to prevail over technical hairsplitting.

That jurors have trouble coping with gobbledygook in instructions is no news. Strangely, the parties make nothing of the behavioral and social science studies demonstrating this fact, which predate the current research Study relied on by Gacy. The Study introduced by Gacy was a survey of persons reporting to a courthouse as potential jurors. They were given the facts of a case and a set of instructions based on the 1987 Illinois Pattern Instructions for capital cases, which were similar, though not identical, to those given to Gacy's jury. Then the research participants were asked a series of questions designed to test their comprehension of the instructions.

The questions most pertinent to Gacy's argument follow:

Question 4. A juror decides that the fact that Mr. Woods was only 25 years of age when he committed the murder is a mitigating factor sufficient to preclude the death penalty. However the other 11 jurors disagree and insist that his age is not a mitigating factor. The one juror believes that she cannot consider a mitigating factor unless the entire jury agrees upon it and votes for the death penalty. She votes for the death penalty. Has that juror followed the judge's instructions?

One quarter of the subjects answered *yes*, leading the researcher to conclude that as much as one third of the pool of jurors would not understand a critical feature of the instructions.

Question 5. A juror decides that the fact that Mr. Woods was good to his family is a mitigating factor sufficient to preclude the death penalty. However, the other 11 jurors disagree. The other jurors insist that no juror should consider the defendant's good relations with his family as a mitigating factor unless they all agree it is a mitigating factor. The one juror accepts this approach and votes for the death penalty. Has the juror followed the judge's instructions?

On this question, 45% gave wrong answers. Gacy contends that these error rates demonstrate that the written instruction is confusing and thus could not have corrected the misimpression created by the oral instruction.

Illinois contends that the reported data are inaccurate. The state points out that perhaps the subjects grasped the instructions but misunderstood the questions. The questions are not free of ambiguity. For example, might a subject understand Question 5 as inquiring whether a juror legitimately may be persuaded by other jurors' arguments? Questions 4 and 5 also involve mitigating factors that were not on the list recited in the instruction. Some subjects may have understood these questions as asking whether a particular factor is appropriate, rather than whether the instructions require unanimity. Finally, the state reminds us that the researcher was a zealous opponent of capital punishment and that the Study was conducted under the auspices of an organization devoted to the defense of capital litigation, which may have influenced the findings no matter how careful the researcher sought to be.

If the validity of the Study was controlling and if the Study was valid, we would give Gacy the hearing he requests. But the Study does not assist Gacy. To understand why, consider the question: Is an error rate of 25% large or small? Such a question has no answer. Large or small, compared to what? Presumably compared with some lesser error rate, reflecting greater comprehension achieved by changing the instructions to the jury. That is, actual levels of comprehension must be compared with achievable levels of comprehension, not with ideal levels. Yet this Study did not test jurors' comprehension of differently worded instructions. Nothing in the work shows that some other set of instructions would do better. By contrast, earlier studies, not cited by Gacy, tried out variations of the instructions to determine which were more comprehensible and the degree of improvement attainable from rewording.

To put this differently, there are many potential reasons why jurors might not grasp what a judge tells them: (a) The instructions may be poorly drafted, with needlessly big and technical words and ambiguous constructions; (b) the instructions may convey rules of some complexity, which cannot be mastered on first exposure; (c) the instructions may use concepts that are inherently complex; and (d) jurors may be unable to grasp thoughts unfamiliar to them. If Explanation a is at work, then the state is responsible and may be called on to improve things, although, as we explain below, the Constitution has but a limited role to play even here. Explanation b, by contrast, attributes misunderstanding to a mixture of Illinois law with the constitutional obligations announced by the U.S. Supreme Court (e.g., consideration of mitigating factors that do not appear in Illinois statutes). Justices of the U.S. Supreme Court occasionally complain that these rules are too complex, and the high reversal rate in capital cases supports this perspective. Yet if the U.S. Constitution requires this convoluted set of rules, then the attendant confusion is a regrettable cost rather than a reason why the Constitution's norms are, in application, unconstitutional. Explanation c, the complexity of the concepts, also plays a role. It is no surprise that research participants being peppered with questions about a complex concept they have encountered for the first time will not give satisfactory answers to lawyers. It cannot be that the U.S. Constitution, which requires judges to tell juries to use these elusive concepts, is self-destructive because laypersons will experience difficulty in answering questions about what they have been told. Then there is Explanation d, human shortcomings. Difficulty in coping with abstract concepts (most jurors spend their lives in the world of the concrete) explains why we have lengthy arguments, why judges give instructions orally as well as in writing (and reinstruct juries that ask questions), and why juries deliberate. Jurors who "don't get it" on first hearing may do better as the process continues.

In sum, it is inappropriate to condemn a jury instruction because of inaccurate answers attributable to Explanations b, c, and d. The U.S. Constitution establishes a system of jury trials, which necessarily tolerates the shortcomings of that institution. Pointing to one of these shortcomings, no matter how vivid, does nothing to undercut the Constitution's own mandates. Even if the Study enabled us to lay some responsibility at the state's doorstep (Explanation a), a federal court cannot take a blue pencil to a state's jury instructions. For as long as the United States has been a nation, judges have been using legalese in instructing juries, with an inevitable adverse effect on the jury's comprehension. Jury instructions are not unconstitutional because of this.

One enduring element of the jury system, no less vital today than two centuries ago, is insulation from questions about how juries actually decide. Jurors who volunteered that they did not understand their instructions would not be permitted to address the court, and a defendant could not upset a verdict against him even if all of the jurors signed affidavits describing chaotic and uninformed deliberations. Instead of inquiring about what juries actually understood and how they reasoned, courts invoke a presumption that jurors understand and follow their instructions. This is not a bursting bubble, applicable only in the absence of better evidence. It is a rule of law—a description of the premises underlying the jury system, rather than a proposition about jurors' abilities and states of mind. A critical assumption underlying the system of trial by jury is that juries will follow the instructions given them by the trial judge. Were this not so, it would be pointless for a trial court to instruct a jury and even more pointless for an appellate court to reverse a criminal conviction because the jury was improperly instructed.

Behavioral and social science has challenged many premises of the jury system. Students of the subject believe, for example, that jurors give too much weight to eyewitness evidence and not enough weight to other kinds. Still, the ability of jurors to sift good evidence from bad is an axiom of the legal system, so courts not only permit juries to decide these cases but also bypass the sort of empirical findings that might help jurors reach better decisions. Juries have a hard time distinguishing junk science from the real thing, but aside from some tinkering with the expert testimony admitted at trial, this shortcoming has been tolerated. Jurors reach compromise verdicts, although they are not supposed to. Juries return inconsistent verdicts, representing irrational behavior or disobedience to their instructions. And sometimes juries do not act like reasonable people. When this occurs, the court can overrule the jury's decision. Yet for all of this, courts do not discard the premises of the jury system.

None of this is to suggest that judges ought to be indifferent to the way they write instructions. Polysyllabic mystification reduces the quality of justice. One of the Illinois 1987 pattern instructions is a quadruple negative: "If you do not unanimously find from your consideration of all the evidence that there are no mitigating factors sufficient to preclude imposition of a death sentence, then you should sign the verdict requiring the court to impose a sentence other than death." Would it not be better for all concerned to give an instruction such as, "If after full discussion any one of you believes that a mitigating factor makes death an excessive punishment, then you must return a sentence of imprisonment"? Even this simplified instruction would leave many jurors dumbfounded; the underlying ideas are not at all simple, and words such as *mitigating* and *excessive* are foreign to jurors' daily discourse.

As there are no perfect trials, so there are no perfect instructions. How best to convey the law to laypersons sitting on juries is in the end a question for state legislatures and trial courts to resolve and not for the federal kibitzers in attacks many years later. The jury is a means to resolve disputes, not a way station by which the controversy at trial is transported to a higher level of generality as a social science dispute about juries. Gacy's jury was instructed within the wide bounds set by the Constitution.

ANALYSIS AND IMPLICATIONS

The U.S. Supreme Court has ruled that juries must be given instructions that prevent the arbitrary and capricious imposition of the death penalty. Arbitrary and capricious death sentences constitute cruel and unusual punishment in violation of the Eighth Amendment to the Constitution and are unconstitutional. To overcome arbitrary and capricious decision making, juries must exercise *guided discretion* when deciding whether a defendant should live or die. According to the Court, guided discretion can be assured through a judge's instructions to the jury. These instructions explain concepts like unanimity, aggravating factors, and mitigating factors.

Gacy challenged the Illinois death penalty instructions on the grounds that jurors in his case could not understand them, particularly those parts focusing on unanimity and mitigation. The law requires that all jurors must agree that there is at least one characteristic of the crime or the defendant that qualifies as an aggravating factor. It must be a specific factor, like the brutal nature of the crime or the future dangerousness of the defendant, that is proven beyond a reasonable doubt by the prosecution. If the jury finds that an aggravating factor exists, it must then decide if there is some characteristic of the crime or the defendant that qualifies as a mitigating factor. A mitigating factor is a reason, like young age or diminished mental capacity, that might be used to argue against a death sentence. If one juror believes there is a single mitigating factor that outweighs the aggravating factors, then the defendant cannot be sentenced to death. Furthermore, while the instructions may provide a list of possible mitigating factors, a juror is free to consider any aspect of the crime or defendant that the defendant offers as a mitigator, even if it is not listed (*Lockett v. Ohio*, 1978). These are called unenumerated mitigators. Unlike aggravating factors, mitigating factors do not have to be agreed on unanimously by the jury. The burden of proving the existence of a mitigating factor falls on the defendant.

The judge in Gacy's trial apparently misread to the jury a portion of the instruction relating to mitigation. He stated, "If, after your deliberations, you unanimously conclude there are mitigating factors sufficient to preclude the imposition of the death penalty, you must sign the verdict form directing a sentence of imprisonment." He should have said, "If, after your deliberations, you are not unanimous in concluding that there are no mitigating factors sufficient to preclude imposition of the death sentence, you must sign the verdict form directing a sentence of imprisonment." The appellate court had to determine if the oral instruction was likely to confuse the jurors about their responsibilities. The court cited several reasons why reasonable jurors would not have been confused.

First, the jury heard preliminary statements made by the judge and the attorneys for both sides. In the appellate court's opinion, these statements were accurate representations of the law and came shortly before the final instructions (when the misreading occurred). Second, the court noted that the jury's deliberation was brief. Apparently, there was little disagreement among the jurors about the existence of aggravating factors and the lack of mitigating factors. If there had been, the court was confident that the jury deliberation was sufficient for working out any disagreements or misunderstandings of the instructions. Deliberations may not guarantee an understanding of all the instruction's nuances, but it can produce a *commonsense understanding* of the law that a jury can use to make its decision. Finally, the jury was provided with a written copy of the instructions, which correctly stated the law that the judge misread. If jurors were confused by what the judge read to them, they could simply refer to the written instructions for guidance.

Gacy's contention was that it does not matter whether the instructions are delivered orally or in writing or if they are read accurately or not; they are incomprehensible in any form. Interestingly, and no doubt maddeningly to Gacy and his lawyers, the appellate court did not strongly dispute this funda- mental assertion. The court was quite willing to acknowledge that jurors have trouble understanding the "gobbledygook" in instructions. Furthermore, they did not need Gacy and the Study to tell them of this fact. Indeed, they wondered why it was that Gacy failed to cite the extensive behavioral and social science literature demonstrating the incomprehensibility of jury instructions.

When the appellate court examined the Study, it was not impressed. First, the court noted that the participants of the Study were potential jurors, not actual jurors. Conclusions based on their performance in the Study, there- fore, may not be generalizable to jurors serving in a real capital case. Second, the test was administered to the potential jurors in writing. The court raised the possibility that some participants may have had difficulty reading and interpreting the questions. The court provided an example from the compre- hension test that they believed was evidence of the questions' ambiguity. Third, even if the court accepted that the Study was consistent with previous empirical research showing that jurors do not understand much of the in- structions, the Study failed to provide alternative instructions that may have been more comprehensible. Perhaps the death penalty instructions used in Illinois could not be made more understandable. But even if they could, how much more understandable would they have to be to ensure their constitu- tionality? Stated another way, at what point would the revised instructions provide the guided discretion that the current instructions lacked?

The court also questioned the value of the Study by noting Illinois's doubts about the motivations of the social scientist who conducted the Study, and the organization that sponsored the Study. The scientist was described as a zealous opponent of capital punishment, and the organization was charac- terized as devoted to defending those facing the death penalty. The court agreed with the state's assumption that bias may have influenced the Study's conclusions.

The court's strongest argument against the usefulness of the Study came in the form of a normative assumption. The Constitution requires that juries receive instructions on, in the court's words, a convoluted set of rules. The court reasoned that it is no fault of the Constitution's if the rules cannot be understood. If the instructions prove incomprehensible as a result of this Constitutional requirement, then it is a regrettable cost of our jury system that must be endured.

The court again used normative reasoning when it considered juries and jury instructions in their historical context. It noted that jury instruc- tions have always been written in legalese and misunderstandings are inevi- table. That does not make them unconstitutional. In addition, the court observed that our laws and legal traditions dictate that, with rare exceptions, what jurors do and how they do it remain beyond the second-guessing of our legal system. If judges were allowed to second-guess jury decision making, there would be little point in having juries serve as the backbone of our judicial system. As a means of protecting the jury from invasion, courts must assume that jurors understand and follow the law. Thus, the appellate court ruled that "as there are no perfect trials, there are no perfect instructions," and neither is guaranteed by the Constitution of the United States. Incomprehensible instructions do not violate the Constitution.

Behavioral and Social Science of Jury Instruction Comprehension

The behavioral and social science demonstrating the incomprehensibility of jury instructions is conclusive. The appellate court knew enough about this body of research to comment on an aspect of it that they found lacking in the Study, namely, the testing of an alternative set of instructions to show how much comprehension could be improved by rewriting the instructions.

Consider the following instruction from Gacy's trial (which was included in the appellate opinion).

> If, after your deliberations, you unanimously determine that there are no mitigating factors sufficient to preclude the imposition of the death sentence on the defendant, you should sign the verdict form directing a sentence of death. If, after your deliberations, you are not unanimous in concluding that there are no mitigating factors sufficient to preclude imposition of the death sentence, you must sign the verdict form directing a sentence of imprisonment.

If you could not understand the instruction, you have no reason to feel bad; you are not alone. It is actually a good example of the serious problem that jurors face. True, most jurors will not have to grapple with death penalty instructions, but jury instructions in general are characterized by abstract, arcane legal concepts and terms, confusing syntax, and bad grammar, all of which make them all but incomprehensible to lay jurors (Elwork, Sales, & Alfini, 1977, 1982; Sales, Elwork, & Alfini, 1977; Severance & Loftus, 1982; Severance, Greene, & Loftus, 1984).

One of the interventions that states have used to try to improve the quality of jury instructions is to introduce pattern instructions. Pattern instructions are typically written under the direction of a state commission made up of lawyers and judges. However, the motivation for writing pattern instructions is not always to improve the comprehension of the instructions. The primary goal of pattern instructions is to ensure that all trial courts within the state use the same instructions. It is obviously unfair, for example, to have different defendants, who are charged with the same crime, judged by juries that heard different sets of instructions. Incorrect or inconsistent instructions are a major source of appeals (McBride, 1969), and pattern instructions represent the legal system's attempt to reduce the number of such appeals (Tiersma, 2001). Unfortunately, with a few exceptions (see Tiersma, 2001), the commissions that write pattern instructions are, first and foremost, after uniformity and legal accuracy. Improved comprehensibility, if it should result, is a fortunate but infrequent by-product.

Evidence of the inadequacy of pattern instructions is extensive in the behavioral and social science literature. For example, one of the comparisons that Elwork et al. (1977) made in a study on Michigan pattern instructions was between one group of jurors who received pattern instructions and another who did not receive any instructions at all. Alarmingly, they found no reliable differences on a comprehension test between the two groups. Similar results were found in a series of studies by Severance and Loftus (1982). In one study, jurors who received pattern instructions and jurors who did not receive any instructions showed the same levels of comprehension (about 35%). Charrow and Charrow (1979) asked prospective jurors to paraphrase several pattern instructions for civil cases that had been recorded on audio and played back. They found that participants could accurately paraphrase just 54% of the most essential parts of the instructions. Strawn and Buchanan (1976) found that jurors did not understand about 30% of certain pattern instructions used in Florida's criminal trials. Ellsworth (1989) tested mock jurors' comprehension on California's criminal pattern jury instructions and found they performed no better than if they had guessed.

Although one study (Luginbuhl, 1992) did find improved comprehension for pattern jury instructions in North Carolina, in general, jurors understand about 50% of the judge's instructions (Elwork, Sales, et al., 1982). The best that might be said for the comprehensibility of pattern instructions is that if jurors are already familiar with some of the concepts contained in them, then pattern instructions may be useful for refamiliarizing jurors with those concepts (Tanford, 1990). They do little, however, to aid jurors in understanding new or complex legal concepts (Tanford, 1990). For a review of the findings on comprehension for specific types of jury instructions, see Lieberman and Sales (1997).

Similarly disappointing results have been found in jurors' comprehension of death penalty instructions. For example, after being presented with the death penalty instructions used in California, only 12% of the participants could correctly define mitigation (Haney & Lynch, 1994). Only 15% defined aggravation correctly. Diamond and Levi (1996) have found marginally more promising comprehension rates, with 35% to 60% of their participants failing to understand some portion of the Illinois death penalty instructions.

There are many factors that may explain why such a discrepancy exists between these rates of comprehension. Experiments on jurors' comprehension may differ from one another on the basis of the type of instruction used, complexity of the evidence, realism of the simulation, type of participant (i.e., simulated vs. real juror), education level of the participants, whether deliberation was permitted, other procedural manipulations (e.g., note taking, preinstruction, and providing written copies of the instructions to participants), dependent measures (i.e., the way comprehension was measured), and the preexisting knowledge that participants brought with them to the experiment (see Lieberman & Sales, 1997, for a review).

Behavioral and Social Science of Improving Comprehension

It is critical to our sense of justice that juries understand the law contained in the judge's instructions. If jurors cannot understand their instructions, then verdicts will be based on nonlegal factors, rather than the law. Fortunately, behavioral and social scientists have been able to significantly improve the ability of jurors to understand a judge's instructions by rewriting them according to some simple principles borrowed from psycholinguistics, which studies how the brain acquires, understands, and produces language.

For example, Elwork et al. (1977; see also Elwork, Alfini, & Sales, 1982) tested participants on a series of original pattern instructions and found a comprehension rate of 51%. When they rewrote the instructions according to psycholinguistic principles, comprehension improved to 80% (Elwork, Alfini, & Sales, 1982). Charrow and Charrow (1979), Severance and Loftus (1982) and Severance et al. (1984) have also used psycholinguistic principles to achieve improvement in comprehension for a variety of criminal and civil jury instructions (For a step-by-step guide on how to use these principles for rewriting jury instructions, see Elwork, Sales, et al., 1982).

Improvements have also been shown in juror comprehension for rewritten death penalty instructions. Frank and Applegate (1998) showed prospective jurors a video of a real judge describing the facts of a real murder case but exposed half of the participants to the actual instructions used in the trial and the other half to the same instructions rewritten by a linguist for clarity. Participants who heard the actual instructions answered about 50% of the questions correctly versus 69% correct for the participants who heard the revised instructions (Frank & Applegate, 1998). Consistent with many studies of death penalty instructions, the prospective jurors in Frank and Applegate had the most trouble with instructions concerning mitigation. An issue for future research is to determine how comprehensible effectively rewritten instructions can be.

Reluctance to Rely on the Science

Although we do not know how high comprehension for jury instructions can go if the lessons of past behavioral and social science research are applied, the research clearly proves very poor comprehension rates and the existence of a technology to improve those rates. So why do courts choose not to rely on this research in decision making?

First, judges fear reversal on appeal (Steele & Thornburg, 1988). As already noted, jury instructions mostly consist of laws taken directly from either statutes passed by a state legislature or from rulings handed down by higher courts (Tiersma, 2001). They are, therefore, accurate statements of the law. Rewriting the instructions becomes problematic for judges because they may revise the law to a degree that it no longer represents what the legislature or a higher court intended. Similarly, it is safer for judges to simply read the instructions verbatim than to try and explain them in more understandable language. Paraphrasing can lead to reversal by a higher court (Tiersma, 1993). A defendant or a party in a lawsuit could legitimately complain in an appeal that the jury was incorrectly instructed on the law.

These arguments are supported by research. In Wyoming, 62 state and federal judges were surveyed, and 58% of them reported that jurors were occasionally confused by the instructions. In addition, 23% said jurors were frequently confused. The judges were unanimous in their view that writing instructions in plain English would improve comprehension, but 55% thought that instructions written for their legal accuracy were more important than instructions written for comprehensibility (Young, 2000).

Second, Steele and Thornburg (1988) have suggested a somewhat cynical reason for the reluctance to make jury instructions more understandable—that some lawyers benefit from juror confusion. If an attorney knows that the law is not on the side of his or her client, the failure of the jury to understand the law may be the client's best hope for a favorable outcome. Unable to comprehend what the law requires, the jury abandons the instructions and decides the case based on emotion or commonsense.

Third, even if comprehension for instructions could be improved dramatically, at what point do we agree that sufficient comprehension has been achieved? Should the law set the level at 60%, 70%, 80%, 90%, 100%? Should this threshold apply to each juror or be averaged across all prospective jurors? Should this threshold apply to each instruction given in a trial or to the most important instructions or be averaged across some subset or all of the instructions? If some subsets of instructions are more critical than others, how should the court determine this, empirically or normatively? What if the attorneys disagree as to the importance of particular instructions in particular trials? And what should the courts do if the critical instruction(s) is(are) poorly understood by the jurors but the rest of the instructions are perfectly understood? Most of the answers to these questions will depend on whether the change in comprehension affects deliberation quality and outcome, and this can only be known through further empirical research.

Fourth, many courts believe that comprehension problems can be corrected either through the deliberative process or through other statements of law made during the trial (e.g., during closing arguments by the attorneys). For example, the appellate court in *Gacy* noted that the jury deliberated only two hours, leading it to conclude that the jurors were not confused. On the contrary, the brief deliberation time may only prove that the jurors were confident in their decision and not that they knew or understood the law. Additionally, the court wrote that not all of the jurors would have misunderstood the instructions because of other correct statements of the law that were made in court by the trial court and attorneys. Without empirical testing of jurors after the trial concluded, the effect of these in-court statements on jury comprehension cannot be known.

A study by Saxton (1998) has shown that the court's assumption is likely false. Saxton tested instruction comprehension on real jurors just as they finished serving in either an actual criminal or civil case. Jurors estimated that they spent 34% of their deliberation time discussing the instructions, suggesting that they were confused by them. And in fact, jurors were confused. They answered, on average, only 66% of the questions about the instructions correctly, suggesting that what they were exposed to during the trial did not correct their misunderstandings.

The U.S. Supreme Court has also endorsed the assumption that jurors both understand and follow the jury instructions (see e.g., *Richardson v. Marsh*, 1987; *United States v. Lane*, 1986). Even in cases in which the Court believes that there is some confusion about the instructions, it is reluctant to second-guess the jury. In *Boyde v. California* (1990), the Court decided that it would not intervene unless it could be proven that there was a *reasonable likelihood* that a jury failed to understand the instructions on mitigation in a death penalty case. This reasoning was affirmed in later cases and reasonable likelihood is now the standard by which all courts are to decide whether a jury misunderstood its instructions. In *Boyde*, the Court hypothesized that, even if the instructions were ambiguous, the context of the trial was likely to have cleared up any misunderstandings the jury may have had. Indeed, the Court has consistently turned to the context of the entire trial as a remedy for miscomprehension of the jury instructions. The Court believes that a jury can derive a "commonsense understanding of the instructions" from all that goes on in the trial (*Johnson v. Texas*, 1993). These cases came before the Saxton (1998) study was published.

Several recent decisions reveal that the Supreme Court is holding to its belief that jurors understand and follow the instructions. A recent Supreme Court case illustrates this point. Lonnie Weeks was convicted and sentenced to die in Virginia for the murder of a state trooper during a routine traffic stop (*Weeks v. Angelone*, 2000). After the jury began deliberating they sent a question to the judge asking for clarification concerning one of the instructions. Ironically, just two years earlier, the Supreme Court heard an appeal from a man who was also sentenced to die in Virginia who argued that the very same instruction was likely to have so confused his jury that their verdict was arbitrary and capricious (*Buchanan v. Angelone*, 1998). The instruction read as follows:

> Before the penalty can be fixed at death, the commonwealth must prove beyond a reasonable doubt that his conduct in committing the murders of [his family] was outrageously or wantonly vile, horrible or inhuman, in that [it] involved torture, depravity of mind or aggravated battery to the above four victims, or to any one of them.
>
> If you find from the evidence that the commonwealth has proved beyond a reasonable doubt the requirements of the preceding paragraph, then you may fix the punishment of the defendant at death, or if you believe from all the evidence that the death penalty is not justified, then you shall fix the punishment of the defendant at life imprisonment.

Buchanan argued that the instruction talked only about aggravating factors (e.g., wantonly vile, horrible, or inhuman) while ignoring the mitigating factors (Buchanan presented evidence of a mental illness). He believed that the instruction was interpreted by the jury to mean that if it decided that one or more of the aggravating factors were proven by the state, then they had to sentence him to death. And, that the only way he could receive a life sentence was if the jury decided that none of the aggravating factors had been proven. Neither of these interpretations is correct. If the jury interpreted the instructions in this manner, then it would in fact have misunderstood them.

A majority of the Court disagreed. They ruled that the instruction sufficiently explained mitigation and the role it was to play in the jury's decision, emphasizing that the jury would see and understand the distinction between the words *may* (as in, may sentence the defendant to death if an aggravator is proven) and *shall* (as in, shall sentence the defendant to life in prison if the evidence—i.e., mitigators—justifies it). The Court also pointed out that the jury was unlikely to have ignored the several days of testimony and argument they heard on why Buchanan should not be sentenced to die. Thus, there was a reasonable likelihood that the jury understood the instruction and considered the mitigating evidence before they sentenced Buchanan to death.

As noted above, it was the very same instruction that the Court was considering in *Weeks*. After ruling that the instruction was understandable in *Buchanan*, the Court may have been a little chagrined when the jury in the *Weeks* case asked the trial judge the following:

> If we believe that Lonnie Weeks, Jr., is guilty of at least one of the alternatives, then is it our duty as a jury to issue the death penalty? Or must we decide (even though he is guilty of one of the alternatives) whether or not to issue the death penalty or one of the life sentences? What is the rule? Please clarify?

This was precisely the misunderstanding that the Court said was not likely to have occurred in *Buchanan*. It is clear from the jury's question that they were confused as to whether they had to sentence Weeks to death after deciding that at least one of the aggravators was proven or if they could sentence him to life in prison in spite of the aggravating factor. Acknowledging only a *slight possibility* that the jury misunderstood the instruction, the Supreme Court reiterated the assumption that juries understand and follow the law.

After the Court made the behavioral assumption that the jury instruction was understandable, researchers tested the assumption. In a study of 154 death-qualified mock jurors, researchers found that, on average, 40% of them believed that the instructions used in *Weeks* required them to sentence a defendant to death if at least one of the aggravators had been proven by the prosecution (Garvey, Johnson, & Marcus, 2000). The study also included a condition that required some participants to reread the same instruction that the judge told the jurors in *Weeks* to reread in response to their question to him. This recommendation only made comprehension of the instruction worse: 46% now believed they were required to sentence a defendant to death if the heinous, vile, or depraved aggravator had been proven (Garvey et al., 2000). However, when participants were provided with the answer to the question that the defense requested in *Weeks* (i.e., that they may consider the mitigating factors and sentence Weeks to life despite deciding that the aggravators had been proven), comprehension of the instruction improved on average to 74% (Garvey et al., 2000).

Fifth, empirical facts may conflict with normative assumptions. In this case, the court may have ignored the Study and the behavioral and social science research on instruction comprehension because Gacy and his crimes were extraordinarily evil. It was the jury's opinion that he deserved the most severe punishment available in Illinois. Implicit in the appellate court's opinion was the assumption that in light of Gacy's crimes, it was doubtful that a jury would need instructions to determine Gacy's punishment, much less have instructions that they could understand. The Court assumed that perfectly understandable instructions were unlikely to have changed the jury's decision.

Sixth, it is also likely that the Court ignored the behavioral and social science because overturning Gacy's decision would open the door for all defendants to challenge the fairness of all criminal trials based on jury miscomprehension. This indeed is a frightening prospect for the criminal justice system because the solution is not immediately in hand. Although the techniques for improving comprehension are known (Elwork, Sales, et al., 1982), no one has yet attempted to apply those techniques to most of the specific instructions in the criminal and civil law.

Finally, if states established rewriting commissions, who would serve on them? Lawyers and judges assuredly, but the pattern instructions produced by commissions composed only of judges and lawyers are often no better than the instructions they replace. Should experts in language comprehension play a role in rewriting the instructions? The answer is obviously yes. It is the behavioral and social scientists who have the expertise to do the rewriting and empirical testing of the revisions to prove their comprehension accuracy. But unless these state and federal commissions pay for this research, it is not likely that the needed revisions will ever get done—a result that will ensure that the research on juror inability to understand the law continues to be ignored.

Hope for Improving Actual Juror Comprehension

Still, there are signs of hope that juror comprehension may improve. Some states (e.g., Arizona, California, Idaho, and Michigan) are requiring that instructions now be written so that they are understandable (Tiersma, 1993, 2001). Although without also requiring empirical testing of comprehension, we cannot be sure the new rules will have a significant effect on juror comprehension and verdicts. A few states are allowing research on real juries to improve the jury system in general and jury instructions in particular. For example, Saxton (1998) obtained the permission of the Wyoming Supreme Court to test the comprehension of jurors on recently revised pattern instructions just as the jurors concluded serving in real criminal and civil trials (if the trial judges, attorneys, and jurors agreed). However, we do not know if the Wyoming Supreme Court's support for this research will lead to changes in Wyoming's jury instructions.

Finally, some courts are finding in favor of defendants who challenge jury instructions. For example, a jury asked the trial judge if choosing to sentence a man to life in prison would mean without the possibility of parole. The judge answered that whether the defendant would ever be eligible for parole was not a proper issue for their consideration and that life in prison and the death sentence were to be understood for their plain meaning. In fact, the jury's concern was well-founded. The defense showed the U.S. Supreme Court a statewide public opinion survey indicating that most people believe that defendants who are sentenced to life in prison will eventually be paroled. The Supreme Court decided that there was a reasonable likelihood that the jury did not understand that life in prison meant no possibility for parole and decided the case in favor of the defendant (*Simmons v. South Carolina*, 1994; see also *Kelly v. South Carolina*, 2002; *Shafer v. South Carolina*, 2001). The use of behavioral and social science research appeared to affect the Supreme Court's decision making in this case.

CHAPTER'S LESSON

In some situations, the course of action that behavioral and social scientists may think is best will not be followed in our courts. Legal and the underlying normative constraints, for example, may preclude the use of the behavioral and social facts in the legal decision. In such situations, the scientist may be able to provide sufficient information to the state legislature or Congress, so it might create a new law that courts would then be obliged to follow in the future (e.g., chap. 5, this volume). But even in these other legal arenas, legal, political, moral, and religious values may result in the adoption of laws and rules that ignore, or run counter to, the behavioral and social facts. The conclusion we draw is that behavioral and social scientists should do what they are most qualified for—produce the best research and educate legal decision makers about its value for understanding human behavior in all contexts.

REFERENCES

Boyde v. California, 494 U.S. 370 (1990).

Buchanan v. Angelone, 522 U.S. 269 (1998).

Charrow, R. P., & Charrow, V. (1979). Making legal language understandable: A psycholinguistic study of jury instructions. *Columbia Law Review, 79,* 1306–1374.

Diamond, S. S., & Levi, J. N. (1996). Improving decisions on death by revising and testing jury instructions. *Judicature, 79,* 224–232.

Ellsworth, P. C. (1989). Are twelve heads better than one? *Law and Contemporary Problems, 52,* 205–224.

Elwork, A., Alfini, J. J., & Sales, B. D. (1982). Toward understandable jury instructions. *Judicature, 65,* 432–443.

Elwork, A., Sales, B. D., & Alfini, J. J. (1977). Juridic decisions: In ignorance of the law or in light of it? *Law and Human Behavior, 1,* 163–189.

Elwork, A., Sales, B. D., & Alfini, J. J. (1982). *Making jury instructions understandable.* Charlottesville, VA: Michie.

Finkel N. J. (1995). *Commonsense justice.* Cambridge, MA: Harvard University Press.

Frank, J., & Applegate, B. K. (1998). Assessing juror understanding of capital-sentencing instructions. *Crime and Delinquency, 44,* 412–433.

Gacy v. Welborn, 994 F. 2d. 305 (1993).

Garvey, S. P., Johnson, S. L., & Marcus, P. (2000). Correcting deadly confusion: Responding to jury inquiries in capital cases. *Cornell Law Review, 85,* 627–655.

Haney, C., & Lynch, M. (1994). Comprehending life and death matters. *Law and Human Behavior, 18,* 411–436.

Johnson v. Texas, 509 U.S. 350 (1993).

Kelly v. South Carolina, 534 U.S. 246 (2002).

Lieberman, J. D., & Sales, B. D. (1997). What social science teaches us about the jury instruction process. *Psychology, Public Policy, and Law, 3,* 589–644.

Luginbuhl, J. (1992). Comprehension of judges' instructions in the penalty phase of a capital trial. *Law and Human Behavior, 16,* 203–218.

Lockett v. Ohio, 438 U.S. 586 (1978).

McBride, R. L. (1969). *The art of instructing the jury.* Cincinnati, OH: W. H. Anderson.

Richardson v. Marsh, 481 U.S. 200 (1987).

Sales, B. D., Elwork, A., & Alfini, J. J. (1977). Improving comprehension for jury instructions. In B. D. Sales (Ed.), *Perspectives in law and psychology: Vol. 1. The criminal justice system* (pp. 23–90). New York: Plenum Press.

Saxton, B. (1998). How well do jurors understand jury instructions? A field test using real juries and real trials in Wyoming. *Land and Water Law Review, 33,* 59–189.

Severance, L. J., & Loftus, E. F. (1982). Improving the ability of jurors to comprehend and apply criminal jury instructions. *Law and Society Review, 17,* 153–198.

Severance, L. J., Greene, E., & Loftus, E. F. (1984). Toward criminal jury instructions that jurors can understand. *The Journal of Criminal Law and Criminology, 75,* 198–233.

Shafer v. South Carolina, 532 U.S. 36 (2001).

Simons v. South Carolina, 512 U.S. 154 (1994).

Steele, W. W., & Thornburg, E. G. (1988). Jury instructions: A persistent failure to communicate. *North Carolina Law Review, 67,* 77–119.

Strawn, D. U., & Buchanan, R. W. (1976). Jury confusion: A threat to justice. *Judicature, 59,* 478–483.

Tanford, J. A. (1990). The law and psychology of jury instructions. *Nebraska Law Review, 69,* 71–111.

Tiersma, P. M. (1993). Reforming the language of jury instructions. *Hofstra Law Review, 22,* 37–78.

Tiersma, P. M. (2001). The rocky road to legal reform: Improving the language of jury instructions. *Brooklyn Law Review, 66,* 1081–1119.

United States v. Lane, 474 U.S. 438 (1986).

Weeks v. Angelone, 528 U.S. 225 (2000).

Young, R. M. (2000). Using social science to assess the need for jury reform. *South Carolina Law Review, 52,* 135–240.

10

RELEVANT FACTUAL KNOWLEDGE DOES NOT YET EXIST

EXAMPLE: DETERRING ILLEGAL POLICE BEHAVIOR

In this chapter, we deal with a second U.S. Supreme Court case involving the Fourth Amendment to the U.S. Constitution. The first, the *Vernonia* case discussed in chapter 2, was distinctive in that one does not typically think of a drug test as constituting a search. Certainly the framers of our Constitution did not have that kind of search in mind when the Fourth Amendment was crafted.

The case that we present in this chapter, *United States v. Leon* (1984), deals with the more traditional type of search that involves a suspect's residence and car being searched by law enforcement. Alberto Leon's arrest and conviction were based on evidence obtained from a search warrant that was issued by a judge. After the warrant was executed and the evidence seized, it was determined that the judge made an error and should not have issued the warrant. Under the exclusionary rule, information obtained pursuant to an invalid warrant cannot be used at trial. This rule is designed to deter police from using illegal tactics in getting a magistrate (i.e., a judge with limited jurisdiction or another official who has responsibility for limited judicial functions) or judge (hereafter judge) to issue a warrant.

The Court in this case had to decide whether to apply the exclusionary rule to the evidence obtained from the search. The police officers acted in good faith when they applied for the warrant. Thus, it is unclear what effect excluding this evidence from trial would have on future police behavior. Unfortunately, there was no social science for the Court to draw on when rendering its decision. Scientists will not always have the information that decision makers want when they want it. In addition, even after a question is posed for scientific inquiry, it takes time to design the appropriate study to answer the question, collect and analyze the data, and finally to put the facts into a form the decision maker can best utilize. The lesson of this chapter is that even when behavioral and social facts could improve legal decision making, they will not always be available when needed.

UNITED STATES V. LEON

United States Supreme Court

In August 1981, a confidential informant of unproven reliability informed a police officer that two persons known to him as Armando and Patsy were selling large quantities of cocaine and methaqualone from their residence in Burbank, California. The informant also indicated that he had witnessed a sale of methaqualone by Patsy at the residence approximately five months earlier and had observed at that time a shoebox containing a large amount of cash that belonged to Patsy. He further declared that Armando and Patsy generally kept only small quantities of drugs at their residence and stored the remainder at another location in Burbank.

On the basis of this information, the Burbank police initiated an extensive investigation focusing first on the Burbank residence and later on two other residences. Cars parked at the Burbank residence were determined to belong to Armando Sanchez, who had previously been arrested for possession of marijuana, and Patsy Stewart, who had no criminal record. During the course of the investigation, officers observed an automobile belonging to Ricardo Del Castillo arrive at the Burbank residence. Del Castillo had previously been arrested for possession of 50 pounds of marijuana. The driver of that car entered the house, exited shortly thereafter carrying a small paper sack, and drove away. A check of Del Castillo's probation records led the officers to Alberto Leon, whose telephone number Del Castillo had listed as his employer's. Leon had been arrested in 1980 on drug charges, and a companion had informed the police at that time that Leon was heavily involved in the importation of drugs into this country.

Before the current investigation began, the Burbank officers had learned that an informant had told a Glendale police officer that Leon stored a large quantity of methaqualone at his residence in Glendale. During the course of this investigation, the Burbank officers learned that Leon was living at a second residence in Burbank. Subsequently, the officers observed several persons, at least one of whom had prior drug involvement, arriving at the first Burbank residence and leaving with small packages. They observed a variety of other activity at the two residences as well as at a condominium in Burbank and witnessed a variety of activity involving automobiles belonging to Sanchez, Stewart, Del Castillo, and Leon. In addition, the officers observed Sanchez and Stewart board separate flights for Miami. The pair later returned to Los Angeles together and consented to a search of their luggage. The search revealed only a small amount of marijuana, and the police allowed the pair to leave the airport.

Based on these and other observations, an experienced and well-trained narcotics investigator of the Burbank Police Department prepared an application for a warrant to search the residences and automobiles registered to Sanchez, Stewart, Del Castillo, and Leon. The purpose of the application for the warrant was to search for an extensive list of items believed to be related to the respondents' drug-trafficking activities. The extensive application was reviewed by several deputy district attorneys.

A *facially* valid search warrant (a warrant that on its surface appears to be valid) was issued in September 1981 by a judge. The ensuing searches produced large quantities of drugs at two of the residences and a small quantity at the third. Other evidence was discovered at each of the residences and in Stewart's and Del Castillo's automobiles. Sanchez, Stewart, Del Castillo, and Leon were indicted by a grand jury and charged with, among other things, conspiracy to possess and distribute cocaine.

Sanchez, Stewart, Del Castillo, and Leon then filed motions to suppress the evidence that was seized pursuant to the warrant. The court ruled that the search warrant was invalid because there was no probable cause for its issuance. Therefore, evidence obtained from the search pursuant to the invalid warrant was excluded based on the U.S. Constitution's Fourth Amendment's exclusionary rule. This rule prohibits the government from using information obtained from an illegal search. The government asks this Court to modify the Fourth Amendment's exclusionary rule so as not to bar the admission of evidence seized in reasonable, good-faith reliance on a search warrant that is subsequently held to be defective.

This case involves inherently trustworthy tangible evidence obtained in reliance on a search warrant. The warrant was issued by a detached and neutral judge but was ultimately found to be defective. Researchers have only recently begun to study the effects of the exclusionary rule on the disposition of felony arrests. One study in California suggests that the rule results in the nonprosecution or nonconviction of between 0.6% and 2.35% of individuals arrested for felonies. The estimates are higher for particular crimes in which the prosecution depends heavily on physical evidence. Thus, the cumulative loss from nonprosecution or nonconviction of individuals arrested on felony drug charges is probably in the range of 2.8% to 7.1%. These comparatively small percentages mask a large absolute number of felons who are released because the cases against them were based in part on illegal searches or seizures.

Despite these numbers, we have not seriously questioned the continued use of the exclusionary rule to suppress evidence in cases in which a Fourth Amendment violation has been substantial and deliberate.[1] Yet, any rule of evidence that denies the jury access to clearly relevant and reliable evidence must bear a heavy burden of justification and must be carefully limited to the circumstances in which it will pay its way by deterring official lawlessness. For example, if police learn that illegal warrants result in evidence not being admitted in court, they presumably would start complying with the law. But, when law enforcement officers have acted in good faith or their transgressions have been minor, the magnitude of the benefit conferred on guilty defendants offends basic concepts of the criminal justice system. Indiscriminate application of the exclusionary rule in those cases may well generate disrespect for the law and the administration of justice. As yet, however, we have not recognized any form of good-faith exception to the Fourth Amendment's exclusionary rule.

The balancing (cost–benefit) approach that has evolved during the years of experience with the rule provides strong support for the modification currently urged upon us. A search warrant provides the detached scrutiny of a judge, which is a more reliable safeguard against improper searches than the hurried judgment of a law enforcement officer engaged in the often competitive enterprise of ferreting out crime. Thus, we have a strong preference for warrants and have declared that in a doubtful or marginal case a search under a warrant may be sustainable, whereas without

---

[1]Evidence obtained in violation of the Fourth Amendment, which makes it inadmissible in the prosecution's case, may still be used for some other purposes (e.g., to impeach a defendant's direct testimony).

one it would fall. Reasonable minds frequently may differ on the question whether a particular police affidavit establishes probable cause for the issuance of a warrant, but we have concluded that the preference for warrants requires that great deference be given to a judge's determination.

Deference to the judge, however, is not boundless. A judge's finding of probable cause does not preclude inquiry into the knowing or reckless falsity of the affidavit on which that determination was based. The warrant must be based on an affidavit that provides a substantial basis for determining the existence of probable cause. Bare conclusions in the police affidavit are not sufficient. The judge must perform his neutral and detached function and not serve merely as a rubber stamp for the police. A judge who fails to be neutral and detached when presented with a warrant application, and who acts instead as an adjunct law enforcement officer, cannot provide valid authorization for an otherwise unconstitutional search. Even if the warrant application was supported by more than a bare bones affidavit, a reviewing court may properly conclude that, notwithstanding the deference that judges deserve, the warrant was invalid because the judge's probable-cause determination reflected an improper analysis of the totality of the circumstances or because the form of the warrant was improper in some respect.

There exists no evidence, however, suggesting that judges are inclined to ignore or subvert the Fourth Amendment or that lawlessness among these legal actors requires application of the extreme sanction of exclusion of evidence. Although there are assertions that some judges become rubber stamps for the police, and that the courts may subsequently be unable to effectively screen police conduct, this is not a problem of major proportions. Most important, there is no basis for believing that exclusion of evidence seized pursuant to a warrant will have a significant deterrent effect on the issuing judge. To the extent that the rule is thought to operate as a systemic deterrent on a wider audience, it clearly can have no such effect on individuals empowered to issue search warrants. Judges are not adjuncts to the law enforcement team; as neutral judicial officers, they have no stake in the outcome of particular criminal prosecutions. The threat of exclusion thus cannot be expected significantly to deter them nor is it a meaningful way to inform judicial officers of their errors so they will not repeat their mistakes in the future. If a judge serves merely as a rubber stamp for the police or is unable to exercise mature judgment, closer supervision or removal provides a more effective remedy than the exclusionary rule.

If exclusion of evidence obtained pursuant to a subsequently invalidated warrant is to have any deterrent effect, it must alter the behavior of law enforcement officers or the policies of their departments. One could argue that applying the exclusionary rule promotes the ends of the Fourth Amendment and deters future inadequate police affidavits in cases in which the police failed to demonstrate probable cause in the warrant application or in cases in which police attempted to find a judge who would rubber stamp a warrant application. Suppressing evidence obtained pursuant to a technically defective warrant that was supported by probable cause also might encourage officers to scrutinize more closely the form of the warrant and to point out suspected errors to the judge. But such arguments are speculative. This Court, therefore, concludes that suppression of evidence obtained pursuant to a warrant should be ordered only on a case-by-case basis and only in those unusual cases in which exclusion will further the purposes of the exclusionary rule.

The question here is whether the exclusionary rule can have any deterrent effect when the offending officers acted in the objectively reasonable belief that their conduct did not violate the Fourth Amendment. No empirical researcher, proponent or opponent of the rule, has yet been able to establish with any assurance whether the rule has a deterrent effect. But even if the rule effectively deters some police misconduct and provides incentives for the law enforcement profession as a whole to conduct itself in accord with the Fourth Amendment, it cannot be expected and should not be applied to deter objectively reasonable law enforcement activity.

The deterrent purpose of the exclusionary rule necessarily assumes that the police have engaged in willful, or at the very least negligent, conduct that has deprived the defendant of some right. The goal of refusing to allow evidence gained as a result of such conduct to be used in trials is to instill in those particular investigating officers, or in their future counterparts, a greater degree of care toward the rights of an accused. If the official action was pursued in complete good faith, however, the deterrence rationale loses much of its force. If the purpose of the exclusionary rule is to deter unlawful police conduct, then evidence obtained from a search should be suppressed only if it can be said that the law enforcement officer had or should have had knowledge that the search was unconstitutional under the Fourth Amendment. If the officer's conduct is objectively reasonable, excluding the evidence will not further the ends of the exclusionary rule in any appreciable way. Excluding the evidence can in no way affect his future conduct unless it is to make him less willing to do his duty.

The standard of reasonableness is an objective one. Many objections to a good-faith exception to the exclusionary rule assume that the exception will turn on the subjective good faith of individual officers. Grounding the exception in objective reasonableness, however, retains the value of the exclusionary rule as an incentive for the law enforcement profession as a whole to conduct itself in accord with the Fourth Amendment. The objective standard requires officers to have a reasonable knowledge of what the law prohibits. The key to the exclusionary rule's effectiveness as a deterrent lies in the impetus it has provided to police training programs that make officers aware of the limits imposed by the Fourth Amendment and emphasize the need to operate within those limits.

This is particularly true when an officer acting with objective good faith has obtained a search warrant from a judge and acted within its scope. A warrant is a judicial mandate to an officer to conduct a search or make an arrest, and the officer has a sworn duty to carry out its provisions. Accordingly, there should be a rule that states that evidence obtained pursuant to and within the scope of a warrant is prima facie the result of good faith on the part of the officer seizing the evidence. In most such cases, there is no police illegality and thus nothing to deter. It is the judge's responsibility to determine whether the officer's allegations establish probable cause and, if so, to issue a warrant comporting in form with the requirements of the Fourth Amendment. In the ordinary case, an officer cannot be expected to question the judge's probable-cause determination or his judgment that the form of the warrant is technically sufficient. Once the warrant issues, there is literally nothing more the policeman can do in seeking to comply with the law. Penalizing the officer for the judge's error, rather than his own, cannot logically contribute to the deterrence of Fourth Amendment violations.

The marginal or nonexistent benefits produced by suppressing evidence obtained in reasonable reliance on a subsequently invalidated search warrant cannot justify the substantial costs of exclusion. This does not suggest, however, that exclusion is always inappropriate in cases in which an officer has obtained a warrant and abided by its terms. The officer's reliance on the judge's probable-cause determination and on the technical sufficiency of the warrant he issues must be objectively reasonable.

This analysis precludes inquiries into the subjective beliefs of law enforcement officers who seize evidence pursuant to a subsequently invalidated warrant. Sending state and federal courts on an expedition into the minds of police officers would produce a grave and fruitless misallocation of judicial resources. Accordingly, a good-faith inquiry is confined to whether a reasonably well-trained officer would have known that the search was illegal despite the judge's authorization. In making this determination, all of the circumstances, including whether the warrant application had previously been rejected by a different judge, may be considered. It is clear that in some circumstances the officer will have no reasonable grounds for believing that the warrant was properly issued. It is necessary to consider the objective reasonableness not only of the officers who eventually executed a warrant but also of the officers who originally obtained it or who provided information material to determining whether there was the probable cause to seek a warrant.

When these principles are applied to the facts of this case, it is apparent that the lower court judgment cannot stand. In the absence of an allegation that the judge abandoned his detached and neutral role, suppression of the evidence is appropriate only if the officers were dishonest or reckless in preparing their affidavit or could not have harbored an objectively reasonable belief in the existence of probable cause. Only Leon has contended that no reasonably well-trained police officer could have believed that there existed probable cause to search his house; significantly, the other defendants advance no comparable argument. The officer's application for the warrant clearly was supported by much more than a bare-bones affidavit. The affidavit related the results of an extensive investigation. Under these circumstances, the officers' reliance on the judge's determination of probable cause was objectively reasonable, and application of the extreme sanction of exclusion of the evidence is inappropriate.

CONCURRING OPINION[2]

The Court holds that evidence obtained in violation of the Fourth Amendment by officers acting in objectively reasonable reliance on a search warrant issued by a neutral and detached judge need not be excluded from the case in federal and state criminal prosecutions. In so doing, the Court writes another chapter in the volume of Fourth Amendment law. The rule advances the legiti-

---

[2]A Concurring Opinion is an opinion of one or more of the justices concurring with the Majority Opinion but raising one or more issues not considered by the majority.

mate interests of the criminal justice system without sacrificing the individual rights protected by the Fourth Amendment. This Concurring Opinion underscores the unavoidably provisional nature of the decision.

The Court has narrowed the scope of the exclusionary rule because of an *empirical* judgment that the rule has little appreciable effect in cases in which officers act in objectively reasonable reliance on search warrants. There is no way to avoid making an empirical judgment of this sort, and the Court has made the correct one on the information before it. All courts face institutional limitations on their ability to gather information about legislative facts (i.e., facts needed to address questions of law). Nonetheless, this Court cannot escape its responsibility to decide the question in this case, however imperfect its information may be.

What must be stressed is that any empirical judgment about the effect of the exclusionary rule in a particular class of cases necessarily is a provisional one. By their very nature, the assumptions on which the Court proceeds cannot be cast in stone. To the contrary, they now will be tested in the real world of state and federal law enforcement, and the Court will attend to the results. If it should emerge from experience that, contrary to current assumptions, the good-faith exception to the exclusionary rule results in a material change in police compliance with the Fourth Amendment, the Court will have to reconsider their decision. Its logic, which rests on untested predictions about police conduct, demands no less. If a single principle may be drawn from the Court's exclusionary rule decision, it is that the scope of the exclusionary rule is subject to change in light of changing judicial understanding about the effects of the rule.

ANALYSIS AND IMPLICATIONS

The Fourth Amendment to the U.S. Constitution reads as follows:

The right of the people to be secure in their persons, houses, papers and effects, against unreasonable searches and seizures, shall not be violated, and no warrants shall issue, but upon probable cause, supported by oath or affirmation, and particularly describing the place to be searched, and the persons or things to be seized.

The motivation for this Amendment lies in the experience that early Americans had with British soldiers searching their homes. To ensure that no government would ever again unreasonably search homes and seize possessions, drafters of the Constitution stated very clearly that such government action was prohibited, unless there was probable cause to believe that the search would reveal evidence of wrongdoing. Probable cause means that circumstances exist that would lead a reasonable person to believe that a crime has or will be committed. The belief must be based on facts. A hunch is not good enough to obtain a warrant.

In order for a government official to search homes or property, the official must typically obtain a search warrant from a judge. The official must explain to the judge why a search is necessary, and this explanation comes in the form of an affidavit that is a sworn statement that reviews the evidence, including what the police have observed and what physical evidence they have in their possession, what witnesses or informants have told them, and what physical evidence they will be searching for. The judge then has to decide if the evidence that the official has presented constitutes probable cause for the issuance of a warrant.

Regrettably, there have been periods in our nation's history when local, state, and federal officials have not respected this investigative process. Faced with police misconduct in the issuing of improper search warrants, the Supreme Court devised the exclusionary rule in 1914 to strengthen Fourth Amendment rights. The Court ruled that the government was not entitled to use at trial, evidence against a defendant that it had obtained in violation of the Fourth Amendment. The expectation or hope was that when police hear of courts excluding evidence on the basis of improperly obtained or executed search warrants, they will be more likely in the future to produce more truthful and reliable affidavits.

Deterrent Effect of the Exclusionary Rule

Has the exclusionary rule worked as intended? Unfortunately, the Court did not know because there were no empirical studies on it, but there were ample cases to prove that it was not having its intended effect. The Court noted that there were a large number of cases either not being prosecuted or not resulting in convictions because trial judges were excluding evidence based on the exclusionary rule. Therefore, in the Court's opinion, to suggest that the exclusionary rule is a deterrent to police misconduct in this area is pure speculation.

Some critics of the rule feel that these cases justify abolishing the rule because criminals are getting off on mere technicalities (Markman, 1997). It could also be argued that these cases reflect the fact that law enforcement thought the risk of collecting evidence improperly in hopes of getting it admitted outweighed the risk of having it thrown out by a judge. Why would law enforcement take such a risk? Psychology may have an answer in reactance theory. Reactance occurs in people when their sense of freedom is threatened, and they rebel by adopting an even more extreme position than they would otherwise (Brehm & Brehm, 1981). Applying this theory to law enforcement, police may resent what they consider an intrusion by the courts into their legitimate investigatory domain. To prove their autonomy, they will ignore the rules on searches and seizures. Therefore, the exclusionary rule according to reactance theory may produce a boomerang effect in police behavior.

Even if the exclusionary rule were a deterrent, what should be done about excluding evidence from a case in which there was no police misconduct in obtaining a warrant? Should there be some exception when police, through no fault of their own, execute a search warrant that they obtained in good faith but that later turned out to be issued in error? The Court believed that the application of the exclusionary rule in a case like *Leon* was illogical. Here, a police officer approached a judge in good faith and asked that a search warrant be issued, with an objectively reasonable belief that no violation of Leon's Fourth Amendment rights would result. The officer believed that he had sufficient evidence to show probable cause that a crime had or was about to be committed and that issuance of a warrant was justified. The fact that the officer lacked probable cause was something the judge should have detected. That the warrant was issued was the fault of the judge, not the officer seeking it. In the *Leon* case, the judge should have realized that probable cause was lacking because the reliability of the informant could not be established, and the tip he provided was too old (stale, to use the Court's term). The Court could expect the officer to do no less than what the warrant said to do once it had been issued. If the officer sought it in good faith, then he must have expected that the judge issued it in good faith. Thus, there was no improper police behavior that needed to be corrected by implementing the exclusionary rule. It was the judge's behavior that needed correcting, but this is something that the Court said the exclusionary rule could not accomplish.

Potentially Relevant Social Science Research

The Court notified the country that it did not have the kind of behavioral and social facts that it thought would have been useful in reaching a decision in this case, but it had to proceed in its decision making nonetheless. Courts cannot typically wait until the relevant behavioral and social facts are gathered. The Concurring Opinion made it clear that the Court's decision should be a provisional one. As behavioral and social science research yields empirical facts on deterrence, they should become part of the Court's cost–benefit analysis in future cases.

Such research emerged after the Court's decision in this case. So does the exclusionary rule really deter police misconduct during the application process for a warrant? To address this question, several studies have looked at the ability of police officers and recruits to understand search and seizure law. If police cannot understand what the law is requiring of them, then it cannot be a deterrent. Orfield (1987) conducted structured interviews with 26 members of the Narcotics Section of the Chicago Police Department. He found that when officers had their evidence excluded from trial, 85% of them reported that they always learned of the exclusion, and 87% of them usually or always understood the reasons for the exclusion. Orfield (1987) found other reasons for believing that the rule is a deterrent. When officers had evidence excluded, they were required to explain the reasons why during a review session with a supervisor. Furthermore, if officers had evidence excluded two times (except in minor cases), they were subject to demotion or transfer. The rule had an even broader institutional effect; lawyers were brought in from the state attorney's office to review all search warrants for their legality, and training sessions on search and seizure law were given to the officers (Orfield, 1987). Finally, all of the officers reported that they approved of the exclusionary rule, and more than 50% of the officers reported that the rule prevented them from making a search they thought they should make *reasonably often, frequently,* or *very frequently.* Based on the results of the survey, Orfield (1987) concluded that the rule deters illegal police behavior.

Orfield (1987) did report some disturbing findings, however. When the officers were asked if police "shade the facts a little (or a lot)" to establish probable cause to conduct a search, 76% said yes. In a study of defense attorneys, prosecutors, and judges (Orfield, 1992), 81% of the respondents indicated that they felt officers sometimes changed their testimony (i.e., lied) during suppression hearings so that the seized evidence would not be excluded. In addition, 67% believed that police superiors tolerated such lying; 38% believed that police superiors actually encouraged it; and 80% believed that judges allowed evidence to be used at trial despite the fact that the judges believed that the evidence was a result of an illegal search (Orfield, 1992). An implication of these findings is that the rule may not be nearly as effective a deterrent as Orfield argued. For more thorough reviews of this topic, see Slobogin (1996; and Reitz, 1996, for a reply to Slobogin) and McClurg (1999; examining police lying from a psychological perspective).

Heffernan and Lovely (1991) support the conclusion that the exclusionary rule is not a strong deterrent. They presented 500 police officers with hypothetical search and seizure cases based on Supreme Court rulings and asked them to decide if the behavior of the officer described in the hypothetical case was permissible and if they would carry out the described search themselves. Officers were also given multiple-choice questions designed to test their knowledge of search and seizure law. On the hypothetical questions, officers were correct 57% of the time in identifying a lawful search. Lawyers were correct 73% of the time. On the multiple-choice test, officers answered correctly only 48% of the time. The most distressing result of this study was that the officers with advanced training who demonstrated the greatest knowledge of search and seizure law also were the most likely to report that they would carry out the search described in the hypothetical case, although they knew it to be a violation of search and seizure law. The advanced training may have helped them understand the law better, but it did little to convince them to obey it (Heffernan & Lovely, 1991).

If the exclusionary rule is not a deterrent for many officers, what can be done to improve its effectiveness? Stated another way, what are the factors that are most likely to induce police to comply with the exclusionary rule? First, effective education about what the law requires is going to be essential. Hirokawa (2000), based on interviews with police instructors from six Atlanta area police academies, argued that if the training of the cadets teaches the knowledge of the law and the strategy to act cautiously in the field when in doubt about what to do in regard to the law, compliance for new officers is likely to be very high. But new cadets comprise only a part of the workforce. Continuing training is also needed for active officers. For example, Perrin, Caldwell, Chase, and Fagan (1998) showed that officers correctly answered hypothetical questions about the application of search and seizure law 50% of the time, which means that they are poorly trained or do not understand what they are being taught. We consider a third explanation later in our discussion of conformity—officers being properly trained but still refusing to comply with the exclusionary rule.

Second, effective training requires effective communication. In the Perrin et al. (1998) study, 60% of the officers thought that search and seizure law was complex. If the law is difficult for officers to understand, simply telling them about it in legal jargon will not likely lead to understanding. Training with effective communication for effective outcomes is essential and requires using training approaches that have been empirically proven to achieve the desired outcomes.

Third, learning of prior errors is an important part of the learning experience. If officers engage in misconduct in the application for a warrant, it is important that they learn exactly what behaviors were objectionable and what are the ensuing negative consequences (e.g., exclusion of the evidence from trial). Perrin et al.'s (1998) study showed that approximately 30% of the officers did not learn of the results of a suppression hearing from the judge or prosecutor. Although most (but not all) of this group did learn of the results from another source, it is not clear that the source educated the officers about which of their behaviors were objectionable. This type of feedback is essential so that officers can correct their misbehavior in the future.

Fourth, Orfield (1987) reported that some of the officers he studied reported a sense of personal disappointment when the exclusionary rule was invoked because of the time and energy that they had invested in the case. Orfield suggested that the rule successfully deters police misconduct because officers will work harder to obey the law in future search and seizure cases so that they may avoid a recurrence of these feelings of disappointment. Under what conditions officers experience this sense of disappointment or other feelings such as distress and frustration and how these feelings will affect future compliance deserve further study.

Fifth, compliance with the law may also be affected by the officers' desire to conform in some way. When we change either our behavior or the way we think as a result of what others do or think, we are conforming. (See Eagly & Chaiken, 1993.) Two classic psychological studies illustrate this phenomenon.

One such experiment was conducted by Sherif (1935), who placed several volunteers in a darkened room and asked them to estimate, out loud, the distance that a point of light moved. In fact, the light did not move at all. The participants were really experiencing a visual illusion known as the autokinetic phenomenon: the apparent ability of light to move on its own when seen in the dark. At first, the estimates varied widely among the participants. However, after repeated trials, participants' judgments started to converge toward one another. That is, participants who guessed the light was moving perhaps eight inches lowered their estimates if other participants initially guessed the light was moving only a few inches. Conversely, participants revised their estimates upward in the presence of others who made higher initial estimates.

Asch (1951, 1955, 1956) conducted a second classic set of experiments on conformity. His research was a little different from Sherif's in that Asch removed any ambiguity about the nature of the physical stimulus that participants were asked to judge. Asch showed his participants lines of various lengths drawn on cards. On one card there was a single line called a standard. On a second card, there were three lines, one of which was the same length as the standard and two of which were obviously different in length from the standard. Participants were asked to select the line from among the three that matched the standard line. The task was performed in groups, and participants did not know that the other members of the group were members of the experimental team (confederates). When it was the confederates' turn to make their selection of the matching line length, they picked a line that was clearly wrong (i.e., did not match the standard line). The research question was, what line length would the real experimental participants pick in the presence of others who were giving blatantly incorrect answers? Nearly 40% agreed with the confederates and made an incorrect selection, although it was obviously wrong.

Many possible reasons have been offered for why people conform, and each may help us understand police behavior in response to the exclusionary rule. French and Raven (1959; Raven, 1965) have tried to explain conformity in terms of the differences in power that exist between people who have it (agents) and people who do not (targets). They have identified several bases of power that people can use over others, one of which is legitimacy. An agent's legitimate power stems from the target's belief that the agent has a legitimate ability to dictate the target's behavior. In this instance, the target believes that the agent has certain rights and responsibilities granted by society that allow it to tell others what to do (Eagly & Chaiken, 1993); "You are the justly elected or appointed official(s) so I will do as you say." Although the point is sometimes overlooked, police officers are citizens too who are just as interested in seeing that laws are obeyed. Perhaps better than most, they also understand the importance of chain of command and how adherence to that chain and the rules handed down by those above them promote public safety and social harmony. At the top of this particular chain sits the U.S. Supreme Court, and what they say is legitimately the law of the land, so the police will obey it.

Another way to characterize the effect of perceived legitimacy is to consider it as obedience to authority, which in the case of the exclusionary rule is the law. Milgram (1963, 1974) conducted a classic study on this topic. He deceived his subjects into believing that they were participating in a learning experiment and that he was interested in the effects of punishment on learning and memory. Each participant was told that it would be his job (all participants in the 1963 study were male) to administer increasing levels of shock to a *learner* (really a confederate) seated in an adjoining room every time the learner made an error. In response to the participant's questions, the learner would purposely provide an incorrect answer. Of course, no shock was actually delivered, but the realism of the situation led the participant to believe that he was really shocking the learner whenever a mistake was made.

The participant saw the other person strapped into a chair while the electrodes were attached, and in some experiments the participant even experienced a mild sample shock to feel what it was he would be doing to the learner (at the lower intensities anyway). In addition, as the shocks supposedly grew in intensity with every mistake the learner made, the participant could hear the learner cry out in pain. On the control panel that the participants used to deliver the shocks, intensities ranged from 15 to 450 volts in 15-volt increments and were labeled with descriptors ranging from "Slight Shock" to "Danger: Severe Shock." The two highest shock intensities were ominously labeled "XXX." The participants were told that although the shocks might be very painful, they would do no permanent tissue damage to the learner.

As the experiment began, participants showed little hesitancy in delivering shocks. As the experiment proceeded and shock intensity grew because of incorrect answers, participants would express doubts about whether it was proper for them to continue. After all, the learner could be heard shouting out in a panic that he wanted the experiment to end because it was too painful. When participants demonstrated reluctance to proceed, they were admonished by the experimenter that they had to go on. Incredibly, 65% of the participants delivered the maximum shock possible to the learners (Milgram, 1963).

Milgram (1974) theorized that the participants recognized a hierarchy in authority within the experimental situation and that as participants they were at the bottom and the men in lab coats were at the top. The experimenters, by virtue of their superior position, had the authority to determine the behavior of the participants, and the participants, by virtue of their inferior position, were obligated to obey. Milgram (1974) said that participants viewed themselves as instruments for carrying out the wishes of the experimenters. When roles of authority and power are clearly delineated, people will display remarkable obedience to perceived authority, and this might explain police compliance with the exclusionary rule.

An important issue for both legitimacy and obedience to authority is what group is perceived as having the legitimacy or authority to command conformity or obedience. If police officers consider the U.S. Supreme Court or the law to have perceived legitimacy or authority, then the police will do as they are told, whether they think the Court's order is reasonable or not. However, if the police officers perceive that their departmental colleagues have the legitimacy to dictate behavior and those colleagues constantly exceed the legal boundaries, then the officers will refuse to comply with the exclusionary rule or the law. This may explain the rigid code of silence that police officers adhere to when one of their own behaves inappropriately or illegally. They are certainly aware that a higher authority has instructed them to act ethically and legally. But if an immediate authority, like a supervisor standing over their shoulder or their partner on the force, who has the power to deliver immediate sanctions or immediate consequences instructs them to alter a report for the purposes of securing an otherwise dubious search warrant, they may remain silent.

Police behavior, then, is partially explained by the norms that they hold. A norm is a practice or custom or a deeply held shared value of a group. We know that people conform to the norms of their group (Eagly & Chaiken, 1993). As group identification becomes stronger, conformity to the group's norms becomes stronger. Applying this explanation, police officers will conform to the rules on search because that is what the norms of the immediate law enforcement group or what the norms of some other group that they identify with (e.g., a national law enforcement group) dictate. The need to be accepted by one's peers is powerful motivation to abide by the norms of the chosen group. No officer wants to be perceived by other officers as being a rogue cop who operates outside the boundaries of the group's norms. If the norms of the group are to abide by the letter of the law, an officer who ignores that law, selectively enforces it, or is too incompetent to know the law, risks losing the respect of his or her peers and acceptance by his or her preferred group. Yet, as we have noted, when the respected norms do not value rigid conformity to the law, the police are less likely to comply with the exclusionary rule.

Police officers may also conform for other reasons. For example, they may be willing to follow the exclusionary rule for what are known as informational reasons (French & Raven, 1959; Raven, 1965). When they do so, they are relying on and will follow the specialized knowledge of the courts and policy makers relating to the search process as it is conveyed in the law enforcement training program. Here the officers may learn of the rationale, logic, or philosophy and certainly the mechanics of the law or policy and incorporate it into their jobs.

Officers may conform as the result of compliance (Eagly & Chaiken, 1993). This explanation posits that while some police officers may disagree with a particular law or policy, they are able to set aside their personal misgivings and enforce the law as they are instructed. Perhaps it is the officers' sense of duty and professionalism, the oath they took to uphold the law, or their personal sense of integrity, which act in combination to compel them to conform despite their personal views of the wisdom of the law or policy. Officers may object to the exclusionary rule but be willing, for one or some of the reasons just noted, to abide by the rules that the courts have set down for obtaining a valid search warrant.

Conformity may occur because of acceptance (Eagly & Chaiken, 1993), which suggests that officers obey laws and policies because they believe that the laws and policies represent a good way of doing things. Perhaps the law or policy is consistent with their values, morals, sense of justice, or experience as a police officer. These officers may believe that the exclusionary rule is a good policy because it protects citizens from bad cops or makes them better officers because they have to be certain that their work product is of sufficient quality to satisfy the legal requirements for obtaining a search warrant.

French and Raven (1959; Raven, 1965) have identified other types of power that people in authority can use over others. One of them, reward power, is the ability of an agent to reward a target group if the target group conforms to the agent's wishes. When the relationship is viewed as one based on reward, the courts are telling law enforcement, "Do as we say, and we will reward you." That is, follow the rules we have for obtaining a search warrant, and we will admit the evidence gathered as a result of the warrant into court. This reasoning can also be seen in the Court's justification for a good-faith exception to the exclusionary rule: The officers in *Leon* followed the rules so the evidence they gathered was admissible. The Court was not going to punish officers with exclusion of the evidence for the failure of a judge to follow the rules. Police officers may secure rewards other than the issuance of a search warrant. They may be rewarded with increased pay, promotion, or commendations for following the law so ably. Officers may also be rewarded with intangibles, such as increased pride in a job well done and good will from a grateful public.

An opposite type of power that can be used to get the target to conform is called coercive power. Here the agent tries to influence the target by using its coercive power to punish the target group (French & Raven, 1959; Raven, 1965). If the relationship between the agent and target is based on coercion, then the agent is saying to the target, "If you don't do as I say, I will punish you." This is one of the primary reasons the Court had for introducing the exclusionary rule. For flouting the Fourth Amendment's proscription against unreasonable searches and seizures, the Court felt it necessary to punish the police by denying them the use of their illegally obtained evidence and in so doing sought to coerce the police to change their behavior. When police departments threaten to reassign officers for noncompliance with the exclusionary rule, they also exemplify the use of coercive power.

How these explanatory mechanisms actually work in police settings and how police departments can decrease police misbehavior by using social science knowledge of conformity are topics for future research and collaboration between law enforcement and behavioral and social scientists. What is known, however, is that there already is a rich behavioral and social science literature that can inform this collaboration and lead to directly relevant research that will explain and predict under what conditions the exclusionary rule is likely to achieve its intended effects.

Sixth and finally, the Court in *Leon* said that the exclusionary rule was adopted only in the absence of a "more efficacious sanction," meaning that if some other method were devised that proved to be a better deterrent of police misbehavior than the rule, the Court would consider adopting it. Other sanctions might include a civil action against the individual officer by the person whose rights were violated by the allegedly illegal search, police department sanctions (e.g., loss of pay, suspension, or demotion), or even criminal prosecution. Researchers need to study the practicality and effectiveness of such alternative methods and compare the outcomes to the use of the exclusionary rule.

Cost–Benefit Analysis

Whether to exclude evidence obtained under illegal circumstances must be viewed in terms of the costs and benefits to society. The costs of not using evidence that may lead to a conviction are obvious: a guilty person may go free. The benefit to society is that future police misconduct will be deterred. But how can it deter police behavior that was undertaken in good faith? There is no police misconduct to deter. The only people who would benefit from the exclusion of evidence obtained in good faith would be criminals who would either escape punishment or receive lesser sentences than they would have had the evidence been presented at their trial.

An additional factor the Court considered in its cost–benefit analysis was that the *indiscriminate application* of the exclusionary rule might lead people to disrespect the law and the administration of justice. If incriminating evidence was excluded from a trial when the police did nothing wrong and the offender was never brought to trial because the good-faith exception to the exclusionary rule did not exist, wouldn't the police and the rest of society lose respect for judges, the legal system, and the law? This hypothesis could be directly tested through empirical research. For example, the attitudes of different respondent groups (e.g., police and adults of varying ages) toward police, judges, the legal system, and the exclusionary rule could be assessed after presenting respondents with vignettes that varied in police and judicial misconduct in issuing warrants and in the court's subsequent decision to admit or exclude the evidence obtained.

CHAPTER'S LESSON

There can be little doubt that legal decision makers would benefit from having proven behavioral and social facts available for their consideration, but sometimes this work has not yet been conducted. Proven behavioral and social facts can be taken from three sources: (a) research that was performed solely to build knowledge of human behavior, (b) research that was performed to specifically understand human behavior in legal contexts, and (c) research that was performed at the request of one of the litigants in a case. The first type of research is ongoing in the behavioral and social sciences because not everything is known about human behavior at any given point in time. The result is that some needed proven facts will not be available to legal decision makers when they require them. The second type of research recognizes that the law and legal system provide a rich source of interesting questions about human behavior. As noted by the Court in this case, this work will also be used by legal decision makers when it is available. Finally, a subset of this type of research raises concern because it may be subtly and not so subtly biased (e.g., see the Court's discussion about the Study conducted on behalf of Gacy in chap. 9, this volume). This subtype of work is necessary but should be carried out and reviewed with caution.

REFERENCES

Asch, S. E. (1951). Effects of group pressure upon the modification and distortion of judgments. In H. Guetzkow (Ed.), *Groups, leadership, and men* (pp. 177–190). Pittsburgh, PA: Carnegie Press.

Asch, S. E. (1955). Opinions and social pressure. *Scientific American, 193,* 31–35.

Asch, S. E. (1956). Studies of independence and conformity: I. A minority of one against a unanimous majority. *Psychological Monographs, 70* (9, Whole No. 416).

Brehm, S., & Brehm, J. W. (1981). *Psychological reactance: A theory of freedom and control.* New York: Academic Press.

Eagly, A. H., & Chaiken, S. (1993). *The psychology of attitudes.* Fort Worth, TX: Harcourt Brace Jovanovich.

French, J. R. P., & Raven, B. (1959). The bases of social power. In D. Cartwright (Ed.), *Studies in social power* (pp. 150–167). Ann Arbor: University of Michigan.

Heffernan, W. C., & Lovely, R. W. (1991). Evaluating the Fourth Amendment exclusionary rule: The problem of police compliance with the law. *University of Michigan Journal of Law Reform, 24,* 311–369.

Hirokawa, C. F. (2000). Making the "law of the land" the law of the street: How police academies teach evolving Fourth Amendment law. *Emory Law Journal, 49,* 295–372.

Markman, S. J. (1997). Six observations on the exclusionary rule. *Harvard Journal of Law and Public Policy, 20,* 425–434.

McClurg, A. J. (1999). Good cop, bad cop: Using cognitive dissonance theory to reduce police lying. *University of California at Davis Law Review, 32,* 389–453.

Milgram, S. (1963). Behavioral study of obedience. *Journal of Abnormal and Social Psychology, 67,* 371–378.

Milgram, S. (1974). *Obedience to authority: An experimental view.* New York: Harper & Row.

Orfield, M. W. (1987). The exclusionary rule and deterrence: An empirical study of Chicago narcotics officers. *University of Chicago Law Review, 54,* 1016–1069.

Orfield, M. W. (1992). Deterrence, perjury and the heater factor: An exclusionary rule in the Chicago Criminal Courts. *University of Colorado Law Review, 63,* 75–161.

Perrin, L. T., Caldwell, H. M., Chase, C. A., & Fagan, R. W. (1998). If it's broken, fix it: Moving beyond the exclusionary rule. *Iowa Law Review, 83,* 669–764.

Raven B. H. (1965). Social influence and power. In I. D. Steiner & M. Fishbein (Eds.), *Current studies in social psychology* (pp. 371–382). New York: Holt, Rinehart & Winston.

Reitz, K. R. (1996). The police: Testilying as a problem of crime control. A reply to Professor Slobogin. *University of Colorado Law Review, 67,* 1061–1073.

Sherif, M. (1935). A study of some social factors in perception. *Archives of Psychology, 27,* 1–60.

Slobogin, C. (1996). Testilying: Police perjury and what to do about it. *University of Colorado Law Review, 67,* 1037–1060.

United States v. Leon, 468 U. S. 897 (1984).

11

FACTUAL KNOWLEDGE PRESENTED IS IRRELEVANT TO THE LEGAL ISSUE

EXAMPLE: DISCRIMINATORY IMPACT OF THE DEATH PENALTY

The struggle to end racial discrimination has been waged in the legislatures, the courts, and the streets. The U.S. Supreme Court has addressed discrimination in housing, voting, employment, education, and the death penalty. On this last topic, the Court ruled that the death penalty was constitutionally permissible if its imposition was not arbitrary, if the decision was guided, and if it was not mandatory for any particular crime. The Court, however, had not addressed whether the death penalty was imposed on Blacks more than Whites, as some suggested was the case. If it was, then a strong argument could be made that the sentencing disparity was a violation of the equal protection clause of the Fourteenth Amendment to the U.S. Constitution and was cruel and unusual punishment, which is a violation of the Eighth Amendment to the Constitution.

The NAACP Legal Defense Fund, a longtime opponent of the death penalty, arranged for a study of prosecution decisions and sentencing patterns in about 2,000 Georgia death penalty cases. Its analysis failed to reveal the glaring disparity between sentences for Blacks and Whites that some were anticipating (Baldus, Pulaski, & Woodworth, 1983). It did reveal, however, that convicted murderers were much more likely to be sentenced to death if their victim was White than if their victim was Black. The NAACP filed appeals in 30 Georgia death penalty cases citing the results of this study as evidence of racial discrimination in death penalty sentences. The NAACP hoped that at least one case would wind its way up through the appellate process to the U.S. Supreme Court. One did, and that case was *McCleskey v. Kemp* (1987).

The authors selected this case because it illustrates a fundamental problem that behavioral and social scientists sometimes have when they present their factual knowledge to a legal decision maker—the behavioral and social factual knowledge will be deemed irrelevant to helping decide the factual issues in the case. In this case, McCleskey's lawyers came to court armed with a study specifically designed to argue that racial bias permeated jury decision making in death penalty cases, particularly when the victim was White. This was not the argument the Supreme Court wanted to hear. The Court wanted to know if McCleskey, as an individual, had suffered from intentional racial bias ("purposeful discrimination") in his sentencing—not if there was some generalized indication of racial discrimination averaged over many cases.

MCCLESKEY V. KEMP

United States Supreme Court

McCleskey, a Black man, was convicted of two counts of armed robbery and one count of murder in Fulton County, GA. McCleskey's convictions arose out of the robbery of a furniture store and the killing of a White police officer during the course of the robbery. The evidence at trial indicated that McCleskey and three accomplices planned and carried out the robbery. All four were armed. McCleskey entered the front of the store while the other three entered the rear. McCleskey secured the front of the store by rounding up the customers and forcing them to lie face down on the floor. The other three rounded up the employees in the rear and tied them up with tape. The manager was forced at gunpoint to turn over the store receipts, his watch, and $6. During the course of the robbery, a police officer answering a silent alarm entered the store through the front door. As he was walking down the center aisle of the store, two shots were fired. Both struck the officer. One hit him in the face and killed him.

Several weeks later, McCleskey was arrested in connection with an unrelated offense. He confessed that he had participated in the furniture store robbery but denied that he had shot the police officer. At trial, the state introduced evidence that at least one of the bullets that struck the officer was fired from a .38 caliber Rossi revolver. This description matched the description of the gun that McCleskey had carried during the robbery. The state also introduced the testimony of two witnesses who had heard McCleskey admit to the shooting.

The jury convicted McCleskey of murder. Under Georgia law, in the penalty (i.e., sentencing) phase of the trial, the jury could not consider imposing the death penalty unless it found beyond a reasonable doubt that the murder was accompanied by one of several possible aggravating circumstances:

- The offense was committed by a person with a prior record of conviction for a capital felony.
- The offense was committed while the offender was engaged in the commission of another capital felony or aggravated battery.
- The offense of murder was committed while the offender was engaged in the commission of burglary or arson in the first degree.
- The offender, by his act of murder knowingly created a great risk of death to more than one person in a public place by means of a weapon or device that would normally be hazardous to the lives of more than one person.
- The offender committed the offense for himself or another for the purpose of receiving money or any other thing of monetary value.
- The murder of a judicial officer, former judicial officer, district attorney or solicitor, or former district attorney or solicitor was committed during or because of the exercise of his official duties.
- The offender caused or directed another to commit murder or committed murder as an agent or employee of another person.
- The offense was outrageously or wantonly vile, horrible, or inhuman in that it involved torture, depravity of mind, or an aggravated battery to the victim.
- The offense was committed against any peace officer, corrections employee, or fireman while engaged in the performance of his official duties.
- The offense was committed by a person in, or who has escaped from, the lawful custody of a peace officer or place of lawful confinement.

- The murder was committed for the purpose of avoiding, interfering with, or preventing a lawful arrest or custody in a place of lawful confinement of himself or another.

The jury found two aggravating circumstances to exist beyond a reasonable doubt: the murder was committed during the course of an armed robbery, and the murder was committed upon a peace officer engaged in the performance of his duties.

In making its decision whether to impose the death sentence, the jury was to also consider if any mitigating circumstances existed for McCleskey's conduct. McCleskey, however, offered no mitigating evidence. The jury recommended that he be sentenced to death on the murder charge and to consecutive life sentences on the armed robbery charges. Georgia's law provides that when a statutory aggravating circumstance is found and a recommendation of death is made, the court shall sentence the defendant to death.

McCleskey appealed, raising 18 claims, one of which was that the Georgia capital-sentencing process is administered in a racially discriminatory manner in violation of the Eighth and Fourteenth Amendments to the U.S. Constitution. In support of his claim, McCleskey offered a statistical study (henceforth the Study) that purports to show a disparity in the imposition of the death sentence in Georgia based on the race of the murder victim and, to a lesser extent, the race of the defendant. The Study is actually two sophisticated statistical studies that examine over 2,000 murder cases that occurred in Georgia during the 1970s. The raw numbers indicate that defendants charged with killing White persons received the death penalty in 11% of the cases, but defendants charged with killing Blacks received the death penalty in only 1% of the cases. The raw numbers also indicate a reverse racial disparity according to the race of the defendant: 4% of the Black defendants received the death penalty, as opposed to 7% of the White defendants.

The Study also divided the cases according to the combination of the race of the defendant and the race of the victim. It found that the death penalty was assessed in 22% of the cases involving Black defendants and White victims, 8% of the cases involving White defendants and White victims, 1% of the cases involving Black defendants and Black victims, and 3% of the cases involving White defendants and Black victims. Similarly, the Study found that prosecutors sought the death penalty in 70% of the cases involving Black defendants and White victims, 32% of the cases involving White defendants and White victims, 15% of the cases involving Black defendants and Black victims, and 19% of the cases involving White defendants and Black victims.

The researchers subjected the data to an extensive analysis, taking account of 230 variables that could have explained the disparities on nonracial grounds. One of the statistical models concluded that, even after taking account of 39 nonracial variables, defendants charged with killing White victims were 4.3 times as likely to receive a death sentence as defendants charged with killing Blacks. According to this model, Black defendants were 1.1 times as likely to receive a death sentence as other defendants. Thus, the Study indicates that Black defendants, such as McCleskey, who kill White victims have the greatest likelihood of receiving the death penalty.

The results were actually a bit more complex. The 230-variable model divided cases into eight different ranges, according to the estimated aggravation level of the offense. The results showed that the effects of racial bias were most striking in the midrange cases. As McCleskey's expert testified: When the cases become tremendously aggravated so that everybody would agree that if we are going to have a death sentence, these are the cases that should get it, the race effects go away. Racial factors begin to play a role only in the midrange of cases in which the decision makers have a real choice as to what to do and there is room for the exercise of discretion. Under this model, 14.4% of the Black-victim midrange cases received the death penalty, and 34.4% of the White-victim cases received the death penalty.

McCleskey claims that the Georgia capital punishment statute violates the equal protection clause of the Fourteenth Amendment. He argues that race has infected the administration of Georgia's statute in two ways: Persons who murder Whites are more likely to be sentenced to death than persons who murder Blacks, and Black murderers are more likely to be sentenced to death than White murderers. As a Black defendant who killed a White victim, McCleskey claims that the Study demonstrates that he was discriminated against because of his race and because of the race of his victim. In its broadest form, McCleskey's claim of discrimination extends to every actor in the Georgia capital-sentencing process, from the prosecutor who sought the death penalty and the jury that imposed the sentence to the state itself, which enacted the capital punishment statute and allows it to remain in effect despite its allegedly discriminatory application.

A defendant who alleges an equal protection violation has the burden of proving the existence of purposeful discrimination and that the purposeful discrimination had a discriminatory effect on him. Thus, to prevail under the Equal Protection Clause, McCleskey must prove that the decision makers in his case acted with discriminatory purpose. He offers no evidence specific to his own case that would support an inference that racial considerations played a part in his sentence. Instead, he relies solely on the Study. McCleskey's claim that these statistics are sufficient proof of discrimination, without regard to the facts of a particular case, would extend to all capital cases in Georgia at least those in which the victim was White and the defendant is Black.

McCleskey's logic is problematic. In the capital-sentencing decision, each particular decision to impose the death penalty is made by a jury that is unique in its composition. In addition, the Constitution requires that the jury's decision rest on a consideration of innumerable factors that vary according to the characteristics of the individual defendant and the facts of the particular capital offense. Thus, the application of an inference drawn from the general statistics to a specific decision in a trial and sentencing simply is not appropriate.

For example, the Study seeks to deduce a state policy by studying the combined effects of the decisions of hundreds of juries that are unique in their composition. It is difficult to deduce a consistent policy by studying the decisions of these many unique entities. It is also questionable whether any consistent policy can be derived by studying the decisions of prosecutors. The voters elect the district attorney in a particular county. Because decisions about whether to prosecute and what to charge necessarily are individualized and involve infinite factual variations, coordination among district attorneys' offices across a state would be relatively meaningless. Thus, any inference from statewide statistics to a prosecutorial policy is of doubtful relevance. Moreover, the statistics in Fulton County alone (the county where McCleskey was tried) represent the disposition of far fewer cases than the statewide statistics. Even if the Study is statistically valid as a whole, the weight to be given the results gleaned from this small sample is limited. Finally, as McCleskey's own expert testified, statistical models that are developed to talk about the effect on the average do not depict the experience of a single individual. What they say, for example, is that on average, the race of the victim, if it is White, increases the probability that the death sentence would be given. Whether in a given case that is the answer cannot be determined from statistics. Even a sophisticated multiple regression analysis such as performed in this Study can only demonstrate a risk that the factor of race entered into some capital-sentencing decisions and a necessarily lesser risk that race entered into any particular sentencing decision. It does not prove that discrimination occurred.

Another important problem with McCleskey's attempted use of the Study is that the state has no practical opportunity to rebut it in his particular case. Controlling considerations of public policy dictate that jurors cannot be called to testify to the motives and influences that led to their verdict. Similarly, the policy considerations in allowing prosecutors wide discretion in whether to charge and prosecute suggest the impropriety of our requiring prosecutors to defend their decisions to seek death penalties, often years after the decisions were made. If the prosecutor could be made to answer in court each time a person charged him with wrongdoing, his energy and attention would be diverted from the pressing duty of enforcing the criminal law. In addition, requiring a prosecutor to rebut a Study that analyzes the past conduct of scores of prosecutors is quite different from requiring a prosecutor to rebut a contemporaneous challenge to his own acts. Moreover, absent far stronger proof than the current Study provides, it is unnecessary to seek such a rebuttal because a legitimate and unchallenged explanation for the decision is apparent from the record: McCleskey committed an act for which the U.S. Constitution and Georgia's laws permit imposition of the death penalty.

Finally, McCleskey's Study must be viewed in the context of his challenge. McCleskey challenges decisions at the heart of the state's criminal justice system. One of society's most basic tasks is that of protecting the lives of its citizens, and one of the most basic ways in which it achieves the task is through criminal laws against murder. Implementation of these laws necessarily requires discretionary judgments. Because discretion is essential to the criminal justice process, the law demands exceptionally clear proof before inferring that the discretion has been abused. Accordingly, this Court holds that the Study is clearly insufficient to support an inference that any of the decision makers in McCleskey's case acted with discriminatory purpose.

McCleskey also suggests that the Study proves that the state as a whole has acted with a discriminatory purpose. He appears to argue that the state has violated the Equal Protection Clause by adopting the capital punishment statute and allowing it to remain in force despite its allegedly discriminatory application. But discriminatory purpose implies more than intent as volition or intent as awareness of consequences. It implies that the decision maker, in this case a state legislature, selected or reaffirmed a particular course of action in part because of its adverse effects on an identifiable group. For this claim to prevail, McCleskey would have to prove that the Georgia legislature enacted or maintained the death penalty statute because of an anticipated racially discriminatory effect. There is no evidence that the Georgia legislature enacted the capital punishment statute to further a racially discriminatory purpose.

McCleskey relies on historical evidence to support his claim of purposeful discrimination by the state. This evidence focuses on Georgia's laws in force during and just after the Civil War. Of course, the historical background of the decision is one evidentiary source for proof of intentional discrimination. But unless historical evidence is reasonably contemporaneous with the challenged decision, it has little value. Although the history of racial discrimination in this country is undeniable, we cannot accept official actions taken long ago as evidence of current intent.

Nor has McCleskey demonstrated that the legislature maintains the capital punishment statute because of the racially disproportionate impact suggested by the Study. Indeed, McCleskey has introduced no evidence to support this claim. As legislatures necessarily have wide discretion in the choice of criminal laws and penalties and as there were legitimate reasons for the Georgia legislature to adopt and maintain capital punishment, we will not infer a discriminatory purpose on the part of the state of Georgia. Accordingly, McCleskey's equal protection claims are rejected.

McCleskey also argues that the Study demonstrates that the Georgia capital-sentencing system violates the Eighth Amendment to the U.S. Constitution, which applies to the states through the Due Process clause of the Fourteenth Amendment. The Eighth Amendment prohibits infliction of cruel and unusual punishments. This Court's early Eighth Amendment cases examined only the particular methods of execution (electrocution and public shooting) to determine whether they were too cruel to pass constitutional muster. Subsequently, this Court identified a second principle inherent in the Eighth Amendment, that punishment for crime should be graduated and proportioned to the offense. The basic concept underlying the Eighth Amendment in this area is that the penalty must accord with the dignity of man. In applying this mandate, we have been guided by the statement that the Amendment must draw its meaning from the evolving standards of decency that mark the progress of a maturing society.

Thus, constitutional decisions are informed by contemporary values concerning the infliction of a challenged sanction. This Court recognized that the constitutional prohibition against cruel and unusual punishments may acquire meaning as public opinion becomes enlightened by a humane justice. In assessing contemporary values, subjective judgment is avoided. Instead, objective indicia are sought that reflect the public attitude toward a given sanction. First among these indicia are the decisions of state legislatures because the legislative judgment weighs heavily in ascertaining contemporary standards. The sentencing decisions of juries are also a relevant consideration because they are a significant and reliable objective index of contemporary values.

In light of this analysis, is the punishment of death for murder under all circumstances cruel and unusual in violation of the Eighth Amendment of the Constitution? The imposition of the death penalty for the crime of murder has a long history of acceptance in the United States. Respect for the ability of a legislature to evaluate, in terms of its particular state, the moral consensus concerning the death penalty and its social utility as a sanction leads inescapably to the conclusion, in the absence of more convincing evidence, that the infliction of death as a punishment for murder is not without justification and thus is not unconstitutionally severe. Indeed, 37 states now have capital punishment statutes, and a federal statute authorizes the death penalty for aircraft piracy in which a death occurs.

When a sentencing body has discretion to determine whether a human life should be taken or spared, that discretion must be suitably directed and limited so as to minimize the risk of wholly arbitrary and capricious action. The Georgia system bifurcates guilt and sentencing proceedings so that the jury can receive all relevant information for sentencing without the risk that evidence irrelevant to the defendant's guilt will influence the jury's consideration of that issue. The statute narrows the class of murders subject to the death penalty to cases in which the jury finds at least one statutory aggravating circumstance beyond a reasonable doubt. It also allows the defendant to introduce any relevant mitigating evidence that might influence the jury not to impose a death sentence. The procedures require a particularized inquiry into the circumstances of the offense together with the character and propensities of the offender. Thus, although some jury discretion still exists, the discretion to be exercised is controlled by clear and objective standards so as to produce nondiscriminatory application. The Georgia system adds an important additional safeguard against arbitrariness and caprice. The law provides for an automatic appeal of a death sentence to the State Supreme Court. The statute requires that court to review each sentence to determine whether it was imposed under the influence of passion or prejudice, whether the evidence supports the jury's finding of a statutory aggravating circumstance, and whether the sentence is disproportionate to sentences imposed in generally similar murder cases. To aid the court's review, the trial judge answers a questionnaire about the trial, including detailed questions as to the quality of the defendant's representation and whether race played a role in the trial.

In sum, there is a constitutionally permissible range of discretion in imposing the death penalty. First, there is a required threshold below which the death penalty cannot be imposed. In this context, the state must establish rational criteria that narrow the decision maker's judgment as to whether the circumstances of a particular defendant's case met the threshold. Moreover, a societal consensus that the death penalty is disproportionate to a particular offense prevents a state from imposing the death penalty for that offense. Second, states cannot limit the sentencer's consideration of any relevant circumstance that could cause it to decline to impose the penalty. In this respect, the state cannot channel the sentencer's discretion, but must allow it to consider any relevant information offered by the defendant. McCleskey cannot argue successfully that his sentence is disproportionate to the crime in the traditional sense. He does not deny that he committed a murder in the course of a planned robbery, a crime for which the Court has determined that the death penalty constitutionally may be imposed.

McCleskey further argues that the sentence in his case is disproportionate to the sentences in other murder cases. This Court disagrees. On automatic appeal, the Georgia Supreme Court found that McCleskey's death sentence was not disproportionate to other death sentences imposed in the state. The court supported its conclusion with an appendix containing citations to 13 cases involving generally similar murders. And the statutory procedures adequately channel the sentencer's discretion, such proportionality review is not constitutionally required. Finally, absent a showing that the Georgia capital punishment system operates in an arbitrary and capricious manner, McCleskey cannot prove a constitutional violation by demonstrating that other defendants who may be similarly situated did not receive the death penalty. Opportunities for discretionary leniency by sentencers do not render capital sentences arbitrary and capricious. Because McCleskey's sentence was imposed under Georgia's sentencing procedures that focus discretion on the particularized nature of the crime and the particularized characteristics of the individual defendant, McCleskey's death sentence was not wantonly and freakishly imposed. Thus the sentence is not disproportionate within any recognized meaning under the Eighth Amendment.

Furthermore, McCleskey contends that, because racial considerations may influence capital-sentencing decisions in Georgia, the Georgia capital punishment system is arbitrary and capricious in application, and therefore his sentence is excessive. But even McCleskey's expert does not contend that his statistics prove that race enters into any capital-sentencing decisions or that race was a factor in McCleskey's particular case. According to the expert, McCleskey's case falls in a gray area where you would find the greatest likelihood that some inappropriate consideration may have come to bear on the decision. In an analysis of this type, obviously one cannot say to a moral certainty what it was that influenced the decision. Statistics at most may show only a likelihood that a particular factor entered into some decisions. There is, of course, some risk of racial prejudice influencing a jury's decision in a criminal case. There are similar risks that other kinds of prejudice will influence other criminal trials. The question is at what point that risk becomes constitutionally unacceptable. This Court refuses to accept the likelihood allegedly shown by the Study as the constitutional measure of an unacceptable risk of racial prejudice influencing capital-sentencing decisions.

The inestimable privilege of trial by jury is a vital principle underlying the whole administration of criminal justice. It is the jury that is a criminal defendant's fundamental protection of life and liberty against race or color prejudice. A capital-sentencing jury that is representative of a criminal defendant's community assures a diffused impartiality in the jury's task of expressing the conscience of the community on the ultimate question of life or death.

Individual jurors bring to their deliberations qualities of human nature and varieties of human experience, the range of which is unknown and perhaps unknowable. The capital-sentencing decision requires the individual jurors to focus their collective judgment on the unique characteristics of a particular criminal defendant. It is not surprising that such collective judgments often are difficult to explain. But the inherent lack of predictability of jury decisions does not justify their condemnation. On the contrary, it is the jury's function to make the difficult and uniquely human judgments that defy codification and that build discretion, equity, and flexibility into a legal system.

McCleskey's argument that the Constitution condemns the discretion allowed decision makers in the Georgia capital-sentencing system is antithetical to the fundamental role of discretion in our criminal justice system. Discretion in the criminal justice system offers substantial benefits to the criminal defendant. Not only can a jury decline to impose the death sentence, it can decline to convict or choose to convict of a lesser offense. Whereas decisions against a defendant's interest may be reversed by the trial judge or on appeal, these discretionary exercises of leniency are final and unreviewable. Similarly, the capacity of prosecutorial discretion to provide individualized justice is firmly entrenched in American law. A prosecutor can decline to charge, offer a plea bargain, or decline to seek a death sentence in any particular case. Of course, the power to be lenient also is the power to discriminate, but a capital punishment system that did not allow for discretionary acts of leniency would be totally alien to the law's notions of criminal justice.

At most, the Study indicates a discrepancy that appears to correlate with race. Apparent disparities in sentencing are an inevitable part of our criminal justice system. The discrepancy indicated by the Study is a far cry from major systemic defects in the system. The Study in fact confirms that the Georgia system results in a reasonable level of proportionality among the class of murderers eligible for the death penalty. The system sorts out cases in which the sentence of death is highly likely and highly unlikely, leaving a midrange of cases in which the imposition of the death penalty in any particular case is less predictable.

Any mode for determining guilt or punishment has its weaknesses and the potential for misuse. There can be no perfect procedure for deciding in which cases governmental authority should be used to impose death. Despite these imperfections, constitutional guarantees are met when the mode for determining guilt or punishment itself has been surrounded with safeguards to make it as fair as possible. When the discretion that is fundamental to our criminal process is involved, this Court declines to assume that what is unexplained is invidious. In light of the safeguards designed to minimize racial bias in the process, the fundamental value of jury trials in our criminal justice system and the benefits that discretion provides to criminal defendants, this Court rules that the Study does not demonstrate a constitutionally significant risk of racial bias affecting the Georgia capital-sentencing process.

Taken to its logical conclusion, McCleskey's claim throws into serious question the principles that underlie our entire criminal justice system. The Eighth Amendment is not limited in application to capital punishment, but applies to all penalties. Thus, if McCleskey's claim that racial bias has impermissibly tainted the capital-sentencing decision is accepted, this Court could soon be faced with similar claims as to other types of penalty. Indeed, studies already exist that allegedly demonstrate a racial disparity in the length of prison sentences. Moreover, the claim that his sentence rests on the irrelevant factor of race easily could be extended to apply to claims based on unexplained discrepancies that correlate to membership in other minority groups and even to gender. Also, there is no logical reason that such a claim need be limited to racial or sexual bias. If arbitrary and capricious punishment is the touchstone under the Eighth Amendment, such a claim could, at least in theory, be based on any arbitrary variable, such as the defendant's facial characteristics or the physical attractiveness of the defendant or the victim, that some statistical study indicates may be influential in jury decision making. As these examples illustrate, there is no limiting principle to the type of challenge brought by McCleskey. The Constitution does not require that a state eliminate any demonstrable disparity that correlates with a potentially irrelevant factor in order to operate a criminal justice system that includes capital punishment.

McCleskey's arguments are best presented to the legislative bodies. It is not the responsibility—or indeed even the right—of this Court to determine the appropriate punishment for particular crimes. It is the legislatures, the elected representatives of the people, that are constituted to respond to the will and consequently the moral values of the people. Legislatures also are better qualified to weigh and evaluate the results of statistical studies in terms of their own local conditions and with a flexibility of approach that is not available to the courts.

ANALYSIS AND IMPLICATIONS

McCleskey argued that race (both of the victim and the offender) influenced the administration of the death penalty in Georgia, and thus violated the Fourteenth Amendment's guarantee of equal protection of the law. McCleskey also argued that a death sentence under these circumstances would amount to cruel and unusual punishment because of the racial disparities in sentencing, and thus would be a violation of the Eighth Amendment.

Fourteenth Amendment

Attempting to Apply the Study to McCleskey's Case

McCleskey introduced a social science study of capital sentencing in Georgia to prove that his constitutional rights were violated (Baldus et al., 1983). The Study used multiple regression, which allows one to predict the value of a dependent variable (the thing being measured) from the value of two or more independent variables (things that might influence the value of the dependent variable). This, and newer related techniques not available at the time of the Study, is an important tool for explaining phenomena because rarely is it the case that something has but a single cause. For example, if one wanted to measure the success of a particular cancer-fighting drug, one could compare the number of cancer cells (the dependent variable) in patients who received the new drug (the independent variable) with that of patients who were not administered the medication. Such a simple design would tell a lot about the effectiveness of the drug, but not tell all that one would want to know. There are many more factors that might contribute to a cancer patient's recovery besides the medication he or she is taking (e.g., genetic predisposition, prior history with cancer, prior treatments, age, gender, ethnicity, socioeconomic status, access to health care, support groups, and nutrition). Regression allows a researcher to determine how much of patient recovery is attributable to each of these factors. The Study used a multiple regression analysis to identify which factors were most predictive of death penalty decisions. The Study included in its analysis the effects of 39 factors (e.g., if the murder was committed during the commission of another felony, the type of weapon used, the relationship between the killer and victim, and past criminal record) on sentencing.

Will data drawn from a group of cases (i.e., nomothetic decision) be sufficient to prove discrimination about one individual (i.e., idiographic decision)? Remember that McCleskey argued that he was discriminated against. He did not argue on behalf of all prisoners sentenced to death in Georgia. The Court ruled that for McCleskey to show that his equal protection right had been violated, he would have to prove that he personally suffered intentionally motivated racial discrimination in his sentencing. McCleskey, however, offered no direct evidence on this point, other than the Study. The Court rejected the Study for this purpose. First, it reasoned that even if the Study indicated that a sentencing disparity exists in Georgia, it could not prove that McCleskey suffered from the same problem. The Court noted that each prosecutorial decision, each defendant, each case, and each jury is unique. Second, the factors considered by a jury deciding a death penalty case are *innumerable*, and they are different for each defendant and each crime. Finally, the Court noted that jurors, as a matter of public policy, cannot be made to explain their decisions. This applies whether the crime is the most severe or the most trivial. Nor should prosecutors be made to explain why they or other prosecutors did or did not charge someone with a capital offense (a crime for which one can be sentenced to death if convicted). Having to explain their prosecutorial decisions and actions for past cases would be difficult enough, but having to explain the actions of other prosecutors would be an impossible task. Thus, the Court concluded that a study based on averages could not address the specific factors of any one case, including McCleskey's. At most, the Study demonstrated that there was a risk that race played a role in a Georgia jury's sentencing decision. The fact that there was a risk of discrimination could not be interpreted to mean that discrimination existed in McCleskey's sentencing.

What the court did not address was the fact that nomothetic data is used to make individual predictions all of the time. For example, insurance companies are allowed to set individual insurance rates based on group data, and physicians give patients recommendations for surgery based on similar information. Why should the Court not rely on such data in this case? The Court's answer was that a general study could not address whether there was intentional discrimination in McCleskey's case. Although this seems reasonable, it is odd that the Court noted with approval the Georgia Supreme Court's conclusion that McCleskey did not suffer from racial bias, citing that court's evaluation of 13 cases "involving generally similar murders." This appears to be the same rationale that McCleskey wanted to take advantage of by using the Study, namely generalizing from the many to the few to prove that his death sentence was based on race.

Discretion in the Death Penalty

The Court emphasized the importance of criminal laws in protecting citizens and how these laws will fail to work unless discretion is allowed in their implementation. For example, when a crime is committed and an arrest is made, a decision has to be made on how the suspect will be handled by the judicial system. It must be determined what charges to file, if bail should be opposed, if plea bargains should be offered, or if charges should be dropped because of insufficient evidence or because the case is deemed *unwinnable*. And in capital crimes, a decision must be made if the death penalty should be sought, assuming it is an option in that state. Because prosecutors make these decisions, they have tremendous influence and discretion in deciding the fate of the defendant even before a trial begins.

Yet, if the exercise of discretion is really a subterfuge for making racially discriminatory decisions, then otherwise permissible discretion becomes unconstitutional. So are there disparities in prosecutorial decisions to seek the death penalty that are based on race? Many social scientists examining this question think so. Baldus, Woodworth, and Pulaski (1990) identified prosecutorial discretion as the main reason for the disparity in death sentences handed out to defendants whose victims were White as opposed to Black. In the Study, it was reported that Georgia prosecutors were nearly five times more likely to seek the death penalty for Blacks whose victims were White than if their victims were Black. Radalet and Pierce (1985) reviewed more than 1,000 homicide cases in Florida to see how prosecutors classified the cases according to the circumstances of the crime and whether the classification would lead to a decision that the case should be *upgraded* to a capital case or downgraded from being a death penalty case. They found that upgrading and downgrading were significantly related to the race of the defendant and victim: Blacks whose victims were White were most likely to be upgraded to capital cases (i.e., cases in which the death penalty would be sought) and least likely to be downgraded. Between 1977 and 1991, prosecutors in Missouri were also more likely to seek the death penalty for Blacks who killed Whites than they were for those who killed Blacks (Sorenson & Wallace, 1995).

The Supreme Court also considered the importance of discretion in jury decision making in capital cases. Determining the penalty in a capital case is really a two-step process. First, the jury is provided a list of aggravating factors, which are characteristics of the crime that if present may lead a jury to decide that the defendant deserves death. The Court noted that two of the aggravating factors were present in McCleskey's case: The murder was of a peace officer while doing his duty, and the murder was committed during a robbery.

The mere presence of aggravating factors, however, is not sufficient to sentence a defendant to death. Mitigating factors must also be considered. These are characteristics of the crime or of the defendant that may lead a jury to decide that, despite the presence of one or more aggravating factors, the defendant does not deserve the death penalty. Mitigating factors do not excuse the crime, but their presence may be used as justification for not applying the ultimate punishment. A mitigating factor might include, for example, a defendant's history of being abused as a child or the actions of the victim that in some way provoked the defendant. The law gives wide latitude to what jurors may consider as a mitigating factor. If a single juror believes that a single mitigating factor exists that outweighs the aggravating factor(s), then the defendant cannot be sentenced to death. McCleskey's lawyer did not present the jury with any mitigating evidence. In the absence of any mitigating factors and in the presence of two aggravating factors, the Court concluded that McCleskey was in a poor position to argue that he was the victim of a racially biased application of the law. He was, in other words, more than deserving of the punishment he was about to get.

As a cold-blooded killer of a police officer who was married with one child, it would be difficult to overlook the facts of McCleskey's crime. Under these facts, it would be hard for any court to conclude that McCleskey received the death penalty because of discrimination. Not surprisingly, some opponents of the death penalty have criticized the NAACP for *wasting* the otherwise compelling findings of the Study on the McCleskey case (see Lazarus, 1998).

Moreover, the Court felt that a defendant's best protection against the risk of racial prejudice was the jury's right to exercise discretion in sentencing. McCleskey felt that it was this very discretion that allowed juries to use race in their decision making. The Court reacted strongly to this contention, arguing that discretion represented a major advantage for defendants. Juries have the discretion not to impose the death penalty or even not to convict at all. And a jury that decides in favor of leniency is beyond review.

Finally, McCleskey suggested several other equal protection violations. He argued that the state of Georgia and its legislature were guilty of a violation because they permitted a capital punishment law to remain in effect when they knew it was unfairly applied. The Court said there was no evidence for this. The death penalty is constitutional, and Georgia legislators had the right (discretion) to continue it, revise it, or repeal it. In fact, the Court was explicit in its view that the best and proper forum for overturning the death penalty was in Georgia's legislature and not the courts. The Court felt that the legislature was better qualified to evaluate the Study presented by the NAACP. The most obvious resource available to the legislature that courts lack is the former's ability to hold hearings and conduct lengthy investigations. Here, individuals or groups who have either an interest in the matter or information to offer may be invited or sometimes subpoenaed to testify on the matter. In addition, legislative committees often have staff who can research the pertinent issues. The Court also was concerned that if it accepted the Study and its conclusion that race had infected jury and prosecutorial decision making, it could lead to legal paralysis. If one could argue racial disparity in the death penalty, then one could argue disparities in other sentences and for reasons other than race. There would be no end to the number of factors that defendants could say were improperly influencing jurors. Each conviction and each sentence handed down in a case containing a particular factor would have to be reviewed. Thus, the Study belonged not before the courts, but the legislature. If, in the opinion of the legislature, the Study was evidence of an unacceptable risk of racial bias, then the legislature could enact whatever law it thought appropriate to remedy the problem.

Committees of the U.S. Congress have, in fact, used their resources to address race and prosecutorial discretion in federal death penalty cases sought under the Anti-Drug Abuse Act of 1988. They reported that 87% of these prosecutions targeted African-American or Mexican-American defendants (U.S. Congress Judiciary Subcommittee on Civil and Constitutional Rights, 1994). Governmental agencies, perhaps spurred by the legacy of the Study and some of the findings reviewed here, have examined race and the death penalty as well. For example, the Department of Justice conducted a survey of death penalty prosecutions in federal cases and reported that 89% (16 of 18) of the prisoners on federal death row were minorities. Furthermore, in the 682 cases between 1995 and 2000 in which prosecutors recommended to the U.S. Attorney General that the death penalty be sought, 77% involved Black defendants. After these recommendations were reviewed by the Attorney General of the United States, death penalty prosecutions were approved in 45% of the cases involving either Black or Hispanic defendants and 38% of the cases with White defendants (U.S. Department of Justice, 2000). The survey also found that the proportion of minority defendants in federal capital cases was greater than the proportion of minority individuals in the general population. However, according to the survey, this disparity is not attributable to racial bias but to the over representation of minorities in violent criminal enterprises (like drug trafficking) that have been the subject of intensive local, state, and federal law enforcement efforts (U.S. Department of Justice, 2000).

The Department of Justice survey was criticized for failing to consider a potentially important set of data: those cases in which prosecutors chose not to seek the death penalty, although the facts of the case may have supported such a penalty. Were prosecutors seeking lesser penalties in cases with White defendants (in which the death penalty could justifiably be sought) than they were in cases with minority defendants? The Justice Department addressed this question in a follow-up review (U.S. Department of Justice, 2001). The pool of cases was now expanded to include 973 defendants (78% either Black or Hispanic and 17% White). Prosecutors recommended the death penalty in 79% of the cases with Black defendants, 56% of the cases involving Hispanic defendants, and 81% of the cases with White defendants. After review by the Attorney General of the United States, the death penalty was recommended for 17% of the Black defendants, 9% of the Hispanic defendants, and 27% of the White defendants (U.S. Department of Justice, 2001).

Eighth Amendment

The Court looked on McCleskey's Eighth Amendment claims with similar disfavor. The Court noted that the death penalty has long been an accepted part of American jurisprudence and comported with evolving standards of decency and contemporary values as found in the actions of state legislatures and the decisions of juries in death penalty cases. Presumably, if legislatures passed laws allowing the death penalty and juries used these laws to sentence defendants to death, then the contemporary values of those states must reflect an acceptance of the death penalty. If legislatures thought that the death penalty was cruel and unusual punishment, they would not pass laws permitting it. Even if such laws were passed, juries would not use them if they believed that the death penalty was cruel and unusual.

Although the death penalty might be constitutionally permitted, the Court has ruled in earlier decisions that it cannot be handed out in an arbitrary or capricious manner. It is true that juries have discretion in returning a death sentence, but the discretion must be guided. The Court once feared that juries were being too inconsistent in who was sentenced to death. Some defendants who committed the most heinous of murders were receiving prison terms, whereas others who committed less egregious murders were receiving the death penalty. States that wanted the death penalty responded by introducing several innovations. First, trials became bifurcated, meaning that the trial is split into a guilt or innocence phase and a punishment phase. In some jurisdictions, separate juries sit in judgment of each phase. This way, the jury that decides the defendant's punishment will not have been biased by the evidence that was presented in the guilt or innocence phase. Second, the sentencing (punishment) jury is instructed on the appropriate use of aggravating and mitigating circumstances in reaching their decision. Third, there is an automatic appeal from a death sentence so that legal procedures and rulings can be reviewed for any errors. Georgia had such a system in place with all the necessary safeguards, and McCleskey had full benefit of them.

The Court here acknowledged that the Study might accurately reflect the risk of racial prejudice in death sentences, but that the risk, if it existed, did not rise to the level of a constitutionally unacceptable one. The criminal justice system is always at risk for apparent disparities in sentencing, but the Court seemed to be saying that is just part of the costs of doing business. The Study showed that the system is not perfect, but perfection is not constitutionally guaranteed.

Revisiting the Race of the Defendant and Victim on Capital Sentencing

Although the Supreme Court was not persuaded by the Study, its decision led social scientists to conduct more sophisticated studies in many more locales. This research addressed three critical factors for the issues raised by McCleskey: Does imposition of the death penalty depend on the defendant's race, the victim's race, or an interaction between the race of the defendant and the race of the victim?

Considered in isolation, the defendant's race does not appear to be an overly important factor in determining whether a death sentence will be imposed (see e.g., Baldus, Pulaski, & Woodworth, 1986; Nebraska Commission on Law Enforcement and Criminal Justice, 2001), until the race of the victim is considered in conjunction with the defendant's race. Then it becomes a highly salient factor. For example, the Study reported that, regardless of the color of their victim, Blacks were sentenced to death in 4% of all cases surveyed. However, this number jumps to 22% if the Black defendant's victim was White. Conversely, Whites were sentenced to death in 7% of the cases overall, but the number fell to 3% if their victims were Black. More recent research continues to support this finding. For example, Gross and Mauro (1989) looked at death penalty sentencing in Arkansas, Florida, Georgia, Illinois, North Carolina, Mississippi, Oklahoma, and Virginia. Without exception, defendants who killed Whites were significantly more likely to be sentenced to death than were defendants accused of killing Blacks. In Missouri, for the years 1977 to 1991, Black killers of Whites were four times more likely to be sentenced to die than were White killers of Blacks (Sorenson & Wallace, 1995). Thomson (1997) found a similar pattern of racial disparity in Arizona: Black killers of Whites were the most likely group to receive a death sentence, whereas Black killers of Blacks were the least likely.

To fully understand the interactions between the race of the defendant and the race of the victim, one needs to make comparisons between Blacks who kill Blacks, Blacks who kill Whites, Whites who kill Blacks, and Whites who kill Whites. From the Study it was learned that Georgia juries sentenced to death Blacks who killed Whites most frequently (22% of the time) and Blacks who killed Blacks least frequently (1% of the time). Whites who killed Whites (8%) and Whites who killed Blacks (3%) were the second and third most frequent race of defendant and race of victim combinations to receive a death sentence. Similar findings have been reported in more recent studies. In Kentucky, Keil and Vito (1995) tracked all death penalty cases between 1976 and 1991. They too reported that Blacks who killed Whites were significantly more likely to be charged and sentenced to death than were any other combination of defendant and victim. Most recently, Unah and Boger (2001) examined race and death sentences in North Carolina. In what must now seem like an old record, they too reported that Black killers of Whites were more likely to be sentenced to death (11.62% of the time) than were White killers of Whites (6.10%), White killers of Blacks (5.0%), and Black killers of Blacks (4.71%).

These kinds of racial disparities are not found in all states, however. For example, a study of 177 death-eligible homicides that resulted in 27 death sentences in Nebraska revealed that there was no significant evidence that defendants were sentenced to death based either on the race of the defendant or the race of the victim (Nebraska Commission on Law Enforcement and Criminal Justice, 2001). But the fact that in many states, greater value is placed on the victimization of Whites than Blacks is troubling.

The vote by the U.S. Supreme Court Justices against McCleskey was 5 to 4. The strength of the behavioral and social facts revealed in the Study helped four justices conclude that McCleskey's sentence, and probably many more like his, was the product of racial discrimination that was constitutionally repugnant. Ironically, a few years after he retired in 1988, Justice Powell, who wrote the majority opinion in this case, said that he regretted his decision and that if he could do it over again he would vote with the justices who opposed the death penalty (Simon, 1995). Unfortunately for McCleskey, the relevance of the Study did not strike Justice Powell soon enough. After two more appeals to the Supreme Court, McCleskey was executed on September 25, 1991.

Effect of Minority Status on Noncapital Sentencing

Another interesting part of the Court's opinion was its concern that if it approved McCleskey's claim, it would open the door for similar claims by other minorities challenging other types of penalties. It had good reason to have this concern.

Disparities in sentencing are not limited to minority adult offenders or to capital sentencing. Perhaps the most comprehensive study to examine the treatment of minority youths was conducted by the National Council on

Crime and Delinquency (2000). Using data from a half-dozen government agencies including the FBI, they found that Black youths, overall, are six times more likely to be sent to juvenile prison than are White youths. For violent crimes, Black youths will go to jail nine times more often than will White youths and 48 times more often for crimes involving drugs. When Black youths are sentenced to juvenile prison for committing a violent crime, they spend more time there than White youths: 254 days on average for Blacks compared to 193 days for Whites (National Council on Crime and Delinquency, 2000). These results have been duplicated in the laboratory. Gordon, Bindrim, McNichols, and Walden (1988) found that Black defendants receive longer sentences than Whites accused of the same crime (except for white-collar crimes like embezzlement). In a meta-analytic review of simulation studies, Sweeney and Haney (1992) also reported strong support for sentencing disparities according to race.

The racial disparity in noncapital sentencing is not limited to Blacks. Latino youths will spend, on average, 305 days in juvenile prison upon conviction for a violent offense (National Council on Crime and Delinquency, 2000). A similar pattern has been found for misdemeanor offenses. Munoz, Lopez, and Stewart (1998) found that Latinos were significantly more likely to be charged, fined, and sentenced to longer periods of probation than were Whites for the same kind of misdemeanor crimes (e.g., alcohol and drug offenses).

Effect of Other Extralegal Factors on Sentencing

Finally, the Court also expressed a related concern. The Court opined that if it ruled in favor of McCleskey, cases would come before it alleging bias on the basis of the defendant's physical attractiveness or other extralegal characteristics. Once again, the Court had good reason to be concerned.

A judge or jury should not determine a defendant's guilt or innocence or sentencing on the basis of the defendant's race, physical attractiveness, social status, information carried in newspapers, or any other extralegal factor. However, human nature being what it is, this is sometimes easier said than it is to prevent. For example, research has shown a positive linear relationship between the physical attractiveness of a defendant and winning the case; the better looking the defendant is, the more likely he or she will prevail (Zebrowitz & McDonald, 1991).

In fact, researchers have found that juries sometimes use a wide variety of extralegal factors in their decision making. In a simulated study on the effects of pretrial publicity, Otto, Penrod, and Dexter (1994) asked participants to read newspaper articles describing an incident in which police were called to quell a public disturbance for which they had to make an arrest. The articles contained varying accounts of the suspect's character, job status, prior record, and witness statements. The more negative the account of the suspect, the more likely participants were to think that he was guilty. Then, participants watched an edited videotape of an actual trial depicting events similar to what they had just read about. The effects of watching the defendant get a chance to tell his side of the story reduced the biasing effects of the negative pretrial publicity somewhat, but it did not eliminate it entirely. Participants, particularly those who read negative statements about the defendant's character, were still more likely to judge him or her guilty after watching the video than participants who were not exposed to such negative statements.

Jurors also let a defendant's job status affect their decision making. In general, defendants with high-status jobs who commit a minor transgression are judged less harshly than those with low-status jobs who commit the same offense (Rosoff, 1989). However, if the crime is related to the job, then high-status defendants are judged more harshly than defendants with low-status jobs (Shaw & Skolnick, 1996). In addition, jurors are more lenient toward those defendants with whom they are most similar, for example, if they are of the same race (Ugwuebu, 1979) or religion (Kerr, Hymes, Anderson, & Weathers, 1995). This similarity-leniency effect reverses itself, however, if the evidence against the defendant is overwhelming. That is, jurors are more likely to judge a member of their own group more harshly, a type of black-sheep effect, than are jurors who are not a member of the defendant's group when the evidence points indisputably to guilt (Kerr et al., 1995). Finally, Walsh (1990) reviewed the sentencing records of over 400 sex offenders and found that those who received a label indicating a psychiatric pathology were twice as likely to be jailed than those offenders who were not so labeled.

Finally, gender affects sentencing, with men traditionally receiving harsher treatment. In a comparison of men and women who committed substantially similar murders (and controlling for the fact that men commit the vast majority of murders), men were six times more likely than women to be arrested, convicted, and sentenced to death (Streib, 2003; also see Shapiro, 2000). Women also tended to receive more lenient sentences for serious felonies (Nagel, 1969) and more preferable community service assignments (Meeker, Jesilow, & Aranda, 1992) than men.

Some researchers have theorized that judges are making certain behavioral and social assumptions about women and the effects of incarceration on them (Associated Press, 1984, as cited in Wrightsman, Nietzel, & Fortune, 1998). The first is that women do less well in prison than men because of the tough conditions. Second, women are assumed to be the primary, if not the only, caregivers of children and that incarceration will have an obvious adverse impact on the children. Similarly, some have proposed a *chivalry theory*, suggesting that the male-dominated judicial system adopts a protective, chivalrous attitude toward female defendants and thus tends to treat them more leniently (Carroll, 1997).

But whatever the past views about female offenders, we are experiencing a change in them today. According to research by Mauer (1999; see Roberts, 2001), the number of Black women in state and federal prisons increased more than 200% between the years 1985 and1995, and Black women now represent the single fastest growing segment of the prison population. To explain this phenomenon, an *evil woman theory* has been proposed to suggest that when women are punished they are punished for violating societal expectations of how women should act, that is, for being *unladylike* (Carroll, 1997).

CHAPTER'S LESSON

Because the Court focused on the search for discrimination in McCleskey's case, and not in all similar cases, the Court saw the Study introduced by McCleskey as irrelevant to the legal issues. To avoid having behavioral and social research being viewed as irrelevant, it is critical that behavioral and social scientists, before conducting a study, understand (a) what the law will view as the relevant factual questions that need answering and (b) what the law will view as the relevant factual information that needs to be provided. This creates an interesting dilemma for behavioral and social researchers who are interested in influencing legal decision making. Either they must learn the relevant law, or they must work closely with attorneys to ensure that their work will be relevant. The former is difficult, but the later raises the specter that their science will be seen as litigation driven and therefore potentially biased (see chaps. 9 and 10, this volume).

REFERENCES

Anti-Drug Abuse Act of 1988, Pub. L. 100-690.

Baldus, D. C., Pulaski, C. A., Jr., & Woodworth, G. (1983). Comparative review of death sentences: An empirical study of the Georgia experience. *Journal of Criminal Law and Criminology, 74*, 661–753.

Baldus, D. C., Pulaski, C. A., & Woodworth, G. (1986). Arbitrariness and discrimination in the administration of the death penalty: A challenge to state supreme courts. *Stetson Law Review, 15*, 133–261.

Baldus, D. C., Woodworth, G., & Pulaski, C. A., Jr. (1990). *Equal justice and the death penalty: A legal and empirical analysis.* Boston: Northeastern University Press.

Carroll, J. E. (1997). Images of women and capital sentencing among female offenders: Exploring the outer limits of the Eighth Amendment and articulated theories of justice. *Texas Law Review, 75*, 1413–1452.

Gordon, R. A., Bindrim, T. A., McNicholas, M. L., & Walden, T. L. (1988). Perceptions of blue-collar and white-collar crime: The effect of defendant race on simulated juror decisions. *Journal of Social Psychology, 128*, 191–197.

Gross, S. R., & Mauro, R. (1989). *Death & discrimination: Racial disparities in capital sentencing.* Boston: Northeastern University Press.

Keil, T. J., & Vito, G. F. (1995). Race and the death penalty in Kentucky murder trials: 1976–1991. *American Journal of Criminal Justice, 20,* 17–36.

Kerr, N. L., Hymes, R. W., Anderson, A. B., & Weathers, J. E. (1995). Defendant–juror similarity and mock juror judgments. *Law and Human Behavior, 19,* 545–567.

Lazarus, E. P. (1998). *Closed chambers: The first eyewitness account of the epic struggles inside the Supreme Court.* New York: Times Books.

Mauer, M. (1999). *Race to incarcerate.* New York: New Press.

McCleskey v. Kemp, 481 U.S. 279 (1987).

Meeker, J. W., Jesilow, P., & Aranda, J. (1992). Bias in sentencing: A preliminary analysis of community service sentences. *Behavioral Sciences and the Law, 10,* 197–202.

Munoz, E. A., Lopez, D. A., & Stewart, E. (1998). Misdemeanor sentencing decisions: The cumulative disadvantage of "gringo justice." *Hispanic Journal of Behavioral Sciences, 20,* 298–299.

Nagel, S. (1969). *The legal process from a behavioral perspective.* Pacific Grove, CA: Brooks/Cole.

National Council on Crime and Delinquency. (2000). *And justice for some.* Retrieved June 25, 2004, from http://www.buildingblocksforyouth.org/justiceforsome/jfs.html

Nebraska Commission on Law Enforcement and Criminal Justice. (2001). *The disposition of Nebraska capital and non-capital homicide cases (1973–1999): A legal and empirical analysis.* Retrieved June 25, 2004, from http://www.nol.org/home/crimecom/homicide/homicide.htm

Otto, A. L., Penrod, S. D., & Dexter, H. R. (1994). The biasing impact of pretrial publicity on juror judgments. *Law and Human Behavior, 18,* 453–469.

Radalet, M. L., & Pierce, G. L. (1985). Race and prosecutorial discretion in homicide cases. *Law and Society Review, 19,* 587–621.

Roberts, D. E. (2001). Criminal justice and Black families: The collateral damage of over-enforcement. *University of California Davis Law Review, 34,* 1005–1028.

Rosoff, S. M. (1989). Physicians as criminal defendants: Specialty, sanctions, and status liability. *Law and Human Behavior, 13,* 231–236.

Shapiro, A. (2000). Unequal before the law: Men, women, and the death penalty. *American University Journal of Gender, Social Policy & the Law, 8,* 427–470.

Shaw, J. I., & Skolnick, P. (1996). When is defendant status a shield or a liability? Clarification and extension. *Law and Human Behavior, 20,* 431–442.

Simon, J. F. (1995). *The center holds: The power struggle inside the Rehnquist court.* New York: Simon & Schuster.

Sorenson, J. R., & Wallace, D. H. (1995). Capital punishment in Missouri: Examining the issue of racial disparity. *Behavioral Sciences and the Law, 13,* 61–80.

Streib, V. L. (2003). *Death penalty for female offenders, January 1, 1973 through June 30, 2002* (last modified July 1, 2003). Retrieved June 25, 2004, from http://www.law.onu.edu/faculty/streib/femdeath.htm

Sweeney, L. T., & Haney, C. (1992). The influence of race on sentencing: A meta-analytic review of experimental studies. *Behavioral Sciences and the Law, 10,* 179–195.

Thomson, E. (1997). Discrimination and the death penalty in Arizona. *Criminal Justice Review, 22,* 65–76.

Ugwuebu, D. C. (1979). Racial and evidential factors in juror attributions of legal responsibility. *Journal of Experimental Social Psychology, 15,* 133–146.

Unah, I., & Boger, J. C. (2001). *Race and the death penalty in North Carolina: An empirical analysis: 1993–1997; initial findings—April 16, 2001.* Retrieved June 25, 2004, from http://www.unc.edu/~jcboger/NCDeathPenaltyReport2001.pdf

U.S. Congress Judiciary Subcommittee on Civil and Constitutional Rights. (1994). *Racial disparities in federal death penalty prosecutions 1988–1994.* Washington, DC: U.S. Government Printing Office.

U.S. Department of Justice. (2000). *Survey of the federal death penalty system (1988–2000).* Washington, DC: U.S. Government Printing Office.

U.S. Department of Justice. (2001). *The federal death penalty system: Supplementary data, analysis, and revised protocols for capital case reviews.* Washington, DC: U.S. Government Printing Office.

Walsh, A. (1990). Twice labeled: The effect of psychiatric labeling on the sentencing of sex offenders. *Social Problems, 37,* 375–389.

Wrightsman, L. S., Nietzel, M. T., & Fortune, W. H. (1998). *Psychology and the legal system* (4th ed.). Pacific Grove, CA: Brooks/Cole.

Zebrowitz, L. A., McDonald, S. M. (1991). The impact of litigants' baby-facedness and attractiveness on adjudications in small claims courts. *Law and Human Behavior, 15,* 603–624.

12

FACTUAL RESEARCH
HAS LIMITATIONS

EXAMPLE: JURY SELECTION

The right to a jury in criminal and civil cases is guaranteed in many types of cases by the U.S. Constitution and is considered essential to ensuring that people receive fair trials. So how do jurors get selected? Typically, the court will call a pool of registered voters to come to the courthouse the morning that the trial is to begin. If there is to be one trial starting that day, the pool may consist of 50 people. If there are several trials scheduled to begin, then 200 to 300 people may be called to the courthouse. From this pool, 30 to 50 people will be randomly assigned to a particular courtroom. Once there, the judge and often the attorneys will ask a series of questions trying to determine if there is some reason that a prospective juror should *not* be allowed to sit either as a juror or an alternate in that trial. Alternate jurors sit in on the trial but do not participate in jury deliberations unless one of the jurors becomes unable (e.g., because of illness) to finish the trial.

This process of questioning and rejecting prospective jurors is known as the voir dire or jury selection process. The use of the latter phrase, although common, is ironic because jurors are not selected from the prospective juror pool; they are rejected. Many trial judges and attorneys consider the voir dire an essential part of the trial because it allows them to eliminate those prospective jurors who cannot or will not be fair in judging the case.

There are two ways that these prospective jurors are struck from the jury pool: a causal challenge or a peremptory challenge. In a causal challenge, the judge will excuse a prospective juror from service because he or she meets a criterion laid out in the law (e.g., does not understand English or is overwhelmingly biased). In a peremptory challenge, the attorneys can remove a prospective juror without giving any explanation, although it cannot be done because of race or gender. There are no limits to the number of causal challenges that can be exercised, but peremptory challenges are limited by the judge and law to a set number (e.g., 3 or 6 per side). Of the remaining prospective jurors, the judge will ask the first 12 who entered the courtroom, or whatever number the jury is to be composed of, to sit as the jurors. The next 4, or whatever number the judge deems appropriate, will be seated as alternates. The rest of the prospective jurors are excused.

In exercising challenges, what if the prosecution eliminated all prospective jurors who would *not* be willing to impose the death penalty in a capital case? Is the resulting jury more prone to convict than if these so-called *excludables* had been allowed to serve? That is the issue the U.S. Supreme Court faced in *Lockhart v. McCree* (1986). To reach its decision, the Court considered relevant empirical research, but it had to decide whether this work was sufficiently well done that it should influence the Court's decision.

LOCKHART V. MCCREE

United States Supreme Court

A combination gift shop and service station was robbed, and Evelyn Boughton, the owner, was shot and killed. Ardia McCree was arrested after a police officer saw him driving a maroon and white Lincoln Continental matching an eyewitness's description of the getaway car used by Boughton's killer. McCree admitted to police that he had been at Boughton's shop at the time of the murder. He claimed, however, that a tall Black stranger wearing an overcoat first asked him for a ride and then took his rifle out of the back of the car and used it to kill Boughton. McCree also claimed that after the murder the stranger rode with him to a nearby dirt road, got out of the car, and walked away with the rifle.

McCree's story was contradicted by two eyewitnesses who saw McCree's car between the time of the murder and the time when McCree said the stranger got out and walked away. These witnesses stated that they saw only one person in the car. The police found McCree's rifle and a bank bag from Boughton's shop alongside the dirt road. Based on ballistics tests, a Federal Bureau of Investigation officer testified that the bullet that killed Boughton had been fired from McCree's rifle.

McCree was charged with murder and, in accordance with Arkansas law, the trial judge at voir dire removed eight prospective jurors who stated that they could not under any circumstances vote for the imposition of the death penalty (i.e., known as *Witherspoon* excludables). The jury convicted McCree of murder but rejected the state's request for the death penalty, instead setting McCree's punishment at life imprisonment without parole.

McCree appealed claiming that *death qualification* (i.e., the process whereby *Witherspoon*-excludable prospective jurors are removed), violated his right under the Sixth Amendment, as applied to the states through the Fourteenth Amendment, to have his guilt or innocence determined by an impartial jury selected from a representative cross section of the community. In support of his claim, McCree introduced into evidence 15 social science studies.

Only six of the studies even purported to measure the potential effects on the guilt–innocence determination of removing *Witherspoon* excludables from the jury. Of the remaining nine studies, eight dealt solely with generalized attitudes and beliefs about the death penalty and other aspects of the criminal justice system, and were thus, at best, only marginally relevant to the constitutionality of McCree's conviction. The 15th and final study dealt with the effects on prospective jurors of voir dire questioning about their attitudes toward the death penalty. McCree conceded that the state may challenge for cause prospective jurors whose opposition to the death penalty is so strong that it would prevent them from impartially determining a capital defendant's guilt or innocence. Because of this fact, the state must be given the opportunity to identify such prospective jurors by questioning them at voir dire about their views of the death penalty.

Of the six studies introduced by McCree that at least purported to deal with the central issue in this case, namely, the potential effects of death qualification on the determination of guilt or innocence, three were also before this Court when it decided *Witherspoon v. Illinois* (1968). This Court reviewed the studies in that case and concluded that the data were too tentative and fragmentary to establish that jurors *not* opposed to the death penalty tend to favor the prosecution in the determination of guilt. In addition, on the basis of the trial court record then, it could not be concluded that the exclusion of jurors opposed to capital punishment resulted in an unrepresentative jury on the issue of guilt or substantially increased the risk of conviction. It goes almost without saying that if those studies were too tentative and fragmentary to make out a claim of constitutional error in *Witherspoon*, the same studies, unchanged but for having aged some 18 years, are still insufficient to make out such a claim in this case.

Nor do the three post-*Witherspoon* studies introduced by McCree on the death-qualification issue provide substantial support for his constitutional claim. All three of the new studies were based on the responses of individuals randomly selected from some segment of the population but who were not actual jurors sworn under oath to apply the law to the facts of an actual case involving the fate of an actual capital defendant. This Court has serious doubts about the value of these studies in predicting the behavior of actual jurors. In addition, two of the three new studies did not even attempt to simulate the process of jury deliberation, and none of the new studies was able to predict to what extent, if any, the presence of one or more *Witherspoon* excludables on a guilt-phase jury would have altered the outcome of the guilt determination.

Finally, and most importantly, only one of the six death-qualification studies even attempted to identify and account for the presence of so-called nullifiers. These are individuals who because of their deep-seated opposition to the death penalty would be unable to decide a capital defendant's guilt or innocence fairly and impartially. McCree concedes that nullifiers may properly be excluded from the guilt-phase jury, and studies that fail to take into account the presence of such nullifiers are fatally flawed. The effect of this flaw on the outcome of a particular study is likely to be significant. The only study that attempted to take into account the presence of nullifiers revealed that approximately 37% of the *Witherspoon* excludables identified in the study were also nullifiers. Surely a constitutional rule as far reaching as the one McCree proposes should not be based on the results of the lone study that avoids this fundamental flaw.

DISSENTING OPINION[1]

Eighteen years ago in *Witherspoon v. Illinois*, this Court vacated the sentence of a defendant from whose jury the state had

---

[1] A Dissenting Opinion is an opinion of one or more judges who do not agree with the Majority Opinion.

excluded all persons expressing *any* scruples against capital punishment. Such a practice violated the Constitution by creating a tribunal for the sentencing phase of a trial that was organized to return a verdict of death during the sentencing phase of a trial. The only persons who could be constitutionally excluded from service in capital cases were those who made it unmistakably clear that they would automatically vote against the imposition of capital punishment.

McCree contends that the death-qualified jury that convicted him, from which the state had excluded all persons unwilling to consider imposing the death penalty, was in effect organized to return a verdict of guilty during the guilt phase of the trial. In support of this claim, he presented overwhelming evidence that death-qualified juries are substantially more likely to convict, or to convict on more serious charges, than juries on which unalterable opponents of capital punishment are permitted to serve.

McCree does not demand that individuals unable to assess culpability impartially (nullifiers) be permitted to sit on capital juries. All he asks for is the chance to have his guilt or innocence determined by a jury like those that sit in noncapital cases—one whose composition has not been tilted in favor of the prosecution by the exclusion of a group of prospective jurors uncommonly aware of an accused's constitutional rights but quite capable of determining his culpability without favor or bias.

With a glib nonchalance ill suited to the gravity of the issue presented and the power of McCree's claims, the Majority Opinion upholds a practice that allows the state a special advantage in those prosecutions in which the charges are the most serious and the possible punishments the most severe. The state's mere announcement that it intends to seek the death penalty if the defendant is found guilty of a capital offense will, under today's decision, give the prosecution license to empanel a jury especially likely to return that very verdict. Such a blatant disregard for the rights of a capital defendant offends logic, fairness, and the Constitution.

McCree is not the first to argue that death qualification poses a substantial threat to the ability of a capital defendant to receive a fair trial on the issue of his guilt or innocence. As one scholar observed, "Jurors hesitant to levy the death penalty would seem more prone to resolve the many doubts as to guilt or innocence in the defendant's favor than would jurors qualified on the 'pound of flesh' approach." In *Witherspoon v. Illinois*, Witherspoon provided empirical evidence to corroborate this opinion. The data on this issue, however, consisted of only three studies and one preliminary summary of a study. Although the data certainly supported the validity of Witherspoon's challenge to his conviction, these studies did not provide the Court with the firmest basis for constitutional decision making. As a result, the Court was unable to conclude that the exclusion of jurors opposed to capital punishment results in an unrepresentative jury on the issue of guilt or substantially increases the risk of conviction. As a result, although this Court reversed Witherspoon's death sentence, it declined to reverse Witherspoon's conviction.

In the wake of *Witherspoon*, a number of researchers set out to supplement the data that the Court had found inadequate in that case. The data strongly suggest that death qualification excludes a significantly large subset of potential jurors who could be impartial during the guilt phase of trial. Among the members of this excludable class are a disproportionate number of Blacks and women.

The perspectives on the criminal justice system of jurors who survive death qualification are systematically different from those of the excluded jurors. Death-qualified jurors are, for example, more likely to believe that a defendant's failure to testify is indicative of his guilt, more hostile to the insanity defense, more mistrustful of defense attorneys, and less concerned about the danger of erroneous convictions. This proprosecution bias is reflected in the greater readiness of death-qualified jurors to convict or to convict on more serious charges. And, finally, the very process of death qualification, which focuses attention on the death penalty before the trial has even begun, has been found to predispose the jurors that survive it to believe that the defendant is guilty. The evidence thus confirms, and is itself corroborated by, the more intuitive judgments of scholars and of judges, defense attorneys, and prosecutors in capital trials.

McCree's case would of course be even stronger were he able to produce data showing the prejudicial effects of death qualification on actual trials. Yet, until a state permits two separate juries (i.e., one death qualified and one not death qualified) to deliberate on the same capital case and return simultaneous verdicts, defendants claiming prejudice from death qualification should not be denied recourse to the only available means of proving their case, re-creations of the voir dire and trial processes. It is the courts that have often stood in the way of surveys involving real jurors, and we should not now reject a study because of this deficiency.

The chief strength of McCree's evidence lies in the essential unanimity of the results obtained by researchers using diverse subjects and varied methodologies. Even the haphazard jabs in the

Majority Opinion cannot obscure the power of the array. When studies have identified and corrected apparent flaws in prior investigations, the results of the subsequent work have only corroborated the conclusions drawn in the earlier efforts. Thus, for example, some studies might be criticized for failing to distinguish between nullifiers (whom McCree acknowledges may be excluded from the guilt phase) and those who could assess guilt impartially. Yet the results of these studies are entirely consistent with other studies that controlled for nullifiers by removing them from the study. And despite the failure of certain studies to allow for group deliberations, the value of their results is underscored by the discovery that initial verdict preferences made prior to group deliberations are a fair predictor of how a juror will vote when faced with opposition in the jury room.

The evidence adduced by McCree is quite different from the tentative and fragmentary presentation that failed to move this Court in *Witherspoon*. Moreover, in contrast to *Witherspoon*, the record in this case shows McCree's case to have been subjected to the traditional testing mechanisms of the adversary process. Testimony by expert witnesses during the trial permitted the trial court, and allows this Court, to understand better the methodologies used here and their limitations. There are no studies that contradict the studies submitted by McCree; in other words, all of the documented studies support McCree's position and the trial court's findings.

The true impact of death qualification on the fairness of a trial is likely even more devastating than the studies show. *Witherspoon* placed limits on the state's ability to strike scrupled jurors for cause, unless they state "unambiguously that they would automatically vote against the imposition of capital punishment no matter what the trial might reveal." It said nothing, however, about the prosecution's use of peremptory challenges to eliminate jurors who do not meet that standard and would otherwise survive death qualification. There is no question that peremptory challenges have indeed been used to this end, thereby expanding the class of scrupled jurors excluded as a result of the death-qualifying voir dire challenged here. The only study of this practice has concluded that, for the 5-year period studied, a prima facie case (i.e., a case that, on its face, is presumed to be true unless other evidence can disprove it) has been demonstrated that prosecutors in Florida's Fourth Judicial Circuit systematically used their peremptory challenges to eliminate from capital juries persons expressing opposition to the death penalty.

Judicial applications of the *Witherspoon* standard have also expanded the class of jurors excludable for cause. Although the studies produced by McCree generally classified a subject as a *Witherspoon* excludable only on his or her unambiguous refusal to vote death under any circumstance, the courts have never been so fastidious. Trial courts have frequently excluded jurors even in the absence of unambiguous expressions of their absolute opposition to capital punishment. And this less demanding approach will surely become more common. It thus seems likely that this law will lead to more conviction-prone panels because scrupled jurors (those who generally oppose the death penalty but do not express an unequivocal refusal to impose it) usually share the prodefendant perspective of excludable jurors.

Faced with the near unanimity of authority supporting McCree's claim that death qualification gives the prosecution a particular advantage in the guilt phase of capital trials, the majority of this Court makes a weak effort to contest that proposition. This disregard for the clear import of the evidence tragically misconstrues the settled constitutional principles that guarantee a defendant the right to a fair trial and an impartial jury whose composition is not biased toward the prosecution.

ANALYSIS AND IMPLICATIONS

Death penalty cases involve two distinct issues. The first is whether the defendant was guilty of a crime, and the second is whether the defendant deserves the death penalty or a sentence of life imprisonment if found guilty. This means that the trial is split into two phases: the guilt phase during which the defendant's guilt or innocence is decided, and the penalty (i.e., sentencing) phase during which, if the defendant has been found guilty, his or her punishment is decided (i.e., death or life imprisonment). Some states have the same jury decide both the defendant's guilt or innocence and the sentence if guilty. Other states empanel separate juries for the two phases.

What if a prospective juror's reservations about capital punishment would prevent him or her from making an impartial decision about the defendant's guilt during the guilt phase of the trial, or what if he or she could never vote to impose the death penalty during the penalty phase of trial? Should he or she be excluded for cause from the jury because he or she was too biased to reach a decision based on the law and evidence? In 1968, the U.S. Supreme Court, in *Witherspoon v. Illinois*, addressed this question. Witherspoon appealed his criminal conviction and death sentence because the judge excluded prospective jurors who said that they had *some* opposition to capital punishment or indicated that they had conscientious scruples against inflicting it. Witherspoon contended that the resulting jury, unlike one chosen at random from a cross section of the community, would ignore the presumption of innocence, would accept the prosecution's version of the facts, and would be more likely to return a guilty verdict. The Court disagreed:

> The [social science] data adduced by [Witherspoon] . . . are too tentative and fragmentary to establish that jurors not opposed to the death penalty tend to favor the prosecution in the determination of guilt. We simply cannot conclude . . . that the exclusion of jurors opposed to capital punishment results in an unrepresentative jury on the issue of guilt or substantially increases the risk of conviction. (p. 1774–1775)

The Court, however, felt differently about Witherspoon's argument in regard to the penalty phase of the trial:

> Guided by neither rule nor standard, "free to select or reject as it sees fit," a jury that must choose between life imprisonment and capital punishment can do little more—and must do nothing less—than express the conscience of the community on the ultimate question of life or death. . . . Culled of all who harbor doubts about the wisdom of capital punishment— of all who would be reluctant to pronounce the extreme penalty—such a jury can speak only for a distinct and dwindling minority. . . . If the State had excluded only those prospective jurors who stated in advance of trial that they would not even consider returning a verdict of death, it could argue that the resulting jury was simply "neutral" with respect to penalty. But when it swept from the jury all who expressed conscientious or religious scruples against capital punishment and all who opposed it in principle, the state crossed the line of neutrality. In its quest for a jury capable of imposing the death penalty, the state produced a jury uncommonly willing to condemn a man to die. (p. 1775–1776)

The Court went on to rule that it is unconstitutional to exclude prospective jurors from the penalty phase simply because they voiced general objections to the death penalty or expressed conscientious or religious scruples against its infliction. It is only appropriate to excuse those jurors from the penalty phase when their opposition to the death penalty prevents them from being impartial in the penalty phase or if they would never vote for the death penalty (i.e., *Witherspoon* excludables).

In 1985, the Supreme Court in *Wainwright v. Witt* was faced with a similar case. Johnny Paul Witt was convicted of first-degree murder and sentenced to death in Florida. In that state, prospective jurors whose views were thought to "substantially impair their ability to do their job as jurors" were eligible to be excused for cause. The Supreme Court used this opportunity to clarify their holding in *Witherspoon*. This time the Court held that the standard is "whether the juror's views would prevent or substantially impair the performance of his duties as a juror in accordance with his instructions and his oath" (p. 424).

The next year, in *Lockhart v. McCree* (1986), the Supreme Court revisited the issue of excluding *Witherspoon* excludables from the guilt phase of a death penalty trial. The Court noted that the term *Witherspoon* excludable was "something of a misnomer" because the proper standard was laid out in *Wainwright v. Witt* (1985). Because the parties used the phrase *Witherspoon* excludable, however, the Court decided to continue using it with the understanding that it was referring to the *Witt* standard. McCree argued that death qualification of prospective jurors, which in his trial resulted in the removal of eight jurors whose opposition to the death penalty would automatically prevent them from voting for it in a penalty phase hearing, would violate the U.S. Constitution. McCree reasoned that if these *Witherspoon* excludables were prevented from serving in the guilt phase of a trial, then the resulting jury would not represent a fair cross section of the views of the community in which the crime was committed and would result in a partial jury (i.e., one that was more prone to convict). This would violate the Sixth Amendment to the U.S. Constitution as applied to state action through the Fourteenth Amendment.

Methodological Concerns With the Social Science Studies

In support of his appeal, McCree relied on 15 social science studies, three of which were originally presented in *Witherspoon*. The Court found all of the studies unconvincing.

Simulated Jurors and Juries

The Court faulted three of the studies because they did not use actual jurors serving in an actual trial sitting in judgment of an actual defendant. The studies were simulations in which the Court felt that the lack of anything at stake limited their application to the question that confronted them in *Lockhart*. How could data based on people pretending to be jurors be used to predict how real jurors would act in a real trial?

The answer is that simulations allow the experimenter to control most of the extraneous variables that might occur in a real trial (e.g., there are no mistrials in simulations). The ability to control what mock jurors see, hear, and do permits the researcher to specifically address the issues that are most relevant to both the legal system (e.g., trying out a procedural innovation such as death qualification) and social science (e.g., testing a theory that explains group decision making). In what must come as a surprise to legal critics, this degree of experimental control can actually improve the accuracy of the findings.

Failure to maximize simulation characteristics, however, can harm a simulation's external validity (i.e., the degree to which its findings describe what is occurring in the real world; Diamond, 1997). This is an issue that social scientists who study jury decision making have grappled with for years (e.g., Diamond, 1997; Weiten & Diamond, 1979). Ideally, researchers would like to be able to study real jurors as they serve in an actual trial, but in only the most rare instances has this been permitted. And even when it has been permitted, courts dramatically limit what researchers can vary in their experiments in order to protect the rights of defendants. Thus, researchers are left to use simulations (sometimes with prospective jurors or with people who have served as jurors in a past trial) of varying verisimilitude (i.e., trying to make something as close to the real thing as possible). The best trial simulations use realistic reenactments (usually on videotape but sometimes acted out live before the participant jurors) in a realistic setting (e.g., in a courtroom as opposed to a classroom), employ large samples (to detect any experimental effects) with participants who have been randomly selected from a real jury pool, and allow the participants to deliberate until they reach a verdict (Devine, Clayton, & Dunford, 2001; Diamond, 1997).

Unfortunately, not all researchers are able to study jury behavior under the ideal simulation circumstances described here. Many still recruit college undergraduates as their *jurors* who are given short written vignettes as the *trial* stimulus in an unrealistic setting (e.g., a psychology laboratory) and are not given the opportunity to deliberate. In fact, in a review of jury simulation studies published over the last 20 years in the major American journals dedicated to empirical psycholegal research, Bornstein (1999) found that these kinds of studies were becoming more prevalent.

Although Bornstein (1999) also advocates the use of the best methodologies, his review suggests that we need not be overly alarmed at the trend among researchers to use these quick, less realistic, and inexpensive simulation methods (specifically the use of written materials in place of videotape and college students as jurors). As part of his review, Bornstein looked at jury simulation experiments in which researchers compared the verdict choices of college undergraduates and community residents (e.g., participants selected from voter registration lists, potential jurors or jurors who completed their jury service, and participants recruited from other community sources). There were 25 such studies and in only 5 of them was there a significant difference between the student and community samples. In the five studies in which differences were detected, the student jurors were found to be more lenient in verdict choice and monetary rewards (in civil case simulations) than their community cohorts. Jury simulation experiments that compared the effect of method of trial presentation (i.e., live reenactments, videotape, written, and audiotape) on verdict were also reviewed. This comparison comprised 11 studies, and Bornstein found that in only 3 was there a difference, and in these the results were conflicting. The failure to find reliable differences between simulations that use students as jurors and simulations that employ a sample more closely resembling real jurors and between simulations that vary the method of trial presentation led Bornstein to conclude that it is appropriate to generalize from the simulations to actual jury behavior.

Diamond (1997) has touted the methodological improvements available to jury researchers as well but notes two areas that should be addressed further. First, she recommends more corroborative field data. Although she concludes that there is little inconsistency between what laboratory and field research demonstrates, the generalizability of the simulations would be enhanced if researchers could confirm in the field (i.e., in real trials) what they have learned in the lab. Second, researchers need to know more about the nature of the kinds of decisions that mock jurors are making during the simulations. We do know that most of the decisions that mock jurors make are not consequential; no matter what the mock jurors decide, no one is going to go to jail. This issue really gets to the heart of the Court's criticisms that there is nothing at stake in the simulations. There are potential solutions, however. For example, actual judges from the state or federal courts can participate in the research and instruct mock jurors about the importance of their work to the courts. In addition, the mock jurors could be informed that they will be participating in a simulation that mirrors a real trial that was already held and that their results will be compared with the results of the original trial (Elwork, Sales, & Alfini, 1982).

Although some of the studies that McCree introduced into evidence may have accurately measured the attitudes and decisions of potential jurors toward capital punishment, they could not make the leap (i.e., generalize), in the Court's estimate, to actual juror behavior. The challenges for behavioral and social scientists are to work cooperatively with the legal community so that each may better understand the benefits and limitations of the other's process and product and for social scientists to employ designs that would be both valid and meet the particular concerns of the law. In this way, the facts that behavioral and social scientists provide to legal decision makers are less likely to suffer from the limitations, real or perceived, that the Supreme Court concluded were present in the social science that was presented to them in *Lockhart v. McCree* (1986). Finally, although there is much to be learned about jury simulation processes, the value of simulations must be considered in light of the alternative—not doing the simulation and relying instead on *armchair* speculation of how one thinks that a real jury behaves (Diamond, 1997). Jury simulations are a much better approach for discovering facts about and explaining real jury's behavior.

Deliberation on Verdict

Another criticism that the Court made of the social science research was its failure to include deliberations as part of the experimental design. The Court concluded that the studies were just not realistic enough or persuasive enough without deliberations.

Integrating deliberations into studies of jury decision making is problematic. Studies using deliberating juries require more participants because it takes 12 jurors to produce a single data point (e.g., a guilty or not guilty verdict). However, if the 12 jurors are tested as individuals, 12 data points are produced. Thus, it would take 144 participants deliberating in 12-person juries to produce the same number of data points as 12 nondeliberating participants. A researcher may have to test many hundreds of participants to detect modest group effects.

Deliberation, however, may not be as crucial a factor as the Court assumes it to be because how jurors feel about a case before they even begin to deliberate is the best predictor of how they will vote after deliberation. The seminal work in this area was done by Kalven and Zeisel (1966). In interviews of former jurors, they found that a jury's verdict was overwhelmingly determined by the distribution of votes for guilt or innocence taken on the first ballot. For example, if jurors voted unanimously either for conviction or acquittal on the first ballot, then the final verdict always reflected that initial vote. This result seems obvious. However, even if as many as five jurors voted for conviction and the other seven jurors voted for acquittal on the first ballot, 91% of the final verdicts resulted in acquittal. If the distribution of votes on the first ballot was seven guilty and five not guilty, then the final group verdict was for guilt in 86% of the cases. Sandys and Dillehay (1995) reported results remarkably similar to those found by Kalven and Zeisel. First ballot verdicts predicted final verdicts 93% of the time. And similar results have been obtained for jury-eligible participants who deliberated in simulated trials (Tanford & Penrod, 1986). Finally, Bowers (1996) has reported data from the Capital Jury Project, an investigation into how real jurors behaved in actual death penalty trials. Based on comprehensive interviews of randomly selected jurors, the project found that many jurors begin to consider what the defendant's punishment should be before the defendant's guilt has been determined. Half of the jurors interviewed said they had decided the defendant's punishment before the penalty phase and thus before they heard any aggravating or mitigating evidence. Researchers are confident, therefore, that if they can determine how an individual juror will vote on the first ballot before deliberation begins, they can predict with reasonable accuracy what the group verdict will be (e.g., Hastie, Penrod, & Pennington, 1983) and that the failure to include deliberations should not disqualify the use of a study by the Court.

One study that McCree offered did include deliberations in its design (Cowan, Thompson, & Ellsworth, 1984). But the Court criticized it because the simulated jurors, although asked to deliberate, were not asked to provide a *group* verdict. Although this study did include *Witherspoon* excludables in its mock juries (the failure of which was another shortcoming of all of the other studies, according to the Court), the Court concluded that the study shed little light on the influence that the presence of *Witherspoon* excludables has on *jury* decision making. But this complaint is somewhat mitigated by the research noted above—namely, that predeliberation verdicts of individual jurors are very good predictors of how the entire jury will vote.

Attitudes Versus Behavior

Of the 15 studies cited in the Court's opinion, 8 were surveys of death penalty attitudes and beliefs. The Court did not see how the responses of anonymous citizens to questions about their attitudes on the death penalty related to the behavior of the jurors sitting in judgment of McCree's guilt or innocence. After all, what could facts about attitudes and beliefs tell them about the behavior of death-qualified juries in general and McCree's jury in particular? According to the Court, nothing at all. The surveys were only *marginally relevant* and provided little insight into whether McCree was unconstitutionally convicted.

Do attitudes predict the behavior of prospective jurors in death penalty cases? This is not a theoretical question because attorneys are legally allowed to probe the attitudes of prospective jurors during the voir dire. With this information, lawyers for each side can then determine the prospective juror's suitability to sit on the jury and decide whether to exercise a causal or peremptory challenge. The Court had already decided in *Witherspoon* that removal of jurors who were unalterably opposed to capital punishment was constitutional. Therefore, questions during voir dire concerning attitudes and beliefs on the death penalty had to be constitutional as well. Why let attorneys question jurors about their attitudes if there is no relationship, as the Court suggests, between attitudes and behavior?

One study introduced by McCree addressed the effect that questioning prospective jurors on their death penalty beliefs had on subsequent jury decision making. This study showed that merely questioning a jury on the death penalty during the voir dire focuses their attention on the possible guilt of the defendant. A juror might ask, "Why would the judge and the attorneys be questioning me so closely about my views on capital punishment if they did not already believe that the defendant was guilty?" Haney (1984) randomly assigned participants to one of two groups: a group that went through a typical voir dire or a group that went through a typical voir dire plus death qualification. Participants who went through death qualification turned out to be more conviction prone and more likely to sentence a defendant to death than participants who were not subject to death qualification. They were also more likely to believe that the law does not approve of opposition to the death penalty. Haney concluded that the emphasis placed on death qualification during voir dire biased the jury toward favoring the death penalty. The effects that Haney described were later supported by a meta-analysis of 14 studies on attitudes and the death penalty (Allen, Mabry, & McKelton, 1998). It was found that the voir dire as practiced in the 14 studies tended to produce juries that were more conviction prone and more amenable to sentencing a defendant to death (see also Filkins, Smith, & Tindale, 1998).

Effect of Nullifiers on Juries

Finally, the Court singled out the Cowan et al. (1984) study for special consideration because it attempted to account for the presence of nullifiers. The term nullifier describes jurors who do not follow the law as explained in the jury instructions. Rather, when rendering the guilty–innocent decision, they decide the case according to some other reason or principle (e.g., their conception of justice). No one disputes that jurors who express an unwillingness to follow the law may be removed from the jury.

But would people who could never impose the death penalty (i.e., *Witherspoon* excludables) be unable to follow the law and vote for a guilty verdict during the guilt phase of a trial if that was the appropriate verdict? Haney, Hurtado, and Vega (1994) questioned nearly 500 Californians in depth in much the same way as judges and lawyers would during voir dire in a capital case. They discovered that about 4.5% of their sample were so strongly opposed to the death penalty that they would not convict in the guilt phase knowing that the death penalty was a possibility (i.e., these are the so-called nullifiers). This contrasts with estimates of between 8% and 12% found in earlier research (e.g., Fitzgerald & Ellsworth, 1984, as described in Haney et al., 1994). Assuming no other jurors held intractable views in favor of never voting for innocence, the presence of nullifiers would make a jury less than impartial.

This is not quite the same, however, as removing all *Witherspoon* excludables. Some, and perhaps most, *Witherspoon* excludables might vote to convict the defendant if he or she were allowed to sit on a jury. Although they may be opposed to the death penalty, they may be strong supporters of law and order and want criminals convicted of their crimes.

With only the Cowan et al. (1984) study attempting to take into account the effect of nullifiers on the guilty–innocent decision, the Court was not going to create a rule that could later be used to overturn the convictions of every inmate sitting on death row who had been convicted by a death-qualified jury. The lack of other studies on nullifiers was in the Court's opinion a fatal flaw.

The Court's concern was reasonable. Surely, when answering a constitutional question that will have an impact on many more lives than McCree's, it is not unreasonable for the Supreme Court to look for a replication of the study's findings or for other studies on the same issue. The Cowan et al. (1984) study was not the most realistic simulation. Before considering these problems, in fairness to Cowan et al., it should be noted that their study did possess some important attributes that made it relevant to the question before the Court. Among those good attributes were the following: The mock jurors were death qualified; the trial stimulus was a detailed 2.5-hour videotape based on the transcripts of a real murder trial; and the mock jurors were permitted to deliberate. Among the study's shortcomings was the fact that only 37 of the 288 participants came from an actual jury pool (after completing their jury service). The rest responded to an ad in the paper or were referred by friends. As volunteers, the entire sample of participants was self-selected, and only residents of California participated. These research participants very probably represented a far different kind of sample than would have been obtained in Arkansas where McCree was tried and convicted. Participants also watched the videotape in groups as large as 36 people in an auditorium rather than in groups the size of real juries. After watching the videotape, the participants were asked to provide an initial verdict. In real trials, jurors are instructed (although they may have a hard time complying) not to reach a decision until they have heard all the evidence and have deliberated with their fellow jurors. Before deliberating, an experimenter instructed the participants that deliberations usually begin with a straw vote (i.e., an unofficial vote whose purpose is to get an idea of where the group stands). Although this is often the case, the instruction may have needlessly influenced the course of the deliberations. It should have been left up to the participants to decide how to structure their deliberations, as is the case with real jurors. Deliberations were videotaped with visible camera and microphones. The presence of these devices may have affected deliberations and the behavior of the participants, although based on their review of the tapes, the experimenters suggested that the mock jurors soon forgot the presence of the cameras. Finally, participants were told that they would be allowed only one hour to deliberate. Knowledge of this time constraint may also have influenced the deliberations.

CHAPTER'S LESSON

The research introduced in *Lockhart* would be relevant to the factual issues in the case if it had been done properly, but the Court in this case concluded that it was plagued by methodological limitations. As we noted in our analysis of the Court's opinion, social scientists who conduct research in this area would disagree and support the Dissenting Opinion's views on this matter. Perhaps when two very different disciplines, law and the behavioral and social sciences, interact, such disagreements are inevitable. As Sales and Shuman (2005) argue, there clearly is a need for lawyers and judges to be educated about how to accurately evaluate expert information in litigation and for behavioral and social scientists to be educated about the law and legal decision making that they wish to study. This is a new lesson, and perhaps the ideal one, on which to end this book.

REFERENCES

Allen, M., Mabry, E., & McKelton, D. (1998). Impact of juror attitudes about the death penalty on juror evaluations of guilt and punishment: A meta-analysis. *Law and Human Behavior, 22,* 715–731.

Bornstein, B. H. (1999). The ecological validity of jury simulations: Is the jury still out? *Law and Human Behavior, 23,* 75–91.

Bowers, W. J. (1996). The capital jury: Is it tilted toward death? *Judicature, 79*, 220–223.

Cowan, C. L., Thompson, W. C., & Ellsworth, P. C. (1984). The effects of death qualification on jurors' predispositions to convict and on the quality of deliberation. *Law and Human Behavior, 8*, 53–79.

Devine, D. J., Clayton, L. D., & Dunford, B. B. (2001). Jury decision making: 45 years of empirical research. *Psychology, Public Policy and Law, 7*, 622–727.

Diamond, S. S. (1997). Illuminations and shadows from jury simulations. *Law and Human Behavior, 21*, 561–571.

Elwork, A., Sales, B. D., & Alfini, J. (1982). *Making jury instructions understandable.* Charlottesville, VA: Michie.

Filkins, J. W., Smith, C. M., & Tindale, R. S. (1998). An evaluation of the biasing effects of death qualification: A meta-analytic/computer simulation approach. In R. S. Tindale, L. Heath, J. Edwards, E. Posavac, F. Bryant, & Y. Suarez-Balcazar (Eds.), *Theory and research on small groups: Social psychological applications to social issues* (pp. 153–175). New York: Plenum.

Haney, C. (1984). The biasing effects of the death-qualification process. *Law and Human Behavior, 8*, 121–132.

Haney, C., Hurtado, A., & Vega, L. (1994). "Modern" death qualification: New data on its biasing effects. *Law and Human Behavior, 18*, 619–633.

Hastie, R., Penrod, S., & Pennington, N. (1983). *Inside the jury.* Cambridge, MA: Harvard University Press.

Kalven, H., & Zeisel, H. (1966). *The American jury.* Boston: Little, Brown.

Lockhart v. McCree, 476 U.S. 162 (1986).

Sales, B. D., & Shuman, D. W. (2005). *Experts in court: Reconciling law, science, and professional knowledge.* Washington, DC: American Psychological Association.

Sandys, M., & Dillehay, R. C. (1995). First ballot votes, predeliberation dispositions, and final verdicts in jury trials. *Law and Human Behavior, 19*, 175–195.

Tanford, S., & Penrod, S. (1986). Jury deliberations: Discussion content and influence processes in jury decision making. *Journal of Applied Social Psychology, 16*, 322–347.

Wainwright v. Witt, 469 U.S. 412 (1985).

Weiten, W., & Diamond, S. S. (1979). A critical review of the jury simulation paradigm: The case of defendant characteristics. *Law and Human Behavior, 3*, 71–93.

Witherspoon v. Illinois, 391 U.S. 510 (1968).

INDEX

unconscious transfer and, 158, 159–160, 161, 166

Facts
  from behavioral and social sciences, 9–10
  complexity of, 4
Federal courts, 7–8
Fourteenth Amendment
  abortion as constitutional right under, 39, 50
  drug testing and, 19
Fourth Amendment
  drug testing and, 18, 19
  search and seizure and, 195–196, 197, 203, 212

Gacy v. Welborn. See also Jury instruction comprehension
  jury instruction comprehension in
    aggravating factors and unanimity, 178
    challenge of, 183–184
    constitutionality of, 180, 181
    mitigating factors and unanimity in, 177–178, 179
    oral vs. written version and, 177
    presumption of comprehension of, 181
    reasons for failure of, 180–181
    state rebuttal of study, 179–180
  jury instruction comprehension study, 178–179, 184
    appellate court rebuttal of, 184–185
    behavioral and social science of, 185–187
    commonsense understanding of law and, 183
    incomprehensibility of instructions in, 184
Good faith
  in issuance of search warrant, 205
  of officer in seeking search warrant, 201, 203, 205

Informed consent to abortion
  antiabortion arguments and, 53
  "governmental interest in," 51
  impact on woman's decision
    persuasion literature in, 53
  minors and, 49

under Pennsylvania Abortion Control Act, 42–43
  exception to compliance with, 43
  prevention of psychological consequences and
    research in minors, 52
    research on adults, 52
Interviewer and child testimony
  emotional tone of, 76
  status of, 77
Interview(s)
  in children's testimony
    factors affecting, 75–76
    coercive or suggestive techniques in, 67–68, 69, 71
    environment and, 118–119
    face-to-face, 118
    multiple, 71
    in New Jersey v. Michaels, 69–72
    rigid versus conversational conduct of, 119
    suggestibility of child witnesses and, 69–70, 71
    telephone, 118
    threats and bribes in, 69, 70, 75

Joy v. Penn-Harris-Madison, testing for tobacco use, 33
Jurors
  feelings predeliberation and vote after deliberation, 253
  predeliberation juror verdicts predict and group vote after deliberation, 253
Jury instruction comprehension. See also Gacy v. Welborn
  aggravating circumstances and
    burden of prosecution to establish, 176
  behavioral and social science of, 185–187
  in Buchanan v. Angelone, 190–191
  in death penalty, 186–187
  in Gacy v. Welborn, 176–182
  improvement of
    states' requirements for and, 192
    through defendants' challenges of, 192
    through rewritten instruction, 187
    through science, reluctance to, 187–188

judicial notice in, 115
social science survey in, 115–121
testimony from behavioral and social scientific research, 115
Volkswagen and Audi v. Uptown Motors, 106–112

Undue burden
Pennsylvania Abortion Act and, 51
of spousal notification of abortion, 47, 55
state interests and abortion, 41–42
state right to restrict abortion and, 51
United States Supreme Court, 7–8
United States v. Leon, 195–202
concurring opinion and, 202–203
exclusionary rule and, 195–196, 197
suspected drug trafficking in, 196–197
United States Supreme Court and, 196–202

Veronia School District v. Acton (mandatory drug testing of student athletes)
compellingness of district's interest, 21–23, 32
constitutional claim of Acton, 18–19
custodial and tutelary responsibility of District and, 19–20, 23, 32
district drug-testing policy and, 17–18
drug use problems and, 16–17
privacy interest of student athletes and, 19–21
United States Supreme Court case, 16–23
Viability of fetus
Roe v. Wade and, redefinition of, 51
state's interest and, 41, 49
Virginia Military Institute (VMI). *See also* Sex differences and higher education
admission of women
and destruction of, 149–150
effect on egalitarianism and, 149
reasons for, 128
adversative education at, 126, 127–128
admission of women and, 136–137
coeducation effect on, 136
versus cooperative method of VWIL, 130
effect on women, 136–137
coeducation and
effect on physical training, adversative approach, privacy, 129, 130

exclusion of women
adversative education and, 126, 127–128
adverse effects of, 148
appellate court decision, 129–130
equal protection challenge to, 126–150
justifications for, 133
and mission, 126–127
successful accommodation of women to professional schools and military academies *versus*, 150
trial court ruling in favor of VMI, 128–129
mission of, 127–128
and accommodation of women, 138
to produce citizen-soldiers and leaders, 126–127
remedial plan for single-gender policy, 130, 138–143. *See* Virginia Military Leadership Institute (VMLI)
single-gender education as contribution to diversity in state system
appellate court findings, 135–136
trial court findings, 129
single-gender education as objective, 131–132
single-gender policy excluding women. *See* VWIL
benefits of, 133–134
history of higher education and, 134
remedial plan for, 130–131
as single sex (male) state military college, 126–127
Virginia Military Leadership Institute (VMLI)
comparison with VMI
cooperative *versus* adversative education, 130
funding, 130
differences from VMI program, 139–142
lack of substantial equality in, 142–143
limitations of, 141–142
as parallel to VMI program, 130–131, 138–139
satisfaction of Equal Protection Clause, 130–131
Volkswagen and Audi v. Uptown Motors
degree of similarity between VW's trademark and Uptown's mark, 107
likelihood of confusion issue, court resolution of, 114–115

ABOUT THE AUTHORS

Peter W. English, PhD, is a visiting scholar in the Department of Psychology at the University of Arizona and an adjunct professor of psychology at Pima Community College. Professor English has published and continues to conduct research on topics related to psychology, public policy and law, such as comprehension of jury instructions. Professor English has also published and presented nationally on topics related to cognitive psychology, such as the distribution of attention within visual fields. Professor English has served as an editorial assistant on the journal *Psychology, Public Policy, and Law* and is a member of the American Psychological Association, American Psychology–Law Society, and the American Psychological Society.

Bruce D. Sales, PhD, JD, is professor of psychology, sociology, psychiatry, and law at the University of Arizona, where he is also director of its Psychology, Policy, and Law Program. Among his other works are *Experts in Court: Reconciling Law, Science, and Professional Knowledge* (with D. Shuman), *Laws Affecting Clinical Practice* (with M. Miller & S. Hall), *Courtroom Modifications for Child Witnesses: Forensic Assessment and Testimony* (with S. Hall, in press), *Family Mediation: Facts, Myths, and Future Prospects* (with C. Beck), *Treating Adult and Juvenile Offenders With Special Needs* (coedited with J. Ashford & W. Reid), *Ethics in Research With Human Participants* (coedited with S. Folkman), *Doing Legal Research: A Guide for Social Scientists and Mental Health Professionals* (with R. Morris & D. Shuman), *Law, Mental Health, and Mental Disorder* (coedited with D. Shuman), and *Mental Health and Law: Research, Policy and Services* (coedited with S. Shah). Professor Sales, the first editor of the journals *Law and Human Behavior* and *Psychology, Public Policy, and Law*, is a fellow of the American Psychological Association and the American Psychological Society, and an elected member of the American Law Institute. He received the Award for Distinguished Professional Contri-

271

butions to Public Service from the American Psychological Association, the Award for Distinguished Contributions to Psychology and Law from the American Psychology–Law Society, and an Honorary Doctor of Science degree from the City University of New York for being the "founding father of forensic psychology as an academic discipline."